Also by Barry Took
The Best of *Round the Horne* (Equation, 1989)

COMEDY
GREATS

A Celebration of Comic Genius Past and Present

B·A·R·R·Y · T·O·O·K

EQUATION

© Barry Took 1989

British Library Cataloguing in Publication Data

Took, Barry
Comedy greats.
1. Comedy. Biographies. Collections
I. Title
791'.092'2
1. Comedians — biography
ISBN 1–85336–039–2

Equation is an imprint of the Thorsons Publishing Group,
Wellingborough, Northamptonshire, NN8 2RQ, England

Printed and Bound in Great Britain by
Biddles Limited, Guildford, Surrey

1 3 5 7 9 10 8 6 4 2

To John Fisher who encouraged me to write this book.

PICTURE
ACKNOWLEDGEMENTS

The illustrations were supplied and/or reproduced by kind permission of the following:

Popperfoto: 16, 24, 68 (top right; centre), 74, 170, 206.
©Thames Television: 36 (top left; bottom left).
Rex Features: 36 (top right), 68 (top left; bottom right), 128, 136, 148, 156, 188, 196.
Sunday Times: 36 (bottom right).
International Creative Management: 48.
Brooksfilms: 58.
The Richard Stone Partnership: 68 (bottom left).
National Film Archive, London: 88, 104, 114, 178.
John Timbers: 218.

Every effort has been made to trace the ownership of all illustrations. We apologize for any error or omission that may have occurred.

CONTENTS

INTRODUCTION

I t has truly been said that 'No man is a hero to his valet', and it's probably as true to say that no comedian is a hero to his scriptwriters.

One pleasantly sultry January day in 1988 I sat in the famous Polo Lounge of the Beverly Hills Hotel in Los Angeles and talked to four leading exponents of scriptwriting art. They were Allan Manings, Hal Kanter, and a couple of Bobs who'd written together for years, Bob Schiller and Bob Weiskopf. This quartet had created comedy shows on radio and television, had worked on movies and in the theatre, and between them had written for almost every American comedy star of major consequence. I completed the quintet and brought a similar dossier of experience from Great Britain. So between us there was something over 300 years of writing know-how, disappointment and success, award-winners and flops.

My own association with comedy and comedians dates from my childhood, when visiting the music-halls of North London I was enthralled and delighted by the atmosphere generated by such big names of the day as Max Miller, Sid Field, Vic Oliver, and Flanagan and Allen. Later, I went into the business via the small-time London pubs and clubs which offered entertainment (of a sort), and where an aspiring comedian could learn, albeit painfully, the business of making people laugh.

In 1951 I won a radio talent contest and became a professional comedian. For the next five years I toured the length and breadth of the British Isles, from Truro in Cornwall to Edinburgh in Scotland, from Clacton on the east coast to Llanelli in west Wales ... and just about everywhere in between. As stand-up comedian, comedian–compère, and manager of touring companies I learned what Bob Hope, Jack Benny, the Marx Brothers, Tony Hancock, Tommy Cooper, George Burns and the rest had learned before me: that it's a tough life with small compensations and only the occasional weeks when audiences love you keep you from despair. I invented new routines — which were stolen by other comics! This was only fair I suppose, as I had started by stealing from others, but it sharpened my desire to write, and in time, after a three-year spell in West End revue, and cabaret in the classier West End nightclubs—The Blue Angel, The Cascade, Quaglinos, and The Dorchester—I more or less gave up performing and concentrated on scriptwriting, writing for many well-known British comedians. Marty Feldman and I teamed up in 1960 and wrote a number of successful comedies, but after 10 years or so, whilst staying with friends, we ended our writing partnership and went our separate ways.

I describe Marty's career in more detail in this book. My own writing career led me into educational TV, journalism, and books, and this in turn led me eventually to the Polo Lounge of the Beverly Hills Hotel on that warm January day in 1988.

One of the writers in the group, Allan Manings, was an old friend from my days working on *Rowan and Martin's Laugh-In*. Bob Weiskopf, Bob Schiller, and Hal Kanter I knew only by reputation, but such is the freemasonry of scriptwriters that within minutes of meeting it was as if we'd all known each other for years.

So we sat there, reminiscing, and while the Bloody Marys went down and the decibel level went up, I learned a lot about some of the comedy greats and not so greats who have been part of all our listening and viewing lives. But, as the valet who sees his master naked and undignified, before the dressing and grooming that enable him to face the world with suave assurance, so the writers remembered the odd difficult, hilarious moments when the comedy stars were without the armoury of bright scripts and, for a moment, vulnerable.

I can't remember to whom Hal Kanter was referring when he described one comedian as 'a lewd capon' (at least I can, but I'm not repeating it here) but that seemed to get things going. Bob Schiller and Bob Weiskopf had written for Lucille Ball for many years and had one story I particularly liked. It seems that Lucy was the complete professional, who learned her lines, didn't ad lib, didn't need those cue cards so aptly named 'idiot boards', and always gave a sparkling performance. Except on one occasion when Tallulah Bankhead was a guest on the show. All through the week's rehearsal Miss Bankhead was never on time, fluffed her cues, forgot her lines and appeared to be wearing a perfume more reminiscent of Gordon's Gin than Chanel No. 5. By showtime, perfectionist Lucille Ball was in a highly nervous state — but on recording Tallulah Bankhead was sober, word-perfect and charming, and it was Lucy who fumbled. It was, say Schiller and Weiskopf, the only time they'd seen her thrown. It must be said that their admiration for Lucille Ball and Desi Arnaz knows no bounds, and they were part of the *Lucy* team for many years, only quitting when they felt they had no more to contribute.

The two Bobs, grey-haired, chubby, each with a mischievous gleam in his eye, are kind men who understand the traumas that beset comedians, as does Hal Kanter, who many years before had worked for Ed Wynn, a radio great and one of the first stars of TV comedy in the USA.

Kanter told the following anecdote:

> Ed Wynne and I were talking once about who was and who wasn't funny, and I said, 'Ben Blue is a very funny man but he's never achieved star-

dom'. Ed Wynn said, 'You're right, Ben is a very funny man but there's a problem with Ben. The reason he's never become a star is that if Ben has to be on stage and be funny at 8.15 he starts getting funny at about 8.12, in the wings — three minutes before he has to go on. If I have to be funny,' Wynn continued, 'I start getting funny at four o' clock in the afternoon.'

Hall Kanter was puzzled by that:

> But [he said], some years later I was working at Paramount and Charlie Chaplin was filming on the back lot — a New York street. The film was *Limelight* and I rushed out to watch the great man at work. They were shooting a scene where Chaplin was supposed to be walking along the sidewalk. There are some little children in the foreground — he stops to pat one on the head — then he goes up a flight of stairs, fumbles trying to put his key in the door — and that's the end of the shot. He was supposed to be drunk, incidentally. When I got there he was saying, 'Let's try it one more time', and the director said, 'Ok, here we go — take 14', and Charlie started off camera and came staggering in. By the time the camera picked him up he was 'drunk', he went through the same routine and then said, 'One more time'. By the time I left [says Kanter] they were on take 34. Each time he did the shot he would start further and further back from the camera, and each time he went back further he would get progressively drunker ... until the scene was perfect. It was then I realized what Ed Wynn had said to me all those years before about the preparation that goes into being funny.

I remarked, having met Dudley Moore a few days previously, that he too was a thoughtful actor who prepared his comic scenes. That drew the comment, 'When he's doing his thing he's wonderfully funny but he needs editing. Sometimes he goes too far.' But how far any comedian goes is a matter of opinion, and many different techniques are effective. Chaplin was possibly the most accomplished of all comedians and conceivably the most painstaking, but improvisation and the inspiration of the moment can be devastatingly effective. The only true criterion is how long the funny person stays funny to his or her public.

The conversation at the table in the Polo Lounge — a venue where, I should think, more conversations about show business have taken place than anywhere else on the planet — drifted to talk of many comedians, including Robin Williams, who got a general thumbs up from our group, and John Cleese. 'We love him', said one of the Bobs, while the other nodded assent. Then the question of grotesques came up: comics such as Marty Feldman and Dandy de Vito. One Bob said, 'I can't stand grotesque people working — just because they are grotesque.' The other Bob argues, 'I think in the case of Danny de Vito his acting outweighs his grotesqueness.' Allan Manings mentioned Jonathan Winters, a comedian who creates grotesque characters but who does so many he forgets some of the things he's created and has to be reminded of them by his writers. One of the problems of versatility is probably that in the excitement of creating a new character old characters get forgotten. Milton Berle seems to have changed little in a long career

— smart, wise-cracking, never at a loss. But — perhaps a slight tendency to over-do the joke.

In one *Lucy Show* he had, for plot purposes, to be dressed as a woman. Bob Weiskopf, remembering the incident, says:

> 'And he gets to the door to walk out and he has to do this funny walk — walking on his ankles. He has high-heeled women's shoes on and women's clothing and lipstick and he had to make it funny! The next day he grabs me and says, 'I hear you didn't like the show last night.' I said, 'All I said was, with all this — the woman's clothing and smoking a cigar you didn't have to walk on your ankles.' He said, 'If you just want someone just to walk you get a 25 dollar a week actor.' So I retorted 'To get someone to write that ankle business you get a 25 dollar a week writer.'

Hal Kanter contributed the thought: 'What you should have said, Bob, was 'Milton, you *are* a 25 dollar a week actor — only you've got a very good agent.'

On the subject of dressing up to get a laugh, the two Bobs, who wrote radio scripts for Fred Allen, who was tops when radio was king, remembered something that Fred had told them about the time he was the straight man in a vaudeville double act. It seems that one night Fred Allen ad libbed something and got a laugh. The comedian of the act was furious. 'In the dressing room afterwards the guy who was the comic comes in and this is how he's dressed: he's got a light bulb for a nose, slap shoes, a toilet plunger for a cane, a mangy fur coat with big patches on it, and he says to Fred, "I'll be goddamned if I'll play straight for anybody." '

That took the conversation on to George Burns, who played straight to Gracie Allen for years and who by so doing made the team of Burns and Allen stars. Right into his 90s he was still inventive and, said Hal Kanter, 'God bless him, he's one of the most refreshing people you could possibly meet on or off stage.' George Burns also scored high marks in our group for being an excellent editor of script material and also, of course, a very effective writer himself.

It seems that Garry Shandling is George Burns's natural heir. Shandling's ability to talk to the audience and to roam in and out of the plot of his situations is reminiscent of the early Burns and Allen TV shows. It's perhaps too early to say if Garry Shandling is an all-time comedy great, but his show is certainly a refreshing and adult addition to the nearly moribund world of the sit com. Talk of Shandling brought Hal Kanter to mention George Gobel, for whom he wrote for many years and whom he liked as a decent, honest man who understood his business and was a big star in his day. A more recent television star — host of a late-night chat show in the USA, was dismissed as a 'half-assed smart ass', and with that we moved on to talk of other, better, men — for instance Carl Reiner. 'A brilliant comedy mind', said Kanter, and who would argue? Among the comedy classics Reiner's creation *The Dick Van Dyke Show* must rate very high. Bob Schiller chipped in with 'We haven't mentioned Woody Allen' — and everybody agreed that he was tremendous and we moved on. On reflection, our meeting at the Beverly Hills Hotel was not unlike the opening of Woody Allen's film *Broadway Danny Rose*, where a bunch of comedians sit around in a New York café, reminiscing about their successes and failures.

Allan Manings then tossed the name of Jackie Gleason into the conversation and we discussed *The Honeymooners*, a TV series which also featured that first-rate comedy actor, Art Carney. Allen next mentioned the almost legendary Henny Youngman — a stand-up comic of the old school — deadpan delivery and an unchanging repertoire of gags. Hal Kanter quipped, 'Sure, Henny is a funny man — but if he was drowning he couldn't ad lib "Help!" '

As I have suggested, no group of comedy writers could get together without starting to tell horror stories of the poor treatment writers sometimes get. After working for a day with one well-known entertainer the writers started to leave. 'Where are you going?' asks the comedian. 'To eat,' comes the reply. 'I'll give you your dinner,' says the comic, 'and while you're eating you can come up with some more jokes.'

It's agreed by us all that in the old days comedians felt that by employing writers they owned them, body and soul, 24 hours a day. I can remember when working on *Rowan and Martin's Laugh-In* in 1969–70 being told: 'George [the producer] doesn't like us taking time off to have lunch.' To be fair, George Schlatter supplied his writers with every need, but when he employed a writer from nine to five he expected him to work nine to five, grabbing snacks along the way.

This is not a practice found in England where, as Denis Norden has said, 'scriptwriting is still a cottage industry'. On the whole, in Britain scriptwriting is, or was, an honourable profession and its practitioners, Frank Muir and Denis Norden, Sid Colin, Ted Kavanagh, Galton and Simpson, Spike Milligan, and the rest, are treated by the public, if not their producers, with a certain amount of respect. There are, of course, comedians' labourers, the itinerants who move from show to show in the manner of Kentish hop-pickers. Not that good American writers are not honoured, but they are very much like maid, chauffeur, or valet to the star or producer they serve.

Employers can be gracious and charming or downright mean. One comedian working at his country home, telling his writers he always dined *en famille*, banished them to an outhouse. They rebelled and went into town on a bender. Another tyrant was said to have locked his writers in a railway coach until they delivered a script. Yet another, a European, was said to lock his writers in the dungeons of his castle until they delivered the goods.

Danny Kaye was not in this group but, although he was a hard-working all-round entertainer, he carried around his fair share of fantasy. As Hal Kanter said, 'Danny Kaye was more than a comedian. He was a musician, he was a surgeon, a flyer, he was a Rabbi, he was a petulant little boy. He was very moody and very mercurial.' Much of his musical material — and it's from his singing we know him best and remember him with the most affection — was written by his wife, Sylvia Fine. A cynic remarked that they had one of the best marriages in Hollywood — they never saw each other.

Danny Kaye could be very funny, and Hal Kanter remembered an occasion some years before in the days of radio when, standing backstage, Goodman Ace, then the head writer of *The Danny Kaye Show*, was with the head of the William Morris agency, Abe Lastfogel. Lastfogel was saying, 'How can we make this man [Kaye] funnier?' And Goodman Ace said, 'I can't hear you.' Lastfogel repeated his remark. Ace said, 'I still can't hear you.' Lastfogel asked, 'Why not?' Ace answered, 'The audience are laughing too loud.' A discreet way of pointing out that Danny Kaye didn't need to be any funnier.

Funny though Danny Kaye could be, he doesn't really come into the category of comedy greats, but would fit into any category of great entertainers, along with Sinatra, Garland, and Crosby. When Danny Kaye first appeared at the London Palladium back in 1947 he dazzled us with his charm, energy, and style. Today he is better remembered for his portrayal of Hans Christian Andersen in the film of that name, and his subsequent work for UNESCO, for which organization he toured the world bringing hope and encouragement and laughter to many thousands of deprived children.

But meanwhile, back at the Polo Lounge, talk turned to writers' nightmares. Bob Schiller and Bob Weiskopf at one time had three pilot scripts on offer, each potentially a series. One morning they heard the news that all three had been optioned. Bob Weiskopf told his wife who was, of course, delighted, but then bearing in mind the impossibility of Bob and Bob writing three series a week simultaneously said, 'What happens if all three pilots are picked up?' Bob replied, 'We'll jump off that bridge when we come to it.'

Another Weiskopf line was when a show that they'd written had been cast but cancelled before the actors had reached the read through. Bob's comment: 'Better Dead than Read.'

Bob Schiller on the subject of Red Skelton: 'It's been said — if he wasn't so rich they'd put him away.' But, Bob added, 'He was a very funny man.' To Skelton it seemed the writers were the enemy. His opening line each week on receiving the script was 'How are they trying to kill me this week?'

Schiller and Weiskopf were Skelton's head writers for three years — but then gave an interview in a Hollywood paper that was far from flattering to Skelton. They were coming to the end of their contract and felt that with just one more show to write 'what the hell'. Not surprisingly Skelton was livid, and decided to teach these traitors a lesson. Schiller and Weiskopf, who had named their successor, took him along to the show to see how Skelton fudged up a script. So, while the new writer was sitting there with the script in his hands, Skelton — and here was the subtlety of his revenge — performed the script verbatim, reckoning that without his additions it wouldn't get many laughs. It was the first time in three years that he'd done it, and the show got so much laughter that it overran by 11 minutes. But, it seems, Skelton, who had an almost pathological hatred of writers, felt deeply for other performers — understanding from his own agony what they, the other comics, must be going through. For when all is said and done, being funny week after week is a frighteningly difficult task, and it's easy to understand how many of them become unbalanced, or heavy drinkers, or even suicidal. Being a professional funny man is not a task you'd wish on your best friend.

Our session at the Beverly Hills Hotel ended for me on a surprising note. Having spent several hours discussing comedians, swapping anecdotes and having, it must be said, a very good time, Hal Kanter suddenly said, 'Probably the most underestimated reader of comedy lines was Bing Crosby. I wrote for him for five years and his timing was impeccable, his delivery was fabulous, his intelligence and his appreciation of writing were superb. He was a wonderful man to work with.' And Kanter topped *that* with *this*: 'Probably the best joke reader among women was Judy Garland. She was magnificent. She would invest the most trivial of comedy lines with a depth, a reality and sincerity. She was a joy.'

And on that note of unstinting praise for two people who were not professional comedians, I address myself to the stern task of writing about people who were, and in some cases happily still are — in my view — comedy greats.

GEORGE BURNS

NOT FORGETTING GRACIE ALLEN

Comedy greatness comes in all shapes and sizes. There's the immaculate invention of Buster Keaton, the balletic finesse of Chaplin, the 'anything goes' approach of the Marx Brothers, the very personal, manic style of John Cleese, the charm and idiosyncratic manner of Dudley Moore, and the brash, no holds barred comedy of Barry Humphries.

What makes George Burns unique is that his contribution for many years was a series of brief questions such as: 'How's your brother?' 'What did your mother say?' 'Where?', 'What was it?' and 'Why?' The fact that he asked questions of that supremely funny, eccentric comedienne Gracie Allen makes all the difference. George Burns's contribution to over 30 years of stage, radio, and TV appearances made by Burns and Allen was immeasurable in spite of what critics of the act might have said.

In his collection of reminiscences, *Living it Up*, George Burns quotes a review that he and Gracie received, in their early days, from a critic of an Oklahoma City newspaper.

> Number four on the Orpheum bill was a man and woman act, George Burns and Gracie Allen. Miss Allen is not only a beautiful young lady, but a great talent. She captivated the audience with her lovely voice, her exciting dancing and her all round stage presence. On top of all this her comedy timing is flawless. There is no telling how far Miss Allen could go if she worked alone.

In another of his collections of autobiographical anecdotes, *The Third Time Around*, George Burns quotes impresario Charles Dillingham, who was at that time putting together a cast for the London production of *Show Boat*. Burns and Allen were playing a date at the Palace Theatre, New York, and Dillingham was considering them for the comedy parts of Eve Puck and Sammy White. Well he caught the act, and next day wired their agent: 'The team of Burns and Allen I'll pay 500 dollars a week. For the girl alone I'll pay 750 dollars.' Needless to say they didn't accept the offer.

The simple truth is that, although Gracie's looks and charm attracted all the attention, it was George Burns who planned it that way, constructing the act,

17

writing the lines, working on their entrances and exits — in short, being a shrewd and unselfish Svengali to her Irish Catholic Trilby. In *Living it Up*, George Burns gives a typical example of the sort of routine he invented.

GEORGE:	Gracie, this family of yours ...
GRACIE:	When Willie was a little baby my father took him riding in his carriage, and two hours later my father came back with a different baby and a different carriage.
GEORGE:	Well, what did your mother say?
GRACIE:	My mother didn't say anything because it was a better carriage.
GEORGE:	A better carriage?
GRACIE:	Yes ... and the little baby my father brought home was a little French baby so my mother took up French.
GEORGE:	Why?
GRACIE:	So she would be able to understand the baby ...
GEORGE:	... when the baby started to talk.
GRACIE:	Yeah.

Not only were they a hit on stage but their married life was near perfect and lasted for 38 years, until in 1964 Gracie died of a heart attack. She had decided to retire in 1958 but George, who was then 62 years old and, he says, 'fresh as a daisy', went on working in cabaret at Las Vegas and Lake Tahoe both solo and with various partners, including Carol Channing. But before that he'd signed to do a TV series. A Burns and Allen television show without Gracie just couldn't work — it was indeed a case of *Hamlet* without the prince. As George Burns realized, 'It was like having dinner; we had the soup, the salad and the dessert, but the main course was home playing with her grandchildren.'

But that flop didn't deter Burns, and he got together with his writers to devise something completely new — a cabaret routine in which *he* got the laughs. It wasn't that he needed the money or the fame as he was one of the best-known entertainers in the USA, but show business was in his blood, and he just couldn't retire.

George Burns, born Nathan Birnbaum on New York's East Side in 1896, one of 12 children, got the show business bug early. By the time he was 8 years old he was singing in saloons, illegally as it happens, with other kids from the locality. They called themselves the 'Peewee Quartet' (with a combined age of 33). When he was 9 the act split up, but George Burns was stuck with show business for the rest of his life. He was destined not to hit the big time until he was 27 and had teamed up with Gracie, but before that he'd been a singer, a dancer, a yodelling juggler, he did an act with a performing seal, a dog act, and various double acts with human partners. He'd used a variety of pseudonyms and only occasionally was successful. But during this time he learned his trade and acquired the strength to carry on in spite of what fate, poor audiences, and unsympathetic theatre managers had to offer. Furthermore he developed a shrewdness that made him and kept him a star from the age of 27 way into his 90s. I don't suppose, to be truthful, that George Burns was ever terrifically funny on his own. Wry, whimsical, engaging, and humorous certainly but never uproarious.

As a writer and producer of radio and television shows he was, on the whole, very successful and gathered around him a team the public liked. Writers worked for George for a long time too — and as a one-time scriptwriter myself I can assure you that the rapport between writer and comedian can wear very thin. Mainly this is due to the fact that everyone's sense of humour is different and when person A thinks a thing is funny and person B thinks it isn't, then friction starts to build. Also, performers and writers see things from a different perspective. Unless the writer is also a performer, as for instance Woody Allen, Mel Brooks, and Carl Reiner, the chances are he can't always see that a joke may look funny on paper but won't work when said aloud. Added to that, when the performer is the writer's employer it's a fifty to one chance that in an argument about the merits of a gag the performer is bound to win. But George Burns kept his peace and kept his writers. Before he used scriptwriters — and not having a literary background — he tells us that although he used to invent the material for him and Gracie, if it needed to be written down and spelt correctly she would correct his longhand scribbles and see that the script was delivered in good order.

In some cases this lack of education and typing skill might give the artiste an inferiority complex towards writers and make him either totally subservient to them (a highly unlikely situation incidentally) or demanding and arrogant (a very common situation). George Burns seems to understand and enjoy the various and differing personalities of his writers and gives them full credit for their contribution to any script.

Since Gracie Allen died, George Burns has emerged as a very talented screen actor in such films as *The Sunshine Boys, Oh God!, Just You and Me Kid* (with the then 14-year-old Brooke Shields), and *Going in Style.* He's written, or perhaps, as he credits various members of his writing staff, co-written, several books of reminiscence. He's appeared on many TV specials and is still, late in life, when most people of his generation just aren't around any more, a potent force in the US entertainment field.

I admire his pluck, stamina, and sheer reasonableness. He doesn't strain for effect, lie about his age, or act in any other way than what he self-evidently is — a gentleman. If life has treated him well then it could be said that he has reciprocated. He is a man for whom I would love to have written — and nearly did on one occasion.

I was approached by the London office of the J. Walter Thompson organization to write a piece for one of their clients for a conference to be held in Miami. The client was the European sector of a big multinational cereal corporation. The idea that the account executive, copy-writer, and I evolved was a deadpan history of Europe, making jokes about the various countries in which they sold their cereal. This was to be filmed in the UK and shipped out to Miami for the conference. When the script was completed it called for an actor to stand in front of a stylized map of Europe and, with the aid of some pretty girls in the national dress of the countries, describe the activities of the Company in that area.

It was a good, witty script and cried out for George Burns to deliver it. At least, *I* cried out for George Burns to deliver it, but was outvoted, and another actor was found. He did a good job but couldn't compare to the cigar-smoking, gravel-voiced star who, there is no doubt, would have been the hit of that Miami conference.

George Burns playing the part of God seemed, on the face of it, a bizarre piece of casting, but seeing the film *Oh God!* (made in 1978, screenplay by Larry Gelbart, directed by Carl Reiner, and co-starring John Denver) you can't image anyone else who could have combined authority with humility, and a wry knowingness with an air of innocence more effectively. I remember seeing the film and saying to myself, well, if there *is* a God I hope he's like that. The film was, of course, sentimental but that dry, crackling George Burns delivery stopped it from becoming maudlin and, it must be said, John Denver in his first screen role was excellent too. Unfortunately a sequel didn't live up to the promise of the original, and is best forgotten.

The Sunshine Boys, which preceded *Oh God!* by three years, was as different as could be. Where one had a supernatural being descending on a small town, the other had two aged vaudeville comedians asked to make a comeback on TV and renewing their relationship — a lifetime spent hating each other. The part George Burns played, Al Lewis, was originally meant for Jack Benny but alas Jack Benny died before he could make the film, and George was offered the part opposite Walter Matthau. The result was a triumph for them both and for Neil Simon who wrote it, and George received an Oscar for Best Supporting Actor of 1975.

In *Just You and Me Kid*, George Burns played another retired vaudevillian who befriends a runaway girl (Brooke Shields), and a grandfather/granddaughter relationship develops.

George also played a cameo role in the 1977 production *Sergeant Pepper's Lonely Hearts Club Band*, and a larger part with Art Carney and Lee Strasberg in *Going in Style*, but *Oh God!* and *The Sunshine Boys* were the peak of George Burns's acting career.

Like so many of the people who figure in this book the Burns and Allen background was in vaudeville, and I suppose it was the toughest training an entertainer could have. Constant travelling, poor hotels, indifferent audiences, the threat of cancellation if the local manager didn't like your act — Burns claims he was once cancelled after the manager had heard him rehearsing with the orchestra at Band Call on Monday morning before he'd actually appeared! — and the need to be self-sufficient made those tough enough to stand it able to face any show business contingency in later life. Burns and Allen more than survived the life and went on from vaudeville to radio, a series of short films for Paramount, some longer films, until at last they became two of the hardiest stars of television and whose shows, up until Gracie Allen's retirement, were among the best to be seen on 'the box'.

As we marvel at the ease with which Garry Shandling moves from set to audience and the way he addresses the viewer directly before moving smoothly back into the plot of his current TV shows, it's easy to forget that George Burns was doing the same thing 30 years earlier. Perhaps both owe a debt to Thornton Wilder's *Our Town*. But, as George Burns would be the first to admit, the thing that stopped him being a small-time vaudevillian and made him a star was his meeting with Gracie Allen.

Gracie Allen came from San Francisco, the youngest of an Irish Catholic family. Her father was an entertainer who specialized in Irish patter, songs, and clog dancing. Gracie's mother was not in show business but loved it and encouraged her four daughters to follow in their father's clog-dancing steps.

Gracie's elder sisters, Hazel, Pearl, and Bessie became champion clog dancers, winning competitions all over the Bay area of San Francisco. When Gracie was old enough she went the same rounds of competitions and concerts, not with her sisters but solo, with her mother acting as chaperone. She sang, danced, and gave dramatic recitations, and was very popular wherever she appeared.

Time went by, and a local star by the name of Larry Reilly asked Gracie and her sisters to join his act. The act was billed as 'Larry Reilly and Co.', and was so successful that Larry Reilly received an offer of a 10-week tour in the Eastern States. Bessie, Hazel, and Pearl didn't want to leave San Francisco as they all had boyfriends, and besides, they wanted to open a dancing school. Gracie, however, was keen to go east and Larry Reilly added a bagpiper to his act and off they went, still billed as 'Larry Reilly and Co.'

All went well until, according to George Burns, Gracie noticed that at one town the act was no longer billed as Larry Reilly and Co., but just Larry Reilly. Gracie was indignant, and at the end of the engagement left the act with the words, 'Mr Reilly, I'll never work with you again because I was humiliated. I didn't get billing.'

This might be an apocryphal story but shortly after she left Larry Reilly, George Burns met Gracie Allen and the rest, as they say, is history.

Looking at old videos and listening to ancient gramophone records you cannot help but be charmed by Gracie and delighted by the droll, self-effacing manner of George Burns, the man who made the big time by asking: 'How's your brother?'

FILMS

These include:

The Big Broadcast   1932
Produced by Paramount
Directed by Frank Tuttle

Written by George Marion Jr, from the novel *Wild Horses*
by William Ford Manley

International House   1932
Produced by Paramount
Directed by Edward Sutherland
Written by Francis Martin, Walter de Leon, Lou Heifetz, and Neil Brant

Love in Bloom   1933
Produced by Paramount
Directed by Elliott Nugent
Written by J. P. McEvoy and Keene Thompson

We're Not Dressing   1934
Produced by Benjamin Glazer
Directed by Norman Taurog
Written by Horace Jackson, Francis Martin, George Marion Jr, from the play
The Admirable Crichton by J. M. Barrie

The Big Broadcast   1937
Produced by Lewis Gensler
Directed by Mitchell Leisen
Written by Edwin Gelsey, Arthur Kober, Barry Travers, Walter de Leon, and
Francis Martin

The Sunshine Boys   1975
Produced by Ray Stark
Directed by Herbert Ross
Written by Neil Simon, from his play

Sergeant Pepper's Lonely Hearts Club Band   1977
Produced by Dee Anthony
Directed by Michael Schultz
Written by Henry Edwards

Oh God!   1978
Produced by Jerry Weintraub
Direct by Carl Reiner
Written by Larry Gelbart, from the novel by Avery Corman

Just You and Me Kid   1979
Produced by Irving Fein and Jerome M. Zeitman
Directed by David Selman
Written by Ford Beebe

Going in Style   1979
Produced by Tony Bill
Directed by Martin Brest
Written by Martin Brest

Oh God! Book Two   1980
Produced by Warner
Directed by Gilbert Cates
Written by Josh Greenfield, Hal Goldman, Fred S. Fox, Seaman Jacobs, and
Melissa Miller

TELEVISION

The Burns and Allen Show   1950–1958   CBS
The George Burns Show   1959–1960   CBS
Wendy and Me   1964   Warner/Natwill

BOB HOPE

Bob Hope has led a full and active life. As a comedian–compère he has few equals. In films with Bing Crosby and Dorothy Lamour, and on quite a different level with a variety of leading ladies, Leslie Towns Hope, to call him by his given names, has delighted the customers and made a mint of money. Beyond that, he is *the* troop entertainer of the twentieth century, visiting America's fighting men wherever they are and bringing that same salty cockiness that he's brought to everything he's done, from small-time vaudeville to Golf Classics.

It's said that Hope is very much what his myriad of writers over the years have made him, but other comics have had a number of scriptwriters and are still desperately unfunny. I can think of ... but no matter — I don't want a libel suit on my hands. It's true that Bob Hope always has had, and still does have, several scriptwriters near to hand, but then he makes so many appearances that he is constantly in need of new material. Hope lives or dies on his topicality and the sharp, quick-witted response to what is currently happening. I have only once seen him put out of his stride and that was at the Miss World finals in London in 1970 when the Women's Liberation Movement staged a protest, and poor Bob Hope, his cue cards in disarray, was forced to beat an undignified retreat.

In the mid eighties, scandal blew up around the Bob Hope Classic Golf Tournament which was staged at Moor Park, a famous course not far from London. Hope himself was not implicated in the rumours of double dealing that went around, but his name was tarnished and the Classic was dropped from the golfing calendar.

At school the young Leslie Towns Hope (nicknamed 'Hope-lessly', and 'Hopeless') learned to fight back when the other boys jeered at his name or appearance but became interested in music and song in the school choir and in a church group, 'The Sambo Minstrels'. After school it seems that he despised mundane jobs, vowing that he'd do something different — be a film star perhaps — but meanwhile preferred hanging round the pool hall.

It's odd when you consider that Bob Hope, probably the hardest-working comedian of all time, came into show business in the mid twenties, when having tried loafing, pool-sharking, and after a brief inglorious stab at boxing, he finally decided that his future was on the stage.

His first stab at stage stardom was as a dancer in a double act with another Cleveland lad, Lefty Durbin. Sadly Durbin died in 1925, after which Hope teamed up with George Byrne, with the act billed as 'Hope and Byrne — Dancing Demons'. Their hoofing was well received but their attempts at comedy weren't, and it was not until Hope split up with Byrne in 1927 and went solo that his career as comedian-compère was set on the course that was to take him to the top.

Bob Hope used a number of stooges in his early days, most importantly Louise Troxell. She would wander on to the stage in the middle of his act and they would perform a sort of Burns and Allen routine after which she would exit, and Hope would conclude the act on his own with a song and dance.

Later, on stage and radio, he worked with a delightful dizzy blonde he called 'Honey Chile' on account of her southern fried accent. Her real name was Patricia Wilder, and she came from Macon, Georgia.

A typical exchange from a 1935 broadcast went:

HONEY CHILE: Mr Hope, I've got two brothers at home that I'm sure would be a big hit on radio.
HOPE: What's their names?
HONEY CHILE: The oldest is Ed.
HOPE: What's the young 'un's name?
HONEY CHILE: Ed.
HOPE: The two boys in one family by the name of Ed?
HONEY CHILE: Yes. Father always said that two Eds were better than one.
HOPE: Your father said that? What's keeping him off the air?

As William Robert Faith says in his comprehensive biography of Bob Hope, *A Life in Comedy*, 'The routines were simple but Hope discovered that regardless of what she said it was much more how she said it' — and I can well believe it.

Before that, two important events had happened. The first and most important was that he met and married Dolores Reade, a night-club singer in the 'low and husky' style — and they were happy ever after. The other event that made the 1933–4 period a bright one for the sprightly Hope was landing a major part in the Jerome Kern musical, *Roberta*.

He was now an established Broadway star with a loving wife, an apartment on Park Avenue, and a chauffeur to drive his Pierce-Arrow car. He was becoming more popular on radio and making short comedy films for Warner Brothers in their Brooklyn studio. When *Roberta* folded he took Dolores and Honey Chile on tour and did great business on the road too.

Then came another Broadway show, *Ziegfeld Follies* (1936), which starred Fanny Brice, Hope, Eve Arden, and Josephine Baker. The show didn't run as long as was expected due to the failing health of Fanny Brice, but as Hope was now doing a weekly radio show — *The Frank Parker Show* — he didn't mind too much. In fact, such was Hope's appeal on the air that it became known as *The Frank Parker–Bob Hope Show*. In June 1936 Frank Parker quit the programme to join

Paul Whiteman's radio show and it became Bob Hope's show. William Robert Faith comments:

> Even with a new visibility as the absolute star of the show Hope was still plagued with personal criticism about the quality of his material.
>
> With the large number of comedians working on radio at the time, all depending on a limited number of gag writers, and using them at high speed, mediocre material and gag larceny were not uncommon. The show had a low rating but Hope was gaining valuable experience for what was coming.

What was coming, of course, was the biggest of the big time on radio, TV, and films, but at that time it seems that Hope was just another gag-cracker and hadn't built the individual personality that served Jack Benny, and Burns and Allen so well. Another comedian with an absolutely characteristic style was Jimmy 'Schnozzle' Durante, and Hope worked with Durante in 1936–7 in a revue starring Ethel Merman, called *Red Hot and Blue*. Hope, with third billing, could watch with amusement as the two tough stars, Merman and Durante, battled for the honours. The battle was over in May 1937 when the show closed in Chicago after a brief Broadway run, and Hope went back to radio — in *The Woodbury's Rippling Rhythm Revue*.

By now Dolores had, to all intents and purposes, retired to become the gracious hostess of the Hopes' frequent parties, and Hope engaged his third Honey Chile. The first had left him on signing a film contract with RKO, the second, Margaret Johnson, signed with Columbia Pictures, and so Clare Hazel from Bennettsville, South Carolina, took on the role of the dumb girl from the sticks.

In June 1937 Hope signed a contract with Paramount Pictures for his first feature film, *The Big Broadcast of 1938*. The film, typically fatuous for that time, was vaguely about a race between two ocean liners, Hope playing the MC on one of them. What wasn't fatuous, and in fact possibly one of the most important moments in Bob Hope's career, was the song written for him and Shirley Ross to sing, 'Thanks for the Memory'. Not only was the song a hit but it became Bob Hope's signature tune, and added that touch of wry sentimentality that his routines had hitherto lacked. Why, people felt, the man wasn't just a joke-teller — he actually felt emotion.

In 1938 Paramount had under contract a large number of stars, both comic and serious, including Jack Benny, Beatrice Lillie, Harold Lloyd, Mae West, Marlene Dietrich, Gary Cooper, Fred McMurray, and Randolph Scott. More important for Bob Hope's future was that the studio also had Bing Crosby and Dorothy Lamour under contract, and those three together were destined to create something special in film comedies — the *Road* pictures.

Before they came, however, Hope scored two major successes. One was as star of the Pepsodent toothpaste radio show, where he followed the previous incumbents, Amos 'n' Andy, and took the already successful show to new heights.

The other was the movie *The Cat and the Canary*, in which he co-starred with Charlie Chaplin's then wife, Paulette Goddard.

Around this time too (1939–41) Bob and Dolores Hope adopted two children, a girl, Linda, and a boy, Tony. After the Second World War the Hopes adopted two more children, Kelly and Nora. It's a strange, somewhat sad, co-incidence that, like Bob and Dolores, neither Jack and Mary Benny, nor George and Gracie Burns could have children of their own — all of them created their families through adoption.

Could it be that Benny, Burns, and Hope, having to question their potency in one area of their lives, compensated through their careers? One can but speculate, but whatever the cause, Hope's drive for success and recognition — and, incidentally, money — became obsessional. Films, radio, vaudeville tours, benefit concerts, troop shows, MC of the annual Academy Awards presentations — Hope was always on the go.

Even before the USA entered the Second World War, Hope was staging his radio shows at Army, Navy and Marine bases in Southern California, and when war came he went into overdrive. Ever since then, whenever and wherever the USA has been at war — Korea, Vietnam, and even in the late eighties where there was an American naval presence in the Persian Gulf — there Hope would go, with a group of actors, singers, and beautiful girls, keeping up morale. He wasn't the only entertainer to do this but he did it more often and more publicly than others; an example of selfless patriotism that is quite remarkable in someone who, in his professional career, was ruthless, domineering, and, to quote *Time* magazine in 1941, 'A hard man with a dollar'.

As I have said elsewhere in this book, no comedian is a hero to his writers; by the early 1940s Hope always had about a dozen working for him and they nicknamed him 'Scrooge'. What they contributed, uncredited, to the *Road* films we shall never know, but with Bing Crosby Hope seemed at ease and on his best form. Their 'insult' routines, where each would denigrate the other, were, of course, a put-up job; both on the studio set and on the golf course they delighted in each other's company, ad libbing and fooling in a most delightful way, while Dorothy Lamour just stood there and looked beautiful.

The first *Road* film was *Road to Singapore* (1940), then came *Road to Zanzibar* (1941), *Road to Morocco (1942), Road to Utopia* (1946), *Road to Rio* (1948), *Road to Bali* (1952), and finally *Road to Hong Kong* (1962). The plots were all much the same. Bob and Bing were in trouble and had to get out of it the best way they could, and both were in competition for the girl — invariably Dorothy Lamour. Bing Crosby always got her in the end! Into that simple formula were fitted many ingenious jokes, special effects, and tuneful songs.

Among the many writers who must have contributed, the following were credited in one or more of the *Road* pictures: Frank Butler, Don Hartman, Harry Hervey, Sy Bartlett, Norman Panama, Melvin Frank, Edmund Beloin, Jack Rose, Hal Kanter, William Morrow, and Harry Tugend.

Hope's pictures with Paulette Goddard were very successful too. *The Cat and the Canary* (1939) was followed by *The Ghost Breakers* (1940), and *Nothing But the Truth* (1941).

Hope's many other successes in the cinema include *My Favorite Blonde* (1942), in which he starred with Madeleine Carroll, *The Paleface* (1948) with Jane Russell, *Beau James* (1957), which was a sanitized life story of the one-time New York Mayor, Jimmy Walker, and *The Facts of Life* (1960) with Lucille Ball. There were many other successes too, and Bob Hope on television continued where Bob Hope on radio left off.

I don't suppose any one comedian in this century has made more personal appearances, radio or TV shows, and films. Nor has any comedian become the friend of so many presidents of the United States. His work for charity has been phenomenal, and his private life a model of decorum. And yet one is left at the end of the day with a feeling that Bob Hope was really two people: one generous and giving, the other mean-spirited and vain.

The other thing that strikes me, having read a lot about the man, having seen him frequently on television and in the cinema, is the curous fact that I cannot remember one thing that he has ever said, one joke of the millions he has cracked or one memorable line he has uttered.

That he is, or certainly was, one of America's favourite funny men cannot be doubted; that he was content with nothing but the best his gag-writers could turn out cannot be disputed, and yet at the end of it all there is no flavour of the man, no individual touch that makes you think: 'Ah — that's Bob Hope', in the way you can with Jack Benny, or W. C. Fields, or Jacques Tati, or John Cleese. Perhaps it's a case not of 'he's a star because he's great' but 'he's great because he's a star'.

Either way, Bob Hope's story is one of hard work and achievement, and for that he deserves our admiration.

FILMS

Short comedies
Going Spanish   1934
Produced by Educational Films
Directed by Al Christie
Written by William Watson and Art Jarrett

Paree, Paree   1934
Produced by Warner Brothers
Directed by Roy Mack
Written by Cyrus Wood, from the musical *Fifty Million Frenchmen* by Herbert Fields, E. Ray Goetz, and Cole Porter

The Old Grey Mayor   1935
Produced by Warner Brothers
Directed by Lloyd French
Written by Herman Ruby

Watch the Birdie   1935
Produced by Warner Brothers
Directed by Lloyd French
Written by Dolph Singer and Jack Henley

Double Exposure   1935
Produced by Warner Brothers
Directed by Lloyd French
Written by Burnet Hershey and Jack Henley

Calling all Tars   1936
Produced by Warner Brothers
Directed by Lloyd French
Written by Jack Henley and Burnet Hershey

Shop Talk   1936
Produced by Warner Brothers
Directed by Lloyd French
Written by Burnet Hershey and Jack Henley

Feature Films
The Big Broadcast of 1938
Produced by Harlan Thompson
Directed by Mitchell Leisen
Written by Walter de Leon, Francis Martin, and Ken Englund

College Swing   1938
Produced by Lewis Gensler
Directed by Raoul Walsh
Written by Walter de Leon and Francis Martin

Give Me a Sailor   1938
Produced by Jeff Lazarus
Directed by Elliot Nugent
Written by Doris Anderson and Frank Butler

Thanks for the Memory   1938
Produced by Mel Shauer
Directed by George Archibaud
Written by Lynn Starling, from the play *Up Pops the Devil* by Albert Hackett and Frances Goodrich

Never Say Die   1939
Produced by Paul Jones

Directed by Elliot Nugent
Written by Don Hartman, Frank Butler, and Preston Sturges, from the play by William H. Post.

Some Like it Hot 1939
(Renamed *Rhythm Romance*)
Produced by William C. Thomas
Directed by George Archibaud
Written by Lewis R. Foster and Wilkie C. Mahoney, from the play by Ben Hecht and Gene Fowler

The Cat and the Canary 1939
Produced by Arthur Hornblow Jr
Directed by Elliot Nugent
Written by Walter de Leon and Lynn Starling, from the play by John Willard

Road to Singapore 1940
Produced by Harlan Thompson
Directed by Victor Schertzinger
Written by Frank Butler and Don Hartman

The Ghost Breakers 1940
Produced by Arthur Hornblow Jr
Directed by George Marshall
Written by Walter de Leon

Road to Zanzibar 1941
Produced by Paul Jones
Directed by Victor Shertzinger
Written by Frank Butler and Don Hartman

Caught in the Draft 1941
Produced by B. G. DeSylva
Directed by Elliot Nugent
Written by Harry Tugend, with additional dialogue by Wilkie C. Mahoney

Nothing But the Truth 1941
Produced by Arthur Hornblow Jr
Directed by Elliot Nugent
Written by Don Hartman and Ken Englund

Louisiana Purchase 1941
Produced by Harold Wilson
Directed by Irving Cummings
Written by Jerome Chodorov and Joseph Fields, from the musical comedy by Morrie Ryskind, based on a story by B. G. DeSylva

My Favorite Blonde 1942
Produced by Paul Jones
Directed by Sidney Lanfield

Written by Don Hartman and Frank Butler, from the story by Melvin Frank and Norman Panama

Road to Morocco 1942
Produced by Paul Jones
Directed by David Butler
Written by Frank Butler and Don Hartman

They Got Me Covered 1943
Produced by Samuel Goldwyn
Directed by David Butler
Written by Harry Kurnitz

Let's Face It 1943
Produced by Fred Kohlmar
Directed by Sidney Lanfield
Written by Harry Tugend

The Princess and the Pirate 1944
Produced by Samuel Goldwyn
Directed by David Butler
Written by Don Hartman, Melville Shavelson, and Everett Freeman

Road to Utopia 1946
Produced by Paul Jones
Directed by Hal Walker
Written by Norman Panama and Melvin Frank

Monsieur Beaucaire 1946
Produced by Paul Jones
Directed by George Marshall
Written by Melvin Frank and Norman Panama, from the novel by Booth Tarkington

Where There's Life 1947
Produced by Paul Jones
Directed by Sydney Lanfield
Written by Allan Boretz and Melville Shavelson

Road to Rio 1948
Produced by Daniel Dare
Directed by Norman Z. McLeod
Written by Edmund Beloin and Jack Rose

The Paleface 1948
Produced by Robert L. Welch
Directed by Norman Z. McLeod
Written by Edmund Hartmann and Frank Tashlin, with additional dialogue by Jack Rose

Sorrowful Jones 1949
Produced by Robert L. Welch
Directed by Sidney Lanfield
Written by Melville Shavelson, Edmund Hartmann, and Jack Rose, from the play by Damon Runyon

The Great Lover 1949
Produced by Edmund Beloin
Directed by Alexander Hall
Written by Edmund Beloin, Melville Shavelson, and Jack Rose

Fancy Pants 1950
Produced by Robert L. Welch
Directed by George Marshall
Written by Edmund Hartmann and Robert O'Brien, from the novel *Ruggles of Red Gap* by Harry Leon Wilson

The Lemon Drop Kid 1951
Produced by Robert L. Welch
Directed by Sidney Lanfield
Written by Frank Tashlin, Edmund Hartmann, and Robert O'Brien, with additional dialogue by Irving Elinson, adapted from Damon Runyon's short story by Edmund Beloin

My Favorite Spy 1951
Produced by Paul Jones
Directed by Norman Z. McLeod
Written by Edmund Hartmann and Jack Sher

Son of Paleface 1952
Produced by Robert Welch
Directed by Frank Tashlin
Written by Frank Tashlin, Robert L. Welch, and Joseph Quillan

Road to Bali 1952
Produced by Harry Tugend
Directed by Hal Walker
Written by Frank Butler, Hal Kanter, and William Morrow

Off Limits 1953
Produced by Harry Tugend
Directed by George Marshall
Written by Hal Kanter and Jack Sher

Here Come the Girls 1953
Produced by Paul Jones
Directed by Claude Binyon
Written by Edmund Hartmann and Hal Kanter

Casanova's Big Night   1954
Produced by Paul Jones
Directed by Norman Z. McLeod
Written by Hal Kanter and Edmund Hartmann

The Seven Little Foys   1955
Produced by Jack Rose
Directed by Melville Shavelson
Written by Melville Shavelson and Jack Rose

That Certain Feeling   1956
Produced by Norman Panama and Melvin Frank
Directed by Norman Panama
Written by Norman Panama and Melvin Frank, I. A. L. Diamond and William Altman, from the play *King of Hearts* by Jean Kerr and Eleanor Brooke

The Iron Petticoat   1956
Produced by Betty Box
Directed by Ralph Thomas
Written by Ben Hecht

Beau James   1957
Produced by Jack Rose
Directed by Melville Shavelson
Written by Jack Rose and Melville Shavelson, from Gene Fowler's biography of James Walker, *Beau James*

Paris Holiday   1958
Produced by Robert Hope
Directed by Gerd Oswald
Written by Edmund Beloin and Dean Riesner, from a story by Robert Hope

Alias Jesse James   1959
Executive Producer Bob Hope
Produced by Jack Hope
Directed by Norman Z. McLeod
Written by William Bowers and Daniel D. Beauchamp

The Facts of Life   1960
Produced by Norman Panama
Directed by Melvin Frank
Written by Norman Panama and Melvin Frank

Bachelor in Paradise   1961
Produced by Ted Richmond
Directed by Jack Arnold
Written by Valentine Davies and Hal Kanter

Road to Hong Kong   1962
Produced by Melvin Frank

Directed by Norman Panama
Written by Norman Panama and Melvin Frank

Critic's Choice 1963
Produced by Frank P. Rosenberg
Directed by Don Weis
Written by Jack Sher, from the play by Ira Levin

Call Me Bwana 1963
Produced by Albert R. Broccoli
Directed by Gordon Douglas
Written by Nate Monaster and Johanna Harwood

A Global Affair 1964
Produced by Hal Bartlett
Directed by Jack Arnold
Written by Arthur Marx, Bob Fisher, and Charles Lederer

I'll Take Sweden 1965
Produced by Edward Small
Directed by Frederick De Cordova
Written by Nat Perrin, Bob Fisher, and Arthur Marx

Boy, Did I Get a Wrong Number 1966
Produced by Edward Small
Directed by George Marshall
Written by Burt Styler, Albert E. Lewin, and George Kennett

Eight on the Lam 1967
Produced by Bill Lawrence
Directed by George Marshall
Written by Albert E. Lewin, Burt Styler, Bob Fisher, and Arthur Marx

The Private Navy of Sergeant O'Farrell 1968
Produced by John Beck
Directed by Frank Tashlin
Written by Frank Tashlin

How to Commit Marriage 1969
Produced by Bill Lawrence
Directed by Norman Panama
Written by Ben Starr and Michael Kanin

Cancel My Reservation 1972
Executive Producer Bob Hope
Produced by Gordon Oliver
Directed by Paul Bogart
Written by Arthur Marx and Robert Fisher

Above Morecambe and Wise

Below Benny Hill

Above Tommy Cooper

Right Marty Feldman

36

SOME BRITISH
LAUGHTER-MAKERS

Comedians come in all shapes, sizes, and temperaments, and their art is embodied not so much in *what* they do but in *how* they do it. Some are loners, others are gregarious. Some drink to excess, others are total abstainers. Some are iconoclasts tilting at the windmills of pomposity, others are in tune with the established order of things. In short, they are like any group of people, and it's only the special nature of their work that makes them any different from, say, a group of doctors or airline pilots or policemen or waiters. But unlike doctors or waiters, to whom we go for a special service and from whom we expect certain things (e.g. a cure, or a meal served quickly and efficiently), we go to the comedian expecting surprise — something new. When we don't get it — if he tells us jokes we have heard before, or do not understand, or dislike — our disappointment is intense.

Laughter is ultimately unexplainable or, if explainable, not entirely comprehensible. All we need to know is what makes us, the unique individuals that we are, laugh. It's the job of the comedian to serve and satisfy us.

The best, some of whom are described in this book, have made a lot of people laugh a lot of the time. There are others too whom I'd like to spend time on now. They are in no way less important or less funny than the men and women who have been given a whole chapter to themselves, but such is the ephemeral nature of their particular brands of comedy that a full-scale analysis of their work would be fruitless.

MORECAMBE AND WISE

When I first met Eric Morecambe and Ernie Wise (born Eric Bartholomew and Ernest Wiseman, the former in Morecambe, in 1926, the latter in Leeds, in 1925) they were a small-time music-hall double act. Not as far down the bill as I was in those days, or playing in such awful theatres, but certainly not in the big time.

In the late 1950s they were given a television series by the BBC and were not terribly good. In fact, one critic of the day described television as 'the box they buried Morecambe and Wise in'. The techniques required in music-halls and in television studios are quite different, and Morecambe and Wise hadn't mastered the latter.

For a time after that they disappeared from the British scene and toured Australia. They came home via the USA where they watched and learned from a number of top-liners. By the time they returned to the UK their act was much improved. Australian audiences in those days were less demanding, and good response down under had built their confidence. Appearing on *The Ed Sullivan Show* in New York had polished their technique. They were on *The Ed Sullivan Show* more than once, but on their first appearance Sullivan had assumed that they were a three-handed act and introduced them as Morry, Cambey, and Wise. Their success on *The Ed Sullivan Show* helped to bolster their confidence still further and by the time they did get back to the British music-halls they'd added considerable polish, not to say poise, and a touch of magic to their routines. Gone was the sharply etched straight man and feed — their act was more integrated, their personalities a harmonious blend. This rapport they'd developed made all the difference, and it was clear that they had a big future.

Their break came with regular appearances on the big Sunday night variety show, *Sunday Night at the London Palladium*. That was followed by their own series of half-hour programmes for ATV, and in 1961 they appeared in *The Royal Variety Show*. More television followed, and by 1963 they were topping the ratings in the UK. Not only were they popular on TV but could, and did, make a considerable amount of money in personal appearances in clubs and theatres all over Great Britain.

In the mid sixties they switched from commercial television to the BBC and went from strength to strength until in 1968 their progress came to a temporary stop when Eric Morecambe suffered a heart attack. They had a long break and then returned to the small screen as good and as popular as ever.

By now the writers who'd helped to steer them into the big time, Sid Green and Dick Hills, had become big names themselves, chiefly because they'd written themselves into many of the Morecambe and Wise sketches. On receiving an offer to write in the USA, they left Eric and Ernie for the greener grass of Hollywood. It's debatable whether the grass *was* greener, as Hollywood regards most writers as hacks and anonymity is their lot. But with Hills and Green's departure Morecambe and Wise were looking for another writer. BBC's then Head of Variety, Bill Cotton, suggested the brilliant northern gag man, Eddie Braben. The trio of Morecambe, Wise, and Braben got together, and a combination of Braben's originality and Eric and Ernie's long experience of show business created even better TV shows.

One of Braben's better ideas was to present Ernie Wise as a playwright, albeit ignorant and illiterate: in each programme big stars would be lured on to the show to take part in these 'plays', which were usually travesties of well-known classics, such as *Hamlet*. The first star to agree was Peter Cushing, and many others appeared in the years that followed: Dame Flora Robson, Eric Porter, Michael Redgrave, John Mills, Glenda Jackson, Vanessa Redgrave, Diana Rigg, Robert Morley, and many more. When the gag was extended to include musical guests, André Previn and Shirley Bassey both delivered delightful comedy performances. They had refusals from Sir John Gielgud among others, but they admitted once that they wouldn't appear as guests on anyone else's show. That is perhaps what kept them so insular and, though big in Britain, virtually unknown in the USA.

Their films — *The Intelligence Men* (1965), *That Riviera Touch* (1966), *The Magnificent Two* (1968) — have been, to quote Leslie Halliwell, 'less than satisfactory'. This is a shame, but I suppose that the lack of spontaneity that inevitably comes with film-making just didn't suit the two lads from the music-halls, who thrived and prospered on the adrenalin produced when working to a live audience. Added to that the scripts were awful.

They left the BBC to join Thames Television in 1978 mainly on the promise of a feature film, but in 1979 Eric Morecambe had his second heart attack. After he recovered, the team soldiered on, doing less than before, but time was running out for Morecambe and Wise. On 28 May 1984 fate caught up with Eric, and Ernie was left to go it alone.

In their working lives, over 40 years together, they'd come from obscurity to being the top comedians in Britain. They were popular too in many parts of the world but in spite of their BBC TV shows being sold to the USA they were never really able to cross the language barrier and make a real impression on the American audiences.

Ernie Wise now works alone — he's rich enough not to have to, but show business is his life and I guess he'll go on until he drops too.

Tommy Cooper

Tommy Cooper was, in the tradition of W. C. Fields, a conjuror–comedian who appeared to be totally incompetent but who entertained millions of people with his brilliant use of magic tricks to inspire laughter. As with Fields, the real trick was his timing — that indefinable essence of every great comedian.

Tommy Cooper, hugely tall with enormous flat feet and an ingratiating giggle to compensate for his earthy cockney voice, the inevitable fez perched on his dark, curly hair, above all, the air of bewilderment when his tricks went wrong, made him a favourite entertainer both on stage and TV for many years.

His jokes were, to put it mildly, 'corny'. For instance:

> I went to the doctor — I said, 'I've swallowed a spoon.' He said — 'Don't stir for a week.'

And:

> I went into this chemist shop. I said to the chemist, 'Have you got anything to cure hiccups?' He went 'Boo!' I said, 'What did you do that for?' He said, 'It's cured your hiccups.' I said, 'It wasn't for me — it's a bloke outside that's got the hiccups.'

Producing a normal-sized skull from among the paraphernalia that always littered his act he'd say. 'This is the skull of Tutenkhamen.' Then he'd produce another skull, a quarter of the size, and say: 'And this is the skull of Tutankhamen when he was a little boy.' Then he'd laugh in a zany way, and cough as he realized the inadequacy of his patter, and move on to worse jokes and the mayhem of ruined tricks that was his stock in trade:

> A Chinaman went into hospital with yellow jaundice — they put him in a bed with yellow sheets and they couldn't find him.

> I said to the doctor 'I've swallowed a billiard ball.' He said, 'Get to the back of the queue.'

The truth of the matter was that his performance, like his material, defied analysis. There had been many bogus magicians before Cooper appeared on the scene, but certainly in Britain no one came near his charisma and legendary reputation for making people burst into spontaneous laughter. Offstage he was a gentle, amiable man, a gargantuan drinker, usually of champagne, and an incorrigible leg-puller.

Working for Thames Television back in the late 1960s I was given the task of script-editing a Tommy Cooper series. Knowing that in previous series he'd really done nothing more than tell jokes and fumble (intentionally, of course) a number of tricks, I thought we could head him in a new direction — towards situation comedy. Two excellent writers, Johnnie Mortimer and Brian Cooke, were engaged to script the series and I explained my scheme to all concerned. What I proposed was that the show would start with Tommy Cooper doing his spoof magic routine; after a few minutes a trick he was doing would remind him of an incident in his past, then through the medium of a 'ripple dissolve' we'd find Cooper in the situation he'd remembered. At its conclusion, again through the device of a ripple dissolve, we'd bring him back to the present at the moment when he'd left the trick, which he would then complete. With a bit of discreet editing and a few special effects I felt that it would work and, what's more, be a new way of presenting the old master laughter-maker.

Well, it did work. Mortimer and Cooke's scripts were good, Tommy found the idea to his liking, and the series worked very well. Tommy, however, could not resist his addiction to eccentric props. In one situation he was in a shoe shop attempting to buy a pair of shoes that fitted him (as I said, his feet were enormous), and one day in rehearsal he brought with him a large, stuffed toy dog with a movable jaw that opened and shut when he pulled a string. I suppose he'd acquired it from an impecunious ventriloquist, but there it was, in the middle of the shoe-shop sketch, giving, at Cooper's prompting, the occasional 'woof'. The crew and the other actors were duly convulsed but I was a bit puzzled. I asked, 'Why the dog?' Tommy said, 'I don't know. I just thought it was funny.' And indeed funny it was, and it stayed, incongruously, in the sketch.

To Tommy Cooper's way of thinking, if a thing was funny it justified its inclusion. He had a hat routine where, in telling a long and largely incomprehensible story, he'd change into the appropriate hat when a new character appeared in the monologue. They came fast and furious and the hat changing took place at top speed. Then disaster would strike and Tommy would forget where he was in the monologue and have to start again in double quick time, mumbling his way through his lines until he reached the place where he'd fluffed.

It's difficult to describe but was very funny to watch. As my examples of his jokes have shown, Tommy Cooper was no suave sophisticate but he touched depths in his audience that few comedians ever reach, and when he died on stage at the end of a television show in 1987, all who loved the anarchic world of comedy mourned the passing of one of the greats — Tommy Cooper.

BENNY HILL

Benny Hill is a loner. He writes his own material, words and music, devises his own TV shows, lives alone, and has become one of the phenomenal successes of recent television. People laugh at Benny Hill in the sophisticated surroundings of Beverly Hills and in workmen's cottages in London's East End. His TV shows are sold to 93 countries and I know no professional scriptwriter who likes his work.

I have known Benny Hill slightly for many years and like him, but I don't understand his amazing and long-running success. Frankly, one piece of his work is much like another, and his jokes bear a startling resemblance not only to each other but to jokes heard many years ago.

His characters range from sly bumpkins to sly know-alls and were we to meet any one of these creatures in real life we would not be amused. Why is it then that Benny Hill is universally popular? I think that possibly it is because he appeals to the naughty child in us. Laurel and Hardy had that same underlying naughtines in their work, and while their humour was of rebellious children defying mother, Benny Hill's naughtiness seems to be inspired by the early stirrings of adolescent sexuality.

Max Miller was the first of the overtly 'blue comedians' who trumpeted his feelings about sex loud and clear to an audience who had thought the same things but had never dared to voice their private views on the matter. I divine similar qualities in Benny Hill. He says, and indeed *does*, what we at one time or another in our lives have thought and felt. His bumpkins understand what goes on in the barnyard and nod and wink in the knowledge that sex is just around the corner.

The women in Benny Hill's shows are, for the most part, supposed to be titillating or sex-hungry, the men are gross, old, incontinent, and all too real!

Benny Hill's jokes, like those of the late George Formby, are full of the sort of innuendo that went into 'When I'm Cleaning Windows', Formby's song about a window-washer recounting what he's seen, including:

> Honeymooning couples too —
> You'd be surprised the things they do
> When I'm cleaning windows

and the song about a Chinese Laundryman:

> Mr Wu — he's got a naughty eye that flickers
> You ought to see it wobble when he's
> ironing ladies'... blouses.

Curiosity is largely what drives men to buy the *Penthouse* and *Playboy* types of magazine and sends them to nude shows and to watch 'blue' movies on stag nights. It's also the knowledge that the fantasy figures on the glossy pages of magazines, in the strip clubs, and the dirty movies are beyond their reach.

Hill's fantasies — his *on-screen* fantasies — seem to follow that same line of thought. Rather like a man who would rather watch a woman undressing through the keyhole than be with her when she disrobes, so Benny Hill *peeps* at sex. His desires, and therefore those of us who are the viewers, are aroused but not satisfied. The speeded-up motion of many of Benny Hill's sketches also adds to the unreality, and the frequent use of schools, hospitals, and so on as backgrounds to the sketches underline, to me at any rate, some of the stereotypic male fantasies.

The film *Personal Services* shows something of the reality of sexual perversion. Benny Hill's comedy removes at least some of the adult sordidness and replaces it with a kind of schoolboy smut. On the screen and far removed from reality it becomes acceptable.

By saying all this I am by no means denigrating Hill or his work. He is an intelligent man who understands how things are in our society and has taken it upon himself to lift a corner of the veil of sexual fantasy that most of us would neither dare nor care to do.

In a democracy one must acknowledge and respect others' wishes, and in that context one says 'Congratulations' to Benny Hill for having the nerve and insight to be so daring and, in the process, I imagine, to bring a lot of pleasure into the lives of millions.

Marty Feldman

I first met Marty Feldman about 35 years ago. We were both on a music-hall bill at the Empire Theatre in York, Marty with an act called 'Maurice, Marty, and Mitch' — I was doing a single act, some jokes and a song. After initial antagonism over our respective spots on the bill (the later you went on, the more appreciative the audience tended to be) we became friends and remained so until the day he died, tragically, of a heart attack (not helped by his addiction to hard liquor and soft drugs) in Mexico City in 1982 at the age of 49.

We started writing together in the late fifties, first in small TV shows where we performed what we'd written, and later on major radio and TV series. By the mid sixties we were extremely successful and moderately affluent, and I was delighted to put stage work behind me. Marty, however, hankered for stardom. It wasn't enough for him to be associated with a success and to write for a star, he wanted to be a star himself. With Marty, I think it's true to say, the cart always came before the horse; and in a curious way he expected applause before he'd earned it.

His lifestyle, too, reflected his ambition. If I'm not a star, he seemed to say, I will at least live like one. Married, but with no children to tie them down, he and his wife Lauretta were great partygoers, night-clubbers, and, as the song says, 'Fancy free and free for anything fancy.'

Our working life was one of simple progress from small (but enjoyable) radio shows to award-winning TV — a *Daily Mirror* award in 1960 for *Bootsie and Snudge*, a series which starred Alfie Bass and Bill Fraser, and later Writers' Guild awards for *Round the Horne*, a major radio success of the mid sixties, which can still be heard today worldwide as it's often repeated, and the TV show in which Marty finally starred, called *Marty*. That also picked up a British Academy of Film and Television Arts prize, and the Silver Rose at the Light Entertainment Festival at Montreux in Switzerland. Before *Marty*, Marty Feldman had returned to performing in the 1960s TV series *At Last the 1948 Show*, in which he co-starred with John Cleese, Graham Chapman, and Tim Brooke-Taylor. In it he made such an impression that he received offers from all sides, the best of which was from BBC 2, which had just gone from black and white to colour.

After two series of *Marty*, largely written by Marty and me but with impor-tant contributions from Michael Palin and Terry Jones, and John Cleese and Graham Chapman (a quartet subsequently to make up the bulk of *Monty Python's Flying Circus*), Marty went into films, and in particular an opus called *Every Home Should Have One*. The story was by Herbert Kretzmer and Milton Shulman, script by Feldman and Took. It was produced by Ned Sherrin for British Lion, and directed by Jim Clark. It was not a success, although, like the curate's egg, parts of it were excellent.

Then Marty became involved with ATV (the company run at that time by

Lew Grade) in a co-production with the American producer, Greg Garrison, in his series *Golddiggers*. Owing to production difficulties the company had to buy several filmed sketches from the BBC — the ones Marty and I had written for *Marty*. Those sketches, long, complex, and in all modesty very funny, made people in Hollywood sit up and take notice of this strange, new, swivel-eyed comedian from England. Marty was getting nearer to his dream of becoming a Hollywood star.

But first came another British TV series, *The Marty Feldman Comedy Machine*, which also starred Spike Milligan. It was written by a miscellany of people and was patchy. ATV, however, put the good patches together in a compilation which won the Golden Rose of Montreux, a partner for the Silver Rose that Marty had won in 1969. Marty Feldman then went to Hollywood, where he made *Young Frankenstein* and *Silent Movie* for Mel Brooks, *The Adventures of Sherlock Holmes' Smarter Brother* with Gene Wilder, and then signed a six-picture deal with Universal.

Marty invited me to join him at Universal but bad health and work commitments in the UK forced me to refuse. His first film for Universal was *The Last Remake of Beau Geste*, a send-up of the heroics of earlier French Foreign Legion films. Marty confessed to me subsequently that he'd accepted the notion of making the film having confused it with *The Four Feathers* (which is about heroics in the British Army in Sudan). As it turned out, *The Four Feathers* might have been a better vehicle for Marty Feldman as his *Beau Geste* picture was a stinker. His next film, *In God We Trust*, was a total disaster, had terrible write-ups, ran for less than a week after its premiere in the US, and was consigned to oblivion.

This was a body blow to Marty as he not only starred in it but directed it, co-wrote it and edited it, and his wife was one of the producers.

The rest of his Universal contract was scrapped and Marty, who had totally misjudged Hollywood and the movie business, found himself something of a pariah.

Meanwhile, however, Eric Idle, Peter Cook, Spike Milligan, John Cleese, and Graham Chapman were in Mexico making a spoof film about buccaneers, *Yellowbeard the Pirate*, and invited Marty to join them. He did, and must have felt among friends again after his recent traumatic experiences in Hollywood.

He was not, however, to survive the filming and died, as one of his heroes, Tony Hancock, had died — alone in a hotel bedroom.

The Marty Feldman story is not all sad. In his heyday he made a lot of money and won many awards for his work. He always had friends, for he was a likeable man. The burden he carried through his life was a craving for stardom which, when it came, didn't satisfy him and when it left him, destroyed him. All actors are vain but when vanity takes over the personality, the ending can only be tragic.

Marty's thyroid condition, the thing that gave him his pop-eyed look, must have helped to destabilize him, and Marty was a mercurial character. As Mel

Brooks says, 'He was heaven and hell to work with', and it's sad to think that although Marty Feldman touched heaven in his lifetime, he also tasted the bitterness of hell at the end of his short, muddled life.

MORECAMBE AND WISE

FILMS

The Intelligence Men   1965
Produced by Hugh Stewart
Directed by Robert Asher
Written by S. C. Green and R. M. Hills

That Riviera Touch   1966
Produced by Hugh Stewart
Directed by Cliff Owen
Written by S. C. Green, R. M. Hills, and Peter Blackmore

The Magnificent Two   1968
Produced by Hugh Stewart
Directed by Cliff Owen
Written by S. C. Green, R. M. Hills, Michael Pertwee, and Peter Blackmore

TELEVISION

The Morecambe and Wise Show   from 1955 BBC Television
The Morecambe and Wise Show   from 1978 Thames Television

TOMMY COOPER

Many TV shows for BBC and Thames Television

BENNY HILL

Many TV shows for BBC and Thames Television

Marty Feldman

FILMS

Every Home Should Have One 1969
Produced by Ned Sherrin
Directed by James Clark
Written by Marty Feldman, Barry Took, and Denis Norden

Young Frankenstein 1973
Produced by Michael Gruskoff
Directed by Mel Brooks
Written by Mel Brooks and Gene Wilder

The Adventures of Sherlock Holmes' Smarter Brother 1975
Produced by Richard A. Roth
Directed by Gene Wilder
Written by Gene Wilder

Silent Movie 1976
Produced by Michael Hertzberg
Directed by Mel Brooks
Written by Mel Brooks, Ron Clark, Rudy De Luca, and Barry Levinson

The Last Remake of Beau Geste 1977
Produced by William S. Gilmore Jr
Directed by Marty Feldman
Written by Marty Feldman, and Chris J. Allen

In God We Trust 1980
Produced by Universal
Directed by Marty Feldman
Written by Marty Feldman, and Chris J. Allen

Yellowbeard the Pirate 1983
Produced by Carter de Haven Jr
Directed by Mel Damski
Written by Graham Chapman, Peter Cook, and Bernard McKenna

TELEVISION

At Last the 1948 Show 1967 Rediffusion
Marty 2 series 1968–9 BBC
The Marty Feldman Comedy Machine 1970 ATV

46

DUDLEY MOORE

It's tough to write about friends. It's all too easy to write a 'press handout' sort of essay, in which your hero glows with an unreal light and whose virtues are lauded beyond the point of belief. Another pitfall is the 'I know him well and he's a good friend but here he is, warts and all' type of piece, which all too often turns out to be totally made up of warts, and criticizes the alleged friend more fiercely than does his most scathing critic.

To be frank, I don't know how nice Dudley Moore *is* deep down. From what I know of him he's as nice as anyone in the shark-infested waters of show business has any right to be. Oh, sure, there's steel in there. You can't be that good a musician — and Dudley Moore is a very fine musician indeed — without developing a quickness of hand, eye, and ear, tremendous self-discipline, and a basic solidity that is often lacking in other, equally talented, comic actors. Perhaps it's the music in the man that makes the difference. It's surprising how many top comedians are also musicians. Jack Benny, Harpo and Chico Marx, Peter Sellers (albeit not very good) were; Mel Brooks in his youth had lessons in drumming from the great Buddy Rich. Even George Burns sings, although whether that can be classed as musicianship or bravado it's hard to say, and anyone who has seen Barry Humphries as Sir Les Patterson playing the guitar will have been deeply moved.

Dudley Moore is, to my certain knowledge, both a fine jazz pianist and a first-rate classical pianist and organist too. In fact, he went to Oxford on an organ scholarship, and that led him eventually to meeting Peter Cook, Alan Bennett, and Jonathan Miller, and becoming part of the intimate revue to end them all — literally so as it turned out — *Beyond the Fringe*.

Dudley Moore says that he felt inferior to the others who were, he thought, vastly his intellectual superiors. They weren't, of course, but today, many years after the event, Dudley still feels that he was different from the others; as he said to me at a recent meeting, 'I didn't think the way they did. I felt the odd man out. I often wondered what I was doing in their company.'

What he was doing, of course, was what he has done throughout his career: bringing warmth and charm and a beguiling innocence to the otherwise somewhat cerebral show. Dudley is, in short, enchanting. Let me demonstrate.

49

Back in the days of the dinosaurs (that's to say 1971) I was a television producer working for the BBC in their comedy department. One project in which I was involved was a TV series for leading comedy actress Sheila Hancock. Each programme had a theme — the theatre, ecology, women's lib, and so forth — and was a mixture of song, sketch, and chat with an appropriate guest.

When it came to the programme on music my first thought was to invite André Previn, at that time resident in London, and the Korean violin virtuoso, Kyung Wha Chung. 'That would be fine,' said Previn's agent, 'both are available to do it. Just one thing — you'll have to take the London Symphony Orchestra as well.' Unfortunately, our budget didn't run to paying an entire orchestra so I had to rethink, and out of the rethinking came the idea of booking Dudley Moore. I was delighted when he said yes to appearing on the show which, for the record, was called *But Seriously — It's Sheila Hancock*, and intended only to be funny in parts.

One sketch that I bought for Sheila and Dudley was a parody of *Brief Encounter*, where a lady singer whose husband would only let her sing melody meets a gentleman whose wife will only let him sing harmony. They sit at separate tables in a railway station buffet, one whistles a tune, the other joins in, they talk, and fall in love, and plan a perfect future where he will sing melody and she will harmonize.

Well, that was the plan. The buffet set was a perfect replica of the one in *Brief Encounter* where Trevor Howard and Celia Johnson had their emotional meetings, and the costumes were to be in that same (1940s) period. All went well at rehearsals, however, when it came to the recording, Sheila looked fine in her tailored suit — but Dudley, in double-breasted fawn raincoat and trilby hat, looked faintly ridiculous. No — come to think of it, he looked ludicrous. They started the sketch and, after a few lines, Sheila giggled. They started again and Dudley giggled. At the third attempt they both giggled, and after that, for at least four more takes, one or the other would break down in tears of unsuppressible mirth. By now the studio audience were screaming with uncontrollable laughter and I decided that, as clearly the sketch was never going to emerge coherently, we might as well abandon it and go on to the next item.

Over 15 years later I can recall the incident clearly. Dudley did his best, but he looked so funny in the forties hat and coat meant for someone of Trevor Howard's stature, and with his innocent face belied by twinkling eyes suggesting a whole world of mischief, we could never have completed the sketch. And if you don't believe me, just try whistling while you're laughing.

Dudley Moore wasn't always laughing. At school, being less than average height, he — like so many before and since — had to survive not through brute strength but by making his fellows laugh. He was born on 19 April 1935 in Dagenham, a working-class suburb of London famous mainly for the Ford motorcar factory, and a music-hall act of the thirties and forties called 'The Dagenham Girl Pipers'. This consisted of a group of girls who dressed in kilt and sporran and played the bagpipes, and was quite an attraction in its day.

When he was young, a club foot made his life a long procession of hospital visits and a good deal of his time was spent, frustratingly, in a wheelchair. He is quoted as saying, 'It was my leg on to which I projected all my feelings of inadequacy and self-loathing.' To have emerged from that ordeal so well-balanced and outgoing is a tribute to his intelligence and sense of humour, and to the loving care of his parents.

At Magdalen College, Oxford, he felt ill at ease with all the ex-public-school boys around him and intimidated by their self-confident middle-class accents. After initially attempting to copy them, he settled for being himself. Today he can talk as he wishes and in fact his easily understood English accent must have played a part in his success with American audiences. It's difficult for an Englishman accurately to imitate an American, and harder still for an American to imitate a Brit.

Mel Brooks on one of his LPs gives a startling impression of an English film director with the most outrageous cockney accent I have ever heard — its accuracy, if a bit overblown, indicates what a good ear Mr Brooks has.

It was Dudley Moore's 'ear' that elevated him above most of his contemporaries. His musicianship developed early, and whilst studying serious music for a degree, he started playing jazz piano for his, and others', pleasure. A blessed habit, which persists to the present day and which, in the Sheila Hancock programme mentioned earlier, revealed itself in the Brahms Variations on a theme by Handel in a series of breathtaking jazz variations of a quite compelling authority and style.

The whole *Fringe* idea came originally from Robert Ponsonby, who was the organizer of the Edinburgh Festival, that annual arts shindig in Scotland's capital city. There had always been plays, revues, etc., outside the main events of the Festival but in 1960 Robert Ponsonby felt that it would be a good idea to have an 'official' revue.

Ponsonby's assistant, John Bassett, an Oxford graduate and a friend of Dudley's, suggested Moore, and Moore suggested fellow Oxford man Alan Bennett, who had done occasional sketches and monologues adding two Cambridge men, Jonathan Miller, who was by now a qualified doctor, and Peter Cook, a fully fledged professional writer suggested by Miller. The four met, 'disliked each other on sight', and decided it might be a worthwhile venture. The show was made up of old sketches, individual monologues, and so on, plus new and topical material.

The word 'satire' was much bandied about at the time, and so it was thought that, with its sketches about capital punishment, black Africa, the H-bomb, and the myths of the Second World War, *Beyond the Fringe*, a title devised by Robert Ponsonby, was *satire* — and thus OK. OK it certainly was, and to people brought up on the older style of West End revue, which was very much name-dropping and poking fun at the English lower middle classes, new and amazing.

To give an example of the old — that is, pre-1960 — style of revue, items from one Shaftesbury Avenue success, *For Amusement Only* (which ran from 1956 to 1958 and for over 700 performances) included a lampoon of Liberace, a parody of *This is Your Life*, a sketch combining Laurence Olivier's *Richard III* with a send-up of a fictional film about Eton College, a number about Marilyn Monroe, and another number called in the programme 'Going our Whey', the details of which, mercifully, I have forgotten, but which gives you the slightly campy flavour of the material that found favour in London's West End in the fifties.

Beyond the Fringe found fresher targets in the politicians of the day and the absurd but well-meant advice from the government that in the event of a nuclear attack, brown paper would guard you against radiation. Dudley Moore's contributions were mainly musical — a version of 'Little Miss Muffet' as it might have been arranged by Benjamin Britten and sung by Peter Pears, and a piano arrangement of 'Colonel Bogey', which Dudley began well but, when nearing its conclusion, seemed unable to resolve with one final, crashing chord. Dudley prolonged the ending by improvising as he went until the audience were convulsed with laughter. He played speaking roles in the show too, but he was, in that area, a minor voice in comparison with Miller, Bennett, and Cook. *Beyond the Fringe* was a success in Edinburgh when it opened in August 1960 and a sensation when it opened at the Fortune Theatre in London in 1961.

The original cast went to New York in 1962 leaving a second company in London, which took the show on until 1966. In New York, Dudley Moore, Peter Cook, Alan Bennett, and Jonathan Miller were a huge success and the show ran for a year. In 1954 a second American company took over and the original group disbanded.

Dudley Moore and Peter Cook teamed up as a television double act in a series called *Not Only ... But Also* which contained such gems as the sketch 'One Leg Too Few', in which Cook as a theatrical producer interviews Dudley as the one-legged actor auditioning for the role of Tarzan.

COOK: Need I point out to you where your deficiency lies as regards landing this role.
MOORE: Yes, I think you ought to.
COOK: Need I say with over-much emphasis that it is in the leg division that you are deficient.
MOORE: The leg division?
COOK: Yes, the leg division, Mr Spiggott. You are deficient in it to the tune of one. Your right leg I like. I like your right leg. A lovely leg for the role. That's what I said when I saw it come in. I said, 'A lovely leg for the role.' I've nothing against your right leg. The trouble is — neither have you.

The dialogue, good as it is, gives only a partial idea of how funny Dudley made the sketch, hopping nimbly about on one leg, convinced he would make an excellent Tarzan.

The two best-remembered characters to emerge from *Not Only ... But Also* were Dud and Pete, two ignoramuses fantasizing in a surreal way about their love lives. Pete was the dominant idiot. Dud the receptive one whose role it was to spin even more foolish and incompetent fantasies than his opposite number. Here's a typical example:

DUD: Did I tell you about that girl Joan Harold who I used to know? She used to travel on the 148 bus route a lot ... Six o' clock every evening she used to get the 148 bus home. I used to leave work about five o' clock, as you know, about ten miles from where she was, but I always felt I had to see her so what I used to do, I used to come out of work, I used to get the 62B up to Chadwell Heath Merry Fiddlers, then I used to go down the hill and get the 514 trolley down to Rainham Crescent. Then I used to go over by the railway bridge and go across those fields by the dye works ... I'd come out the other side by the hedge by which time the 148 bus, the six o' clock one was coming round the corner, Hobbs Hill. Now it used to come round very slowly, 'cos it was a very sharp turn and there's no bus stop there, but it used to be very slow. If it was going too fast I used to lay down in the middle of the road, but what I used to do I used to leap on the platform as it went past 'cos I knew she was on that bus.

PETE: What happened then Dud?

DUD: Well, I used to lay panting on the platform for about ten minutes.

There's reams more and many published collections and LPs have chronicled the doings of Dud and Pete.

The success of Dudley Moore and Peter Cook led to films. Their first, *The Wrong Box*, had a distinguished cast, including Ralph Richardson, John Mills, Peter Sellers, and Tony Hancock, but was neither terribly good nor terribly popular and, in spite of a few neat touches, didn't really do much to enhance their reputation. Their next film together was *Bedazzled*, a reworking by Cook of the Faust story, with Dudley as a short-order chef in a fast-food restaurant, and Peter Cook as the Devil. Here's a snatch of the dialogue. Dudley, in the character of Stanley, asks Spiggott, the Devil's temporarily assumed name, how he got started.

SPIGGOTT: It was pride that got me into this.

STANLEY: Oh, yes, you used to be God's favourite, didn't you?

SPIGGOTT: That's right. 'I love Lucifer' it used to be in those days.

The film wasn't a great hit but for Dudley it was laying the ground for a film career that was eventually to blast him into the orbit of international stardom.

First, however, came a series of movies that were only mildly successful. One of the first was *Thirty is a Dangerous Age, Cynthia*, co-written by Dudley, John Wells (one of the leaders of the post *Beyond the Fringe* satire boom), and Joe McGrath (the first director of *Not Only ... But Also*), who had moved from TV to films and also directed *Thirty is a Dangerous Age*. Dudley was reunited with Peter Cook in *Monte Carlo or Bust*, which was intended as a hilarious follow-up to *Those Magnificent Men in Their Flying Machines*, but flopped, and that was followed by the film version of the Spike Milligan and John Antrobus play, *The Bed Sitting Room*.

In 1971 Dudley Moore and Peter Cook joined forces again in Australia for a couple of television 'specials' and a stage show. They called it *Behind the Fridge*, a title which originated in New York in their *Fringe* days: the owner of a Manhattan delicatessen was forever telling them how much he liked their show the title of which he rendered as 'Behind the Fridge'. It opened in London in 1972 and ran for a time at the Cambridge Theatre. It was patchy but at its best very funny indeed, and in fact did better in New York where, retitled *Good Evening*, it ran from October 1973 to November 1974 and subsequently toured from February to August 1975.

Their next joint film venture was *The Hound of the Baskervilles*, in which they played Sherlock Holmes and Doctor Watson. It was directed by Paul Morrisey, produced by John Goldstone (the man behind most of the *Monty Python* film successes) and was, frankly, awful.

They then added insult to injury with the 'Derek and Clive' tapes. As Derek and Clive, Peter Cook and Dudley Moore are really only doing a dirty version of Dud and Pete and I'm afraid the humour is not to my taste. That there is a market for it I have no doubt, and it says something about what one section of the public wants. But as other sections of the public also seem to want to drive cars when drunk, take drugs, rob banks, infect each other with AIDS, pollute the environment, and beat up or shoot anyone who doesn't conform to their way of thinking, I'm not totally convinced by the 'market-place' philosophy, which accepts that anything that makes a profit or which people care to do is OK. However, 'Derek and Clive' was a fragment of Dudley Moore's professional life and both in music and films he has succeeded beyond most of his contemporaries.

In 1978, he teamed up with Goldie Hawn in a rather mediocre film, *Foul Play*, and a year later, in Blake Edwards's *10*, which co-starred Julie Andrews and Bo Derek, he was able, possibly for the first time, to break away from the eternally comical; in this film his acting has a good deal of reality and moments of genuine sadness and despair. Sessions with a psychiatrist have helped him to realize his ambitions and gain confidence. In consequence his talent has flowered and the sureness of touch that has always characterized his music is there for all to see in his current film work.

In 1981, he made *Arthur*, in which he played a drunken playboy who becomes besotted with a working-class girl (Liza Minelli) and kept from disaster by his poker-faced English butler, played to the hilt by Sir John Gielgud.

I think it polite to mention *Santa Claus, The Movie* and move swiftly on to Dudley's latest film (at the time of writing), a sequel to *Arthur*, entitled *Arthur on the Rocks*. If *Arthur on the Rocks* is half as good as the film that inspired it, success is certain.* The writer/director of the original *Arthur*, Steve Gordon, died tragically, shortly after the film was released, but he did live to see it succeed in a

*N.B. It isn't! B.T., 1989.

remarkable way and confirm what most of us had believed for some time — that Dudley Moore (acting) drunk or (really) sober is a major star.

Arthur, on the face of it, is an unpromising story. A rich young man, chronically drunk, picks up prostitutes. He's asked: 'What are you looking for?' He answers 'VD — I'm into penicillin!' and shrieks with laughter. At first you are repelled by the film's ugliness but before long the skill of the writing and direction take you through the barrier of the film's tastelessness and you begin to see behind the grossness of Arthur's behaviour to the pain he's suffering.

The one solid factor in his life is his valet, Hobson, played with distinction by Sir John Gielgud. Hobson also gets the best lines, as when Arthur informs him he's going to take a bath and Hobson replies disdainfully, 'I'll alert the media.'

Arthur meets Linda in a Park Avenue store. She's shoplifting a tie (for her father's birthday), but when the store detective nabs her, Arthur comes to her rescue and pays for the tie. He then introduces her to Hobson, and the valet courteously remarks: 'How nice to meet you. Usually one must go to a bowling alley to meet a woman of your calibre.' When Arthur suggests a date and she asks, 'What should I wear?' Hobson advises her to 'steal something casual'.

Hobson dies, Arthur is again alone and reverts to his habitual drunkenness; forced into a marriage he doesn't want and desperately in love with Linda. At the last moment he sacrifices all for love, takes a beating from his would-be father-in-law, and winds up with the girl, and the fortune too.

It's a wry, amusing film full of delightful touches of direction, writing, and performance, and Dudley Moore handles the part of Arthur in a way I can imagine no other actor, British or American, would find possible.

That this easy-going, often imposed-upon lad from an English working-class background, with a handicap to balance his musical flair should have overcome so many hurdles in his life to arrive at what is, I'm sure, more than a temporary period of emotional calm, success, and quiet self-confidence, is an inspiration to us all.

And the future? We can only wait and see what heights the 'adorable' Dudley Moore can reach.

FILMS

These include:

The Wrong Box   1966
Produced by Bryan Forbes
Directed by Bryan Forbes
Written by Larry Gelbart, and Burt Shevelove, from the novel by Robert Louis Stevenson and Lloyd Osborne

Thirty is a Dangerous Age, Cynthia   1967
Produced by Walter Shenson
Directed by Joe McGrath
Written by Dudley Moore, Joe McGrath, and John Wells

Bedazzled   1968
Produced by Stanley Donen
Directed by Stanley Donen
Written by Peter Cook

Those Daring Young Men in Their Jaunty Jalopies   1969
also known as *Monte Carlo or Bust*
Produced by Ken Annakin, and Basil Keys
Directed by Ken Annakin
Written by Jack Davies and Ken Annakin

The Bed Sitting Room   1969
Produced by Richard Lester
Directed by Richard Lester
Written by John Antrobus, from the play by John Antrobus and Spike Milligan

Alice's Adventures in Wonderland   1972
Produced by Derek Horne
Directed by William Sterling
Written by William Sterling

Foul Play   1978
Produced by Thomas L. Miller and Edward K. Milkis
Directed by Colin Higgins
Written by Colin Higgins

10   1979
Produced by Blake Edwards and Tony Adams
Directed by Blake Edwards
Written by Blake Edwards

The Hound of the Baskervilles   1980
Produced by John Goldstone
Directed by Paul Morrisey
Written by Peter Cook, Dudley Moore, and Paul Morrisey

Wholly Moses   1980
Produced by David Begelman
Directed by Gary Weis
Written by Guy Thomas

Arthur   1981
Produced by Robert Greenhut
Directed by Steve Gordon
Written by Steve Gordon

Six Weeks   1982
Produced by Peter Guber and John Peters
Directed by Tony Bill
Written by David Seltzer, from the novel by Fred Mustard Stewart

Romantic Comedy   1983
Produced by Walter Mirisch and Morton Gottleib
Directed by Arthur Hiller
Written by Bernard Slade, from his play

Lovesick   1983
Produced by Charles Okun
Directed by Marshall Brickman
Written by Marshall Brickman

Unfaithfully Yours   1983
Produced by Marvin Worth and Joe Wizan
Directed by Howard Zieff
Written by Valerie Curtin, Barry Levinson, and Robert Klane

Best Defense   1984
Produced by Gloria Katz
Directed by Willard Huyck
Written by Gloria Katz and Willard Huyck, from the novel *Easy and Hard Ways Out* by Robert Grossbach

Micki and Maude   1984
Produced by Tony Adams
Directed by Blake Edwards
Written by Jonathan Reynolds

Santa Claus, The Movie   1985
Produced by Ilya Salkind and Pierre Spengler
Directed by Jeannot Szwarc
Written by David Newman

Like Father Like Son   1987
Produced by Brian Grazer and David Valdes
Directed by Rod Daniel
Written by Lorne Cameron and Steven L. Bloom

Arthur II — Arthur on the Rocks   1988
Produced by Robert Shapiro
Directed by Bud Yorkin
Written by Andy Breckman

TELEVISION

Not Only ... But Also   3 series 1965–71 BBC
Goodbye Again   1968 ITV

MEL BROOKS

In 1981 Mel Brooks was filmed in his office at Twentieth Century Fox in Hollywood for the prestigious BBC arts programme, *Arena*. The interview was largely to promote Brooks's latest film, *The History of the World, Part One*, but with the astute prompting of the interviewer, Alan Yentob, who was also the producer of the BBC film, Mel Brooks not only gave a bravura performance but also, incidentally, revealed a lot about himself.

Born Melvin Kaminsky in Brooklyn on 28 June 1926, the fourth son of Jewish immigrants, he grew up into a short, neat, funny young man and by the time he was in his early 20s was one of a band of talented writers (including Larry Gelbart, Neil Simon, Carl Reiner, and Woody Allen) who created the fifties Sid Caesar TV hit, *Your Show of Shows*. In the process Brooks developed an amazing capacity for improvising dialogue which was to bear fruit in the late fifties and early sixties in the recordings of *The 2000-Year-Old Man*, and other delights. What started as a party turn, with Carl Reiner suggesting a character which Brooks would then adopt, developed into a series of best-selling LPs. Here is an example: the 2000-year-old man describing a discovery more important than fire or the wheel — sex. At first ...

BROOKS: We didn't know who was the ladies and who was fellers.
REINER: You thought they were just different types of fellers?
BROOKS: Yes — stronger, or smaller, or softer — the softer ones I think were ladies all the time.
REINER: How did you find out?
BROOKS: A cute fat guy; you could have mistaken him for a lady ... soft and cute.
REINER: Who was the person who discovered the female?
BROOKS: Bernie!
REINER: How did it happen?
BROOKS: He said, 'Hey, there's ladies here.'
REINER: But how did it come to pass?
BROOKS: Well, one morning he got up smiling. He said, 'I think there's ladies here.' So I said, 'What do you mean?' and he said, 'In the night I was thrilled and delighted.' So then he went into such a story — it's hundreds of years later, I still blush.

REINER: Sir, could you give us the secret of your longevity.

BROOKS: Well, the major thing — is that I never ever touch fried food. I don't eat it. I wouldn't look at it, and I don't touch it. And never run for a bus, there'll always be another. Even if you're late for work ... I never ran I just strolled, jaunty, jolly, walking to the bus stop.

REINER: But there were no buses in those days. What was the means of transport then?

BROOKS: Mostly fear.

REINER: Fear transported you?

BROOKS: Yes. You see, an animal would growl — you'd go two miles in a minute.

Reiner and Brooks together cooked up a number of such characters ranging from London-born film directors to a wide variety of psychiatrists, and even a newborn baby — given, for a few moments at least a precocious power of speech. Here is the newborn Brooks talking to Carl Reiner about the mother he is yet to meet face to face.

REINER: Do you hope she is good looking?

BROOKS: I don't care what she looks like. I'm not going to date her. I'm her child. But I know she's good, because you can tell a person by what they are inside ... I remember when I was a little tadpole swimming around.

REINER: Do you remember having a tail?

BROOKS: Sure. That was the best part. I loved the tail.

REINER: Were you unhappy when it disappeared?

BROOKS: When I lost my tail, I got a nose ... The nose is much more important because — you can't blow your tail.

In Alan Yentob's *Arena* film, Brooks muses on his Jewishness. They are talking about his childhood and Yentob asks, 'Was there anything special about being Jewish in Brooklyn at that time?'

BROOKS: No, everybody was. Every single human being in Brooklyn was a Jew at that point. So there was nothing special — it was quite ordinary. A pedestrian thing to be. I went to Manhattan and I met all these Gentiles and it was a little frightening. I said, My God, you mean there are all these people besides Jews in the world? We never felt any anti-Semitism any strangeness — [But] Had we been transported to Nebraska or Kansas or Abilene Texas, yes — we would have felt ...

Here he puts on the Brooks version of a Texas drawl and works himself into a routine as a Texas oil millionaire.

BROOKS: I got myself a Jew. I wanted an Airedale but I got myself a Jew instead, and it can do anything. Ostensibly it's my accountant but it's cuter than an accountant. It can count, it don't even need a pencil.

He develops the theme:

BROOKS: Every night you take a little matzo — that's what they eat — you put that in their dish with a little water to soften them up because it'll cut their gums. You don't want a little Jew bleeding all over your carpet. You give them the matzos and the little Jews they love you for it. They're wonderful people — and I'm going to get another one — a female, and I'm gonna breed them. I'm gonna breed these little Jews and I'm gonna sell them as little Jew accountants all over Texas.

Jew, Jewish, Jewishness comes into everything Mel Brooks says. When I visited him at Twentieth Century Fox in 1988 he peppered his remarks with such references as 'That little Jew we were talking too'. He described an amiable discussion he had with a waiter as to what we should have for lunch as 'that argument between the Jew and the waiter'. A colleague from his writing days — a Jew himself incidentally — once got so irritated by it that he threatened Brooks with terminal violence. Brooks's reaction was to jump on to the table and shout at the top of his voice, 'So, I'm working with God now. A being who holds sway over life and death.' His colleague's anger cooled and he said, 'OK, Mel, forget it.' At which Mel Brooks climbed down from the table and they got back to work, Brooks remarking, 'God is a Jew too, you know.'

I can't imagine a conversation in which Mel Brooks does not have the last word, and though I think he feels he glides through life in a charming and saintly way (a Jewish saint, naturally), he can get people's backs up.

Marty Feldman confessed to me that he hated working with Mel as he'd be put into acting situations for which he wasn't prepared — literally pushed in front of the camera to play the scene. But as both *Young Frankenstein*, and *Silent Movie*, in which Marty Feldman appeared, were big box-office successes and, regrettably, nothing else that Marty did in the cinema was, perhaps in Mel Brooks's madness there is method. Mel says of Marty Feldman, 'He was a genius, a truly surrealistic comic, a living Chagall. He was heaven and hell to work with — heaven because he was so creative and inventive and superbly talented; hell because he was such a compulsive detailist. We often had to do 30 takes to satisfy his obsession with perfection.'

The Brooks philosophy is simple and his advice to actors is: 'Don't take yourself too seriously. You're not made of marble, you're only flesh and blood. We're only here [on earth] fleetingly, so let's enjoy ourselves. We should be humble at the vast temporariness of it all.'

In a brilliant profile of Mel Brooks in the 30 October 1978 edition of the *New Yorker* magazine, the late Kenneth Tynan quotes Woody Allen, who, I suppose, could be said to be of comparable stature to Mel Brooks, as saying: 'I hear there's a sense of enjoyment on Mel's set. I hear the people on his movies love the experience so much that they wish it could go on forever. On my movies, they're *thrilled* when it's over.'

Like Allen, Brooks is concerned with love and death and insists on the seriousness of his work. His first film, *The Producers*, which he wrote and directed, started as a novel that he attempted to write when *Your Show of Shows* was abruptly cancelled in 1959 and his income dropped from 5000 dollars a week to zero. The title of the novel was *Springtime for Hitler* and that was the original title of the film. Brooks was advised that with a title like that no Jew would go to see it, and so the title was changed. It's known as *Springtime for Hitler* in Sweden, however, and many of Brooks's films there have the 'Springtime' tag — e.g. *Springtime for Frankenstein* instead of the generally used title, *Young Frankenstein*.

The Producers, with major performances from Gene Wilder as the young accountant, Leopold Bloom, lured into a theatrical swindle, and Zero Mostel as the swindler, Max Bialystock, is a wild and exciting film. The plot is to make money by inveigling a number of little old ladies into investing in a show that's bound to flop — the various 'investments' being many times what the show costs and can take at the box office if it's a success. The trick is to find a show that is bound to fold, leaving the producers to pocket the surplus donated by the backers. The show they pick, a musical called *Springtime for Hitler*, looks doomed to failure, but to the amazement and horror of Bialystock and Leopold Bloom it becomes a kitch success.

When it was first shown *The Producers* received poor reviews but gained a cult following and made a little profit. It even won an Oscar for Best Screenplay in 1968 and since then, of course, on re-runs and TV sales, it's notched up a fair profit and can be seen to be a very good film indeed. But at the time it opened it wasn't greeted warmly by either critics or public. In fact, like most of Mel Brooks's pictures, it needs to be seen a second or third time to get the full flavour.

His next film, *The Twelve Chairs*, opened in 1970 and was (and still is to my mind) a flop. Watching it on TV recently it seemed joyless and much too *careful* for a comedy. Ron Moody in the leading role doesn't sparkle and the only saving grace is Mel Brooks's appearance as a drink-sodden janitor. The film is set in post-revolution Russia and the plot is simply the search for diamonds thought to be hidden in one of a set of dining chairs.

In spite of a successful TV series co-written with Buck Henry, a spy spoof starring Don Adams and Barbara Feldon called *Get Smart*, which ran for several seasons from 1965, and a cartoon film called *The Critic*, which he concocted with an animator friend, Ernie Pintoff, in 1962, and which consists of a sequence of abstract shapes with Mel Brooks's voice on the sound track, puzzled and suspicious of what he's watching, Mel Brooks was by 1973 still not in the big time.

The big time came with his next film, *Blazing Saddles*. In it he set about destroying every myth about the Old West that still lingered — and just about succeeded in doing so. The black sheriff, the blowsy nightclub entertainer, the drunken gunfighter, the effects on the cowboys of a diet of pork and beans, a group of negro railroad workers harmonizing 'I Get a Kick Out of You' when asked to sing 'one of them nigger songs', the mutton-headed townsfolk revering Randolph Scott, the line-up of baddies, including Nazi stormtroopers, Arab terrorists, and members of the Ku Klux Klan, the hanging judge so obsessed with his mission he sentences both rider and his horse to the big drop — almost every frame of the film contains some raspberry in the direction of the status quo.

The film, in spite of an initially negative reaction from the management was a wow with the public and made a lot of money for both Warner Brothers and Mel Brooks. His next venture was a Brookish version of a thirties Frankenstein film, *Young Frankenstein*. It was shot in black and white (much to the disquiet of the studio bosses), starred Gene Wilder, Madeleine Kahn, Peter Boyle, Marty Feldman, Cloris Leachman, with a guest appearance by Gene Hackman as the blind philosopher.'How strange are the ways of God to send a man who cannot speak to visit a man who cannot see', he says as the monster blunders around causing unimaginable mayhem. It's a film, I suppose like all of Mel Brooks's pictures, that has its longueurs — moments when the comedy doesn't come to life — as if the master was out of breath for a moment, but when he does get his breath back the comedy is brilliant, original, and sparkling.

Having hit the people who call the tune in Hollywood with a Western send-up and a black and white parody of a horror film what could possibly come next? What came next was *Silent Movie*. But ... a *silent* movie? Yes — and, like the story of the man who asks a friend who has just acquired a 350-pound gorilla: 'Where does it sleep?', and gets the reply: 'Anywhere it wants to', so Mel Brooks could, and did, make exactly the film he wanted, *Silent Movie*.

In it he discharged some of his dislike of the big corporations that were taking over the film companies by inventing the fictitious, multinational corporation, Engulf and Devour, whose chairman frothed at the mouth when thwarted and who would go to any lengths to stop the silent movie being made. Based on the all-too-common fact that unless their films make a profit studios get sold to the highest bidder (Columbia is now owned by Coca Cola), the plot of *Silent Movie* is simply that if the film is made the studio will be saved from Engulf and Devour, and the action of the picture is a quest to find guest stars to appear in it.

There are, in addition, scenes where Brooks, Marty Feldman, and Dom De Luise perform a Mexican cabaret act as a means of enticing Anne Bancroft to make an appearance in their film. Mel Funn, the producer (played by Brooks), whose career has been destroyed by drinking, is now 'on the wagon'; but he falls off it, and performs a hilarious drunk scene that climaxes in a tableau of alcoholic down and outs to whom, thanks to a giant bottle of bourbon he has bought for the soirée, Brooks is King.

There are many broad knockabout scenes involving guest stars James Caan, Liza Minelli, Burt Reynolds, and Paul Newman, and perhaps the funniest of all, Brooks's wife, Anne Bancroft, who by doing things with her eyes — swivelling them this way and that as if they are independent of each other — manages to outshine even Marty Feldman. There is also a typical Mel Brooks touch: the only person to speak in the film is Marcel Marceau, the French mime.

As head of the studio Mel Brooks cast his old boss, Sid Caesar, on whose television series, *Your Show of Shows*, Mel had worked back in the 1950s. In his *New Yorker* profile of Mel Brooks of October 1978, Kenneth Tynan calls Mel: 'A member of the renowned menagerie of authors whose scripts as interpreted by Caesar, Imogene Coca and a talented supporting cast had made *Your Show of Shows* a golden landmark in the wasteland of television comedy.'

Another of the menagerie was Carl Reiner, writer/performer and subsequently director of such films as *Oh God!*, and in 1953 Reiner and Brooks met and became, as I mentioned earlier, not only friends but creators of some of the funniest ad lib interviews ever to be heard on record. Reiner said to Tynan apropos these improvisations, 'I never told Mel what it was going to be, but I always tried for something that would force him to go into panic, because a brilliant mind in panic is a wonderful thing to see.' The panic I wouldn't know about, but there's no doubt about the brilliant mind. *Silent Movie* is simple, and brilliant in its simplicity.

High Anxiety, made in 1977, is an uneven but successful film that opens with a twist on an old Charles Addams cartoon in which every member of a theatre audience is crying except for Addams's ghoulish first-nighter, who is laughing his head off. Mel Brooks turns the tables on this by showing us an aeroplane coming in to land with a smiling face at every window except for Brooks, who looks terrified. The film is a compendium of parodies of various Alfred Hitchcock movies, including *The Birds* and *Psycho*, plus a touch of tongue-in-cheek with a send-up of a scene from one of that year's big successes, *Marathon Man*.

In *High Anxiety* Mel Brooks was producer, director — 'In self-defence' — co-author along with Barry Levinson, Rudy De Luca, and Ron Clark, writer of the title song, which he sings in the film in a laudable send-up of the Frank Sinatra/Tony Bennett school of schmaltz and, of course, star. He plays a psychiatrist in San Francisco for a convention, and the comedy bubbles happily along from one crisis to another with what Mel Brooks describes as 'lunatic class'.

Like Woody Allen — of whom Mel Brooks says with genuine regret, 'Why doesn't he want to be funny any more?' — Brooks has made movies in which he doesn't appear, *The Fly*, a horror film, being one, and *My Favorite Year* being another. This was a nostalgic reminiscence of Mel Brooks's own youth when, as a junior member of the *Your Show of Shows* scriptwriting team, he had to cope with the extraordinary but endearing behaviour of Errol Flynn, played with great style in *My Favorite Year* by Peter O'Toole.

The History of the World — Part I was a period romp in which Brooks starred but which was, for all that, to me, something of a disappointment. Brooks says of the film: '*History of the World — Part I* was a great experience for me. I wrote it all by myself except for sharing music and lyric credit with Ronnie Graham for

'The Inquisition'. It's unique in that it's a revue, a form very rarely used in American cinema.' He adds, tongue-in-cheek, 'I was superb as King Louis because I am basically a tyrant and a letch so the character came to me easily. However, in the Roman Empire my character, Comicus, was really just a Bob Hope impression, more or less sticking things together.' But he adds, 'I personally rate it with my best work.'

More recently came a remake of the 1941 Lubitsch picture *To Be or Not To Be*, in which a Polish theatrical troupe attempt to evade the Nazis. The original starred Jack Benny and Carole Lombard, and in the remake Brooks's wife, Anne Bancroft, played opposite him. It's a film full of marvellous moments but the depiction of the Gestapo in a comedy is always fairly dicey (as witness the British TV series *'Allo 'Allo!*) and references to concentration camps in the form of a joke — at one point Brooks/Benny posing as the Gestapo officer has to say, with a note of self-approval, 'Oh, so they call me Concentration Camp Erhardt do they?' — still strikes a chill note because although Nazis may be funny, concentration camps are certainly not. However, this is to quibble about a film in which both Anne Bancroft and Mel Brooks shine.

Mel Brooks's latest film (as I write) is *Spaceballs*, a parody of all the outer space fantasies of the *Star Wars* school, and has some funny moments and tremendous production values. Mel Brooks's mother, wishing him luck with the movie, is supposed to have said, 'Son, I hope it makes a million.' To which he replied, 'But, Ma — it cost *22* million to make.'

Ensconsed in a homely but active suite of offices at Twentieth Century Fox studios, Mel Brooks can contemplate the future with the calm assurance that comes when you know you're financially way ahead of the field. Today he can make the movies he wants and although several times a week he's offered 'a Mel Brooks movie' he's not going to jump until he feels the project is right.

Looking back, he will find few flops in his career. On television there was the Robin Hood spoof, *When Things Were Rotten*, and in all honesty one must include *The Twelve Chairs* in the 'less-than-great' category; but looking further back he'll see *Your Show of Shows*, and remember the making of the comedy records of which *The 2000-Year-Old Man* alone was enough to make him one of the all-time comedy greats.

Anne Bancroft is a great inspiration, being such a good actor herself and bringing an Italian warmth and emotion to both their private and public lives. Her favourites of Mel's films, by the way, are *The Producers* and *Blazing Saddles*.

Their son, Max has been advised by his father to become an author or a film director on the grounds that both earn prestige and respect. Max's response, according to Mel was: 'I would rather skip a generation and do what my grandfather did so successfully — sell herring.' Quite a family.

MEL BROOKS

FILMS

The Producers   1967
Produced by Sidney Glazier
Directed by Mel Brooks
Written by Mel Brooks

The Twelve Chairs   1970
Produced by Michael Hertzberg
Directed by Mel Brooks
Written by Mel Brooks

Blazing Saddles   1974
Produced by Michael Hertzberg
Directed by Mel Brooks
Written by Mel Brooks, Norman Steinberg, Andrew Bergman, Richard Pryor,
and Alan Uger

Young Frankenstein   1974
Produced by Michael Gruskoff
Directed by Mel Brooks
Written by Mel Brooks and Gene Wilder

Silent Movie   1976
Produced by Michael Hertzberg
Directed by Mel Brooks
Written by Mel Brooks, Ron Clark, Rudy De Luca, and Barry Levinson

High Anxiety   1977
Produced by Mel Brooks
Directed by Mel Brooks
Written by Mel Brooks, Ron Clark, Rudy De Luca, and Barry Levinson

History of the World — Part I   1981
Produced by Mel Brooks
Directed by Mel Brooks
Written by Mel Brooks

My Favorite Year   1982
Produced by Brooksfilms/MGM
Producer Michael Gruskoff
Directed by Richard Benjamin
Written by Norman Steinberg and Dennis Palumbo, from an original story by
Dennis Palumbo

To Be or Not To Be   1983
Produced by Mel Brooks
Directed by Alan Johnson
Written by Thomas Meehan and Ronny Graham

The Fly   1986
Produced by Brooksfilms/Twentieth Century Fox
Producer Stuart Cornfeld
Directed by David Cronenberg
Written by Charles Edward Pogue and David Cronenberg, from a short story
by George Langelaan

Spaceballs   1987
Produced by Mel Brooks
Directed by Mel Brooks
Written by Mel Brooks, Thomas Meehan, and Ronny Graham

Above Lily Tomlin
Above right Goldie Hawn
Right Hermione Gingold

Below Victoria Wood
Below right Mae West

FUNNY LADIES

From time to time people ask why there are no funny ladies, or why there are so few. But the truth is that there have always been many funny ladies on radio, TV, and in the movies — and before that on the music-hall and variety stages. One of the most outstanding of these comediennes has been Lucille Ball (who deserves and gets her own chapter), but there are many more besides.

At the turn of the century, and in fact right up until the coming of talking pictures, the comic stage was dominated by the ladies: Vesta Tilley, Vesta Victoria, Nellie Wallace, Marie Lloyd, Florrie Forde, and Hetty King from the UK; Fanny Brice, Sophie Tucker, Mae West, Gracie Allen, from the USA. On the legitimate side were, for example, Beatrice Lillie, Gertrude Lawrence, Hermione Gingold, and Mary Martin.

In recent years television has proved to be a veritable cornucopia of female talent: early stars like Joan Davis and Lucille Ball (a joke of the fifties based on the titles of their shows was 'I love Lucy but I married Joan') together with their respective co-stars Jim Backus and Desi Arnaz, joined Gracie Allen (with George Burns) and Mary Livingstone (with Jack Benny) in the group at the top of the ratings.

Subsequently, they were joined as top entertainers by the zany performances of Phyllis Diller, who bludgeoned her way to stardom with a grotesque make-up and a searing line of put-down gags about her husband, Fang.

Today, Joan Rivers goes still further in search of laughs, making jokes, not only about people but about parts of their bodies and their various frailties, that teeter on that thin dividing line that separates jokey comment from unfunny insult. It's a tense business being a professional funny man and it must be tougher for a woman who, unless like Mae West she leans heavily on her sexual attraction and implies that she despises convention, must cope with the prejudices that surround a woman being funny.

But why are there these prejudices? A great many people think that it's tied up with the natural respect, and indeed reverence, that the majority of men and women have for their mothers. This makes them unwilling to laugh at a female comedian unless she is so unlike anyone's mother that she avoids this unspoken taboo.

Lily Tomlin first came to prominence doing a routine as a telephone operator calling Gore Vidal, but her portrayal of a mean-minded, frustrated spinster was saved from being that of a clichéd old maid by her wit and political satire. Today Miss Tomlin tours in her one-woman show, filling theatres from New York to San Francisco — where, on a rainy day not long ago, I failed to get a seat for the matinée much to my intense irritation.

In that Lily Tomlin finds the theatre a fitting place to play her great range of characters she resembles past women in that line, such as Ruth Draper and Joyce Grenfell. These women were not outspoken enemies of convention — like Mae West, Phyllis Diller, and Joan Rivers — but by gently and thoughtfully reminding us of what we are and how we behave they were rather like the most perfect mother one could imagine, wise, understanding, and caring — teachers. What Lily Tomlin teaches are home truths about our environment and the dark corners of our souls, which on the face of it isn't the job description of a comedienne, but laughter comes from many sources and Ms Tomlin can, when she cares to do it, be as funny as you could wish.

Goldie Hawn is funny through and through. She first delighted us over 20 years ago in that magical TV series *Rowan and Martin's Laugh-In*. Her innocent blonde looks, her stumbling as she read the cue cards, her swagger and bland rejoinders when faced with the (to her) incomprehensible, and her infectious giggle quickly made her a favourite. And she had tough competition from Ruth Buzzi, who ranged from downtrodden spinster to glitzy Hollywood gossip columnist, Judy Carne, the 'Sock it to me' girl, who week by week was drenched with water, hit with rubber mallets, and made to disappear through trapdoors but still had looks, bounce, and pep. Chelsea Brown, who shared some of Goldie's innocence, and Jo Anne Worley, who exuded a sort of benign rage, were both top performers, and there were others too (including in later series Lily Tomlin) who were excellent. But somehow Goldie not only made her presence felt but went on, through movies like *There's a Girl in My Soup, Private Benjamin*, and *Foul Play* (with Dudley Moore), to form her own film company. She is now a top executive of a major corporation and is living proof that you don't have to be square-cut or pear-shaped to make it big in the movie business.

Another lady who has made it to stardom is Mary Tyler Moore: as Dick Van Dyke's wife in *The Dick Van Dyke Show*, through her own series set in Minneapolis, *The Mary Tyler Moore Show* (ah, those unbelievably ingenious titles!) to running MTM Productions and making movies for TV and the big screen.

The Mary Tyler Moore Show developed another engagingly comic actress, Valerie Harper, who went on to play the character Rhoda in many series of that name.

One funny lady I must mention is Hermione Gingold. Her career in theatre, radio, and films spanned over 50 years, and she brought a kind of tremulous acidity to all that she did. On radio, back in the thirties, she impersonated a character called Mrs Pullpleasure, who would give a discourse on the joys of playing stringed instruments. Later she played the character of the materfamilias in the radio equivalent of the Charles Addams cartoons — The Dooms. As Mrs Doom, served by her loyal creature, Trog, a butler of sorts, she was forever at the tea-table, offering her husband the stimulating beverage with a husky, contralto 'Tea ... Edmond? Milluk ... Edmond?', in a manner that became in its day as renowned as Dame Edith Evans's way of saying 'A haaandbag?' in *The Importance of Being Earnest*.

In the theatre Hermione Gingold was at her best in the 1940s revues *Sweet and Low, Sweeter and Lower*, and *Sweetest and Lowest*, written by Alan Melville. In the cinema she graced the screen for over 40 years, beginning in 1936 in *Someone at the Door*, and appearing subsequently in such films as *The Pickwick Papers, Around the World in Eighty Days, Gigi, The Music Man*, and *A Little Night Music*.

There have been many other funny ladies on stage and screen — Bebe Daniels, Martha Raye, Ethel Merman, Shirley Maclaine, Rosalind Russell, Shelley Winters, and the British *Carry On* team (female section): Hattie Jacques, Joan Sims, and Barbara Windsor. Then there are the late and much lamented Irene Handl and Margaret Rutherford, the former better known on radio and TV in a variety of roles. In films she mainly portrayed cockney cleaning ladies or boarding-house keepers, and on one occasion Sherlock Holmes's housekeeper, Mrs Hudson. Margaret Rutherford had a long and distinguished film career, including such movies as Noel Coward's *Blithe Spirit*, in which she played the dotty medium Madame Arcati, *The Importance of Being Earnest*, in which she played Miss Prism the governess, whose inattention many years before had led to Ernest being left at Waterloo Station in the famous 'haaandbag'. She also played Agatha Christie's Miss Marple in *Murder She Said*, and was in many other films. Dame Margaret Rutherford — described by film historian Leslie Halliwell as: 'Inimitable, garrulous, shapeless, endearing, British comedy character actress who usually seemed to be playing someone's slightly dotty spinster Aunt' — could truly be said to be unique. Like so many of the ladies mentioned in this chapter, an adornment to her profession.

One of the most recent British ladies to make her mark and, I suspect, an indelible one too, is Victoria Wood. Already the winner of many awards this likeable, slightly overweight, blonde composer, scriptwriter, and performer, still a long way from her 40th birthday, arrived with a bang on BBC TV back in 1985 with her show *Victoria Wood As Seen on TV*.

She gathered around her a talented cast, including Julie Walters, Susie Blake, Celia Imrie, and Mary Jo Randle (and some talented men too), and created one of the funniest, most observant and stimulating series to be seen on the small screen for many years. In 1979 this versatile girl from Prestwich, Lancashire, had written a stage play, *Talent*, which was subsequently shown on Granada Television. *Talent* was about competitors in a northern club talent contest and in it Victoria Wood co-starred with Julie Walters. She then wrote a sequel, *Nearly a Happy Ending*, and subsequently another stage play, *Happy Since I Met You*. And then came a sketch series for Granada Television, *Wood and Walters*, which she wrote and starred in, and in which she and Julie Walters explored the possibilities of their joint creativity.

Before that, in 1976, Miss Wood had become known on TV as a singer of rather lightweight topical songs on *That's Life*, a series that combined quite serious consumer complaints with smutty jokes. It was hosted, or perhaps that should be hostessed, by a stalwart of BBC Television, the toothy Esther Rantzen.

Victoria Wood had struggled around show business often ignored and almost universally underrated until with *Talent* and *Wood and Walters* she made everybody sit up. Julie Walters has, of course, made a big name for herself as a dramatic actress in such films as *Educating Rita*, with Michael Caine, and *Personal Services*, a film based loosely on the life of the suburban brothel-keeper, Cynthia Payne. Together Wood and Walters achieve heights never before reached by two funny women — each bringing a special talent but together providing a whole greater than the sum of the parts. At their first meeting Victoria Wood described Walters as 'a woman with the smallest eyes I'd ever seen'. An unpromising start to what became a potent on-stage relationship, and a warm personal friendship.

As the 1980s have progressed so Victoria Wood has grown in confidence and pulling power. In a recent season at the London Palladium her one-woman show was a complete sell-out, not a seat available, 'not even for ready money', throughout the run. Her great quality is versatility and whether playing a working-class woman in a launderette looking like a refugee from *Monty Python's Flying Circus*, or doing a stand-up spot that Woody Allen or Bob Hope would not be ashamed of, she is as near perfect as anyone can expect in these troubled times.

Some excerpts from her sketches will help to give the flavour of her humour.

The stage direction of this one, called 'No Gossip', is: '*Tea shop. Two nice ladies.*' (The first lady is Wood, the second is Walters.)

FIRST LADY : Did you go to see *Macbeth*?
SECOND LADY: Mmmm. Wasn't a patch on *Brigadoon*. There was some terrible woman who kept washing her hands, saying she'd never get them clean. I felt like shouting out 'Try Swarfega'. We walked out in the end.
FIRST LADY: Why?
SECOND LADY: Someone said 'womb'.
FIRST LADY: No.

... and so on.

Here are Victoria and Julie again, this time as Faith and Philippa in an Italian restaurant.

PHILIPPA: My mother's ... in Marbella for the winter.
FAITH: Does she like Spain?

> PHILIPPA: She likes the majesty and grandeur of the landscape, but she's not keen on the bacon.

A little later in the sketch it transpires that Philippa's husband, Nick, has left the nuptial bed and now lives in the toolshed.

> PHILIPPA: ... Nick, apparently, is in love with someone else.
> FAITH: How long's that been going on?
> PHILIPPA: Must be yonks, because he told me 'their tune' was 'Chirpy Chirpy Cheep Cheep'.
> FAITH: Who is it?
> PHILIPPA: You know I mentioned a very small neighbour of mine — buys children's clothes and spends the VAT on Tequila?
> FAITH: Mmm.
> PHILIPPA: It's her. I wondered why he'd had that cat flap widened.

Here's a moment from the sketch, 'Men Talking' — just to show she *can* write for men.

> MAN: And she got more and more depressed. So I said, 'Look, Sheila, if you're that desperate go back to work and I'll stay home and look after the baby.' So off she went. And I changed nappies, made the breakfast, did the hoovering, cleaned the cooker, made the beds, went shopping, fed the baby — and by lunchtime I'd had enough. I phoned Sheila at work — I said, 'You'll have to pack your job in, I just can't stand it.'

In her larger-scale, more complex sketches shot mainly on film, Victoria Wood's sure touch with the bizarre commonplaces of everyday life is even more in evidence. The logical absurdity of her writing and her unselfishness in giving the better parts to the rest of her team make her almost unique among her contemporaries.

Like George Burns, she imprints her personality on everything she does. Her comedy performances, sketches, monologues, and songs bring out a waif-like quality that's endearing, and although she can swagger with the best of them Victoria is never better than when being herself and letting her quick wits carry her through the various fantasies she's concocted.

Wide-eyed and street smart but still at rock-bottom vulnerable, Victoria Wood is a very fine artiste indeed.

LUCILLE BALL

W hen the first episode of *I Love Lucy* was shown on American television in 1951, Lucille Ball had been in show business for nearly 30 years. Today, nearly 40 years on, they are still showing episodes of *I Love Lucy* somewhere in the world.

One of the best jokes in *Crocodile Dundee* was when, asked if he'd seen television before, the outback Aussie answered, 'Yes. Once — 20 years ago.' The set is turned on and there is an episode of *I Love Lucy* on the screen. 'Yes,' says Dundee, 'that's what I saw.' The enduring, endearing comic antics of 'America's favourite female clown' as she has been called, *will* endure while television lasts and I suspect that well into the twenty-first century people will be laughing at the redhead from Jamestown, New York.

Lucille Ball was born on 6 August 1911, so she was 40 when her television career took off, and those 40 years had been full of incident.

Shortly after she was born, Lucy's parents moved to Butte, Montana. In 1915 her father died and her mother, Desiree, pregnant with her second child, moved back to Jamestown to live with her father, Fred Hunt. Like most of the archetypal grandfathers of most autobiographies, Fred was something of a character, a jack of all trades, and a socialist who read the *Daily Worker* and was a left-wing activist at a time when revolution was in the air in Europe — and more than just in the air, as the Russian revolution of 1917 was to prove.

The labour movement and the trades union in the USA were idealistic and committed to the improvement of the lot of the working man, and Lucille Ball's grandfather, being both caring and energetic was very much part of this movement. Lucille must have inherited his energy if not his politics for it's clear from her performances in later life that she must have been active, inventive and, once she'd seen the early movies of Tom Mix, William S. Hart, Pickford, Fairbanks, and Chaplin, must have had Hollywood as her goal.

Meanwhile Lucy's mother had her second child, Fred, and remarried — her husband being a sheet-metal worker by the name of Ed Peterson. For Lucy, growing up meant more frequent appearances at local school concerts, in school plays, and dreaming of the future. She left school at 15 and studied for a time at a New

LUCILLE BALL

York drama school. After a while her mother was told that she was 'wasting her money' as her daughter would never make an actress. But Lucille Ball persisted, going for auditions for *Earl Carroll's Vanities* as a showgirl. After two weeks of (unpaid) rehearsal she was told that she wasn't suitable. She auditioned for other shows with much the same result, and tried her hand at modelling. She was tall and skinny, but although that was a drawback for a showgirl where the keynote was a voluptuous figure it was fine for modelling where the flat, flapper look of the twenties demanded a more boyish figure.

Eventually she graduated to a job at Hattie Carnegie's, an up-market couturier, where she made 35 dollars a week and posed for illustrators and photographers on the side. She was working too hard and at the age of 18 became ill; it took two years back in Jamestown to recuperate from her self-imposed regime of hard work mixed with starvation.

Returning to New York in 1933 she started work again at Hattie Carnegie's, went blonde and landed the job as 'poster girl' advertising Chesterfield cigarettes. Later that year, as a qualified poster girl, she went to Hollywood on a contract for Sam Goldwyn.

There is a time in every entertainer's life — every successful entertainer that is — when the privations and hardships give way to a fairly smooth and unruffled way of life, and it's a matter of personality whether the successful star chooses to forget the bad times and early failures and remember only the moments of success in their early and obviously formative years. In Lucille Ball's case the period of privation in comparison with the long years of success was so short that she can be excused for forgetting how tough it was. In Joe Morella and Edward Z. Epstein's excellent biography of Lucille Ball they quote her as saying:

> People keep saying that success came to me the hard way, after a long struggle. This myth is ridiculous. The truth is just the opposite. I have *never* been out of a job. In my early days in New York ... I was making good money as a model. Then I went to Hollywood and Samuel Goldwyn immediately placed me under contract. Some struggle!

In fact, from being a showgirl in Goldwyn pictures in 1933–4 at 150 dollars a week she moved to Columbia for 75 dollars a week; she hoped for more than the small part and extra work she'd been getting but instead became an unbilled adornment to the Three Stooges in their comedy two-reelers.

But there were compensations, like working on Frank Capra's *Broadway Bill, Jealousy, Men of the Night, The Fugitive Lady*, and, in 1935, *Carnival*, where in a small part as a nurse she eventually got billing. From Columbia she went to RKO at a 50 dollars a week, but it was the moment when her career really started to take off. Her first part was as a model in the screen version of the musical *Roberta*, which starred Fred Astaire, Ginger Rogers, Irene Dunne, and Randolph Scott. It wasn't a speaking part, but Lucy's earlier modelling experience plus that something extra she always brought to the screen made her tiny appearance memorable. Seeing a re-run on TV recently I was struck by her beauty and poise.

Well, back in 1935 RKO must have thought so too because they started to groom her, and she attended the acting lessons given by the studio's drama coach, Lela Rogers, Ginger Rogers's mother.

Then came a series of tiny appearances in various RKO epics: *Old Man Rhythm* (one line of dialogue), *Top Hat, The Three Musketeers, Follow the Fleet* — another Astaire/Rogers movie, in which Lucille Ball played a dance-hall hostess with about three lines of dialogue, *The Farmer in the Dell*, and many others.

But, at last, came a decent film in which she could display her talents. It was the 1937 RKO 'biggie' *Stage Door*, based on the Edna Ferber/George S. Kaufman broadway hit, with Katharine Hepburn, Ginger Rogers, Ann Miller, Eve Arden, Gail Patrick, Constance Collier, and, of course, Lucille Ball, and it received the comment from critic Otis Ferguson: 'It is a long time since we have seen so much feminine talent so deftly handled.' I should imagine with that particular group it would *need* a deft touch, and director Gregory La Cava handled the explosive handful of talent with great skill.

The story is of the heartbreaks and daydreams of a group of would-be actresses in a New York theatrical boarding house, and though there *were* men in the cast — Adolphe Menjou, Jack Carson, and Franklyn Pangborn among them — it was very much a 'woman's picture' in every sense. It did a lot for Lucille Ball, who subsequently got a much better contract and good parts in *The Joy of Living* as Irene Dunne's sister, and as a happy summer camper in *Having a Wonderful Time*.

By 1938 she was appearing in a weekly radio show with Jack Haley, and in addition she made seven films, notably *The Affairs of Annabel*, where, as an actress with a press agent (Jack Oakie) full of publicity ideas that fail miserably and land her in jail, she scored a big comedy success. It was so successful in fact that RKO cobbled together a quick follow-up, *Annabel Takes a Tour*, then, as if to give her a final toughening-up course in coping with comedians, she was given a part in the Marx Brothers' comedy *Room Service*.

Lucille Ball was becoming observant, shrewd and tough. She's quoted as saying, after five years in Hollywood: 'I've never been out of work in this town except for two hours once between contracts.' And she was looking after her mother, her eccentric grandfather, her brother, and her cousin Cleo. Mind you, by 1939 her salary had risen to 1500 dollars a week, which in those halcyon days could have supported the entire population of Outer Mongolia, but although she was now 'big in pictures' they were B-pictures, the second features that backed up the main attraction, which as far as RKO were concerned meant Katharine Hepburn and Ginger Rogers.

In 1940 Lucy appeared with Richard Dix and Chester Morris (who later on was to play the private eye much liked by moviegoers, Boston Blackie) in an undemanding picture — *The Marines Fly High*. She also made *You Can't Fool Your Wife*, and *Dance, Girl, Dance* with Maureen O'Hara, Ralph Bellamy, and, more significantly, the up and coming Cuban bandleader, Desi Arnaz. When Lucy and Desi saw each other it was love at first sight. Desi at 23 was handsome, sexy, and Latin. Lucy at 29 was looking for just that combination. They filmed *Too Many Girls* together for RKO and then Desi Arnaz, who had a band to keep, went on tour.

Lucy's next film was one with probably the worst title ever — *A Guy, A Girl and a Gob** — and was produced by the great stunt comedian Harold Lloyd. In it Lucy starred with George Murphy. On its completion Lucy's stormy relationship with Desi resumed — fierce arguments followed by intense reconciliations. They were married on 30 November 1940, a marriage due to last until 1960 when the couple, having built the Desilu empire, were finally divorced.

Their life in the 1940s went on much as before, Lucy in flims and radio, a regular in *The Chase and Samborn Hour*, with Edgar Bergen and his dummy Charlie McCarthy, Desi on tour with his band.

Lucy's final film for RKO was a dramatic role in a Damon Runyon story, as a night-club singer crippled by her gangster boyfriend and cared for by a waiter, played by Henry Fonda. It was called *The Big Street*, and in it Lucy was able to demonstrate her acting range, with the result that she was offered a contract by MGM, then the biggest studio in Hollywood.

Her first film for Metro was *DuBarry Was a Lady*, a period romp in which she played opposite Gene Kelly and Red Skelton. The picture also featured the deadpan singer Virginia O'Brien, Zero Mostel, and Tommy Dorsey's band. It was something of a hotchpotch and did moderately well but not sensationally at the box office. It was Lucille Ball's fortieth film.

By now the USA was at war and, like many other Hollywood stars, Lucy went on bond-selling tours with Fred Astaire, and troop shows with Bob Hope. In 1943 Desi Arnaz joined the Army and was posted to 'Special Services', which meant entertaining the other soldiers. He also played in the war epic *Bataan* and, in fact spent most of his time in Los Angeles.

In 1944, their marriage seemingly on the rocks, Lucy filed for divorce on the grounds of 'extreme mental cruelty', but the divorce was never finalized and the couple went on as before — fighting, making up, and fighting again.

By 1946 MGM's interest in Lucy had dropped to near zero, but in her idleness she spent her time fruitfully with Buster Keaton who was also under contract to MGM but also regarded as 'past it'. He taught Lucy a lot about visual comedy, the use of props and make-up, having seen her in *DuBarry Was a Lady* and recognized the great comedienne in her.

No one else in Hollywood had spotted the funny lady, the role that nature had cast Lucy for, until she appeared in a stage play, *Dream Girl*. On the strength of her performance CBS signed her to co-star in a radio series, *My Favorite Husband*, with Richard Denning. It was similar in format to the later *I Love Lucy* shows — wacky wife putting her husband into embarrassing situations — and it ran for four years.

---

* 'Gob' is American slang for 'sailor'.

In the cinema her next important role was opposite Bob Hope in a remake of another Damon Runyon story, *Little Miss Marker*, which had starred Shirley Temple when it was first made in 1934. Needless to say, Lucille Ball was not in the Shirley Temple role. The 1948 version was called *Sorrowful Jones* and did well at the box office, so well in fact that the studio teamed Bob Hope and Lucille Ball together again in *Fancy Pants*.

By 1951 television was over its teething period and out hunting for star attractions. In many cases they were already there on radio, as with Jack Benny, and Burns and Allen, but television is a thirsty medium and is always on the lookout for new material and new stars, and certainly this was true in 1951.

At that time Lucy had just completed a contract with Columbia, and Desi and his band were headlining at Ciro's Club in Hollywood. There was one small complication — Lucy was pregnant. But pregnant or not, she, along with Desi, was determined to do a husband and wife show on TV. So they formed a company, Desilu, and started planning *I Love Lucy*. With Lucy five months pregnant they made a pilot programme in which Desi played Ricky Ricardo, a downmarket version of himself — that's to say a moderately successful bandleader — and Lucy was a housewife. They brought over the writers of *My Favorite Husband*, Bob Carroll, Madeleine Pugh, and Jess Openheimer, and cast William Frawley and Vivian Vance as their next-door neighbours, the Mertz family. After much argument with the sponsors, the Philip Morris cigarette company and CBS, who both wanted *I Love Lucy* to be transmitted live from New York, Desi won the battle and the show was made on film in Hollywood. (The baby, by the way, was a girl — Lucy II.) Right from the start *I Love Lucy* was a smash hit. For the first time Lucille Ball was able to give her comic talents full rein, and she was nobly supported by Desi, William Frawley, and Vivian Vance.

The success built. Desilu studios started to produce other comedies, notably *Our Miss Brooks*, starring Eve Arden.

When Lucy was having her second baby, the TV *Lucy* shows were geared to the coming event and, thanks to brilliant timing, excellent PR, and good luck, the boy anticipated in the script emerged in reality — Desi Arnaz junior had arrived. The Arnazes now had everything: a top-rated TV show, a big production company, and two children. They were on top of the world, in demand everywhere and for gigantic fees. What could possibly go wrong?

What went wrong was that the fifties witch-hunters of the Un-American Activities Committee discovered that in 1936 Lucille Ball had registered as a Communist voter. The news was actually broken by Walter Winchell, influential newspaper columnist and TV celebrity, on a coast-to-coast broadcast.

In today's moderate climate, when even Ronald Reagan talks openly to Communists, it seems weird that anybody should have bothered, but bother they did and the rumpus filled every newspaper in the land. What Lucy had done in 1936 to please her grandfather had now rebounded in a most unpleasant way. In her testimony, for she was publicly questioned, she said: 'I am not a Communist now. I have never been ... at no time in my life have I ever been in sympathy with anything that even faintly resembled it.' Those of us who admire Lucille Ball for her guts, determination and talent would, I suppose, prefer that she should have told the Un-American Activities Committee to 'go boil their heads' — and take the consequences. But clearly she was never aware of the dangers of non-conformity, and, as Desi Arnaz told the studio audience: 'The only thing about Lucy that's red is the colour of her hair, and even that's not legitimate.' 'At that,' say the biographers of Lucille Ball, Joe Morella and Edward Z. Epstein, 'the studio audience cheered.' In fact, the whole affair was forgotten in a matter of weeks.

The *Lucy* shows won prestigious Emmy awards in 1952, 1955, 1966, and 1967. During this period the Desilu studios produced, in addition to the weekly *I Love Lucy* shows, *Our Miss Brooks*, *Wyatt Earp*, *The Jimmy Durante Show*, *The Red Skelton Show*, a series about helicopter pilots called *Whirly Birds*, and many more. By the end of 1956 Desilu was grossing more than 15 million dollars annually, and employed over 800 people; and it was to get bigger. In 1957 Desi Arnaz who ran the Desilu business with great skill, decided that they needed to expand still further and bought RKO studios. The deal was consummated in 1958, by which time the *Lucy* shows had become 60 minutes long and monthly rather than weekly. Also at this time the rumbustious relationship of Lucy and Desi was heading for deep trouble.

In 1960 Lucille Ball filed for divorce. As the marriage ended so did *I Love Lucy* after 209 episodes. But Lucy kept on working. Her next project was another film with Bob Hope, *The Facts of Life*, and she followed that with a Broadway musical about oil prospectors, *Wildcat*, which did good business in spite of poor notices, but folded when Lucy became ill.

Also in 1960 she met Gary Morton, am amiable stand-up comedian, and their relationship grew to a point where marriage became inevitable. Gary Morton was the antithesis of Desi Arnaz, quiet, accommodating and courteous. He was some years younger than Lucy and his calmness and unaffected fondness for his new wife gave her a confidence that she'd perhaps been lacking; Gary Morton became a companion who soothed rather than inflamed her quite considerable temper.

In October 1962 Lucy returned to the small screen with her new series, *Here's Lucy*, in which she played a widow bringing up two children. With her on the show were Vivian Vance and Dick Martin, in his pre-*Rowan-and-Martin* acting days. Shortly afterwards Lucille Ball bought the Desi Arnaz slice of Desilu Productions for around three million dollars and became, in addition to an on-screen superstar, and off-screen tycoon — president of the company. She was 51.

Then came a radio show, a five mornings a week programme in which Lucy interviewed a variety of show-business stars — her comment: 'It's easy and it's fun.' Not so easy but more profitable was a movie based on a real family, the Beardsleys. A widowed Navy nurse with eight children met and married a naval officer, a widower with ten children. They then had more children together and this remarkable family made the basis of a remarkable film starring Lucy and Henry Fonda, called *Yours, Mine and Ours*.

In the meantime Desilu had been sold to Gulf and Western, the conglomerate that had recently acquired Paramount Pictures, and while Lucy retained her presidency of the now subsidiary Desilu she was a small fish in an enormous pond.

The Lucy Show was made under the Paramount logo in 1967–8 with Gary Morton producing and in which young Lucy II and Desi II also appeared. Lucille Ball's television shows have never stopped being shown, and while her last big movie, *Mame*, was not a top box-office hit she has never lost her popularity with the public, and especially the TV-watching public.

Her life has been one of constant hard work, almost constant success and a good deal of happiness thrown in for good measure. This, I'm sure, has more than compensated for the bad times, the tough breaks, and the inevitable disappointments that come to us all.

In Gary Morton she has a loving, loyal companion and in the declining years of her life she can look back with satisfaction at a career which truly made her 'America's favourite female clown'.

FILMS

These include:
Moulin Rouge   1934
Produced by Darryl F. Zanuck
Directed by Sidney Lanfield
Written by Nunnally Johnson and Henry Lehrman

Nana   1934
Produced by Samuel Goldwyn
Directed by Dorothy Arzner
Written by Willard Mack and Harry Wagstaff Gribble, from the novel by Emile Zola

Bottoms Up   1934
Produced by B. G. DeSylva
Directed by David Butler
Written by B. G. DeSylva, David Butler, and Sid Silvers

Hold That Girl   1934
Produced by Twentieth Century Fox Productions
Directed by William Hamilton
Written by Dudley Nichols and Lamar Trotti

Bulldog Drummond Strikes Back   1934
Produced by Samuel Goldwyn
Directed by Roy Del Ruth
Written by Nunnally Johnson

The Affairs of Cellini   1934
Produced by Darryl F. Zanuck
Directed by Gregory La Cava
Written by Bess Meredyth, from the play *The Firebrand* by Edwin Justus Mayer

Kid Millions   1934
Produced by Samuel Goldwyn
Directed by Roy Del Ruth
Written by George Oppenheimer

Broadway Bill   1934
Produced by Frank Capra
Directed by Frank Capra
Written by Robert Riskin

Roberta   1935
Produced by Pandro S. Berman
Directed by William A. Seiter
Written by Jane Murfin, Sam Mintz, and Allan Scott, from the play by Otto Harbach

Top Hat   1935
Produced by Pandro S. Berman
Directed by Mark Sandrich
Written by Dwight Taylor and Allan Scott

I Dream Too Much   1935
Produced by Pandro S. Berman
Directed by John Cromwell
Written by Edmund North and James Gow

Follow the Fleet   1936
Produced by Pandro S. Berman
Directed by Mark Sandrich
Written by Dwight Taylor, from the play *Shore Leave* by Hubert Osborne and Allan Scott

Bunker Bean   1936
Produced by William Sistrom
Directed by William Hamilton and Edward Kelly
Written by Edmund North, James Gow, and Dorothy Yost, based on a novel by Harry Leon Wilson and play by Lee Wilson Dodd

Stage Door   1937
Produced by Pandro S. Berman
Directed by Gregory La Cava
Written by Morrie Ryskind and Anthony Veiller from a play by Edna Ferber and George S. Kaufman

The Joy of Living   1938
Produced by Felix Young
Directed by Tay Garnett
Written by Gene Towne, Allan Scott, and Graham Baker

Having a Wonderful Time   1938
Produced by Pandro S. Berman
Directed by Alfred Santell
Written by Arthur Kober

The Affairs of Annabel   1938
Produced by Lee Marcus and Lou Lusty
Directed by Lew Landers
Written by Bert Granet and Paul Yawitz

Annabel Takes a Tour   1938
Produced by Lou Lusty
Directed by Lew Landers
Written by Bert Granet and Olive Cooper, based on a story by Joe Bigelow

Room Service   1938
Produced by Pandro S. Berman
Directed by William A. Seiter
Written by Morrie Ryskind, from a play by John Murray

Beauty for the Asking   1939
Produced by B. P. Fineman
Directed by Glenn Taylor
Written by Doris Anderson and Paul Jerrico

Five Came Back   1939
Produced by Robert Sisk
Directed by John Farrow
Written by Jerry Cady, Dalton Trumbo, and Nathanael West

That's Right You're Wrong   1939
Produced by David Butler
Directed by David Butter
Written by William Conselman and James V. Kern

The Marines Fly High   1940
Produced by Robert Sisk
Directed by George Nicholls Jr and Ben Stoloff
Written by Jerry Cady and A. J. Bolton

You Can't Fool Your Wife   1940
Produced by Erich Pommer
Directed by Dorothy Arzner
Written by Tess Slesinger and Frank Davis, from a story by Vicki Baum

Too Many Girls 1940
Produced by Harry Edgington and George Abbott
Directed by George Abbott
Written by John Twist from a play by George Marion Jr, Richard Rodgers, and Lorenz Hart

A Guy, a Girl and a Gob 1940
Produced by Harold Lloyd
Directed by Richard Wallace
Written by Bert Granet and Frank Ryan

Valley of the Sun 1942
Produced by Graham Baker
Directed by George Marshall
Written by Horace McCoy

Seven Days' Leave 1942
Produced by Tim Whelan
Directed by Tim Whelan
Written by William Bowers, Ralph Spence, Curtis Kenyon, and Kenneth Earl

The Big Street 1942
Produced by Damon Runyon
Directed by Irving Reis
Written by Leonard Spiegelgass, from the story *Little Pinks* by Damon Runyon

DuBarry Was a Lady 1943
Produced by Arthur Freed
Directed by Roy Del Ruth
Written by Irving Brechner

Best Foot Forward 1943
Produced by Arthur Freed
Directed by Edward Buzzell
Written by Irving Brecher and Fred Finklehoffe, from the play by John Cecil Holmes

Meet the People 1944
Produced by E. Y. Harburg
Directed by Charles Reisner
Written by S. M. Herzig and Fred Saidy

Without Love 1945
Produced by Lawrence Weingarten
Directed by Harold S. Bucquet
Written by Donald Ogden Stewart, from the play by Philip Barry

Ziegfeld Follies 1946
Produced by Arthur Freed

Directed by Vincente Minelli
Written by several

The Dark Corner   1946
Produced by Fred Kohlmar
Directed by Henry Hathaway
Written by Jay Dratler and Bernard Schoenfeld

Easy to Wed   1946
Produced by Jack Cummings
Directed by Edward Buzzell
Written by Dorothy Kingsley, Maurine Watkins, Howard Emmett Rogers, and
George Oppenheimer

Two Smart People   1946
Produced by Ralph Wheelwright
Directed by Jules Dassin
Written by Ethel Hill and Leslie Charteris

Lover Come Back   1946
Produced by Howard Benedict
Directed by William A. Seiter
Written by Michael Fessier and Ernest Pagano

Lured   1947
Produced by James Nasser
Directed by Douglas Sirk
Written by Leo Rosten, from the French film *Pièges*

Her Husband's Affairs   1947
Produced by Raphael Hakim
Directed by S. Sylvan Simon
Written by Ben Hecht

Sorrowful Jones   1949
Produced by Robert L. Welch
Directed by Sidney Lanfield
Written by Melville Shavelson, Edmund Hartmann, and Jack Rose, from a story by
Damon Runyon

Easy Living   1949
Produced by Robert Sparks
Directed by Jacques Tourneur
Written by Charles Schnee

Miss Grant Takes Richmond   1949
Produced by S. Sylvan Simon
Directed by Lloyd Bacon
Written by Nat Perrin, Devery Freeman, and Frank Tashlin

Fancy Pants   1950
Produced by Robert Welch
Directed by George Marshall
Written by Edmund Hartmann and Robert O'Brien

The Fuller Brush Girl   1950
Produced by S. Sylcan Simon
Directed by Lloyd Bacon
Written by Frank Tashlin

The Magic Carpet   1950
Produced by Ranald MacDougall
Directed by William A. Graham
Written by Ranald MacDougall

The Long Long Trailer   1954
Produced by Pandro S. Berman
Directed by Vincente Minelli
Written by Frances Goodrich and Albert Hackett, from the novel by Clinton Twiss

Forever Darling   1956
Produced by Desi Arnaz
Directed by Alexander Hall
Written by Helen Deutsch

The Facts Of Life   1960
Produced by Norman Panama
Directed by Melvin Frank
Written by Norman Panama and Melvin Frank

Critic's Choice   1963
Produced by Frank P. Rosenberg
Directed by Don Weis
Written by Jack Sher, from the play by Ira Levin

A Guide for the Married Man   1967
Produced by Frank McCarthy
Directed by Gene Kelly
Written by Frank Tarloff

Yours, Mine and Ours   1968
Produced by Robert F. Blumofe
Directed by Mel Shavelson
Written by Mel Shavelson and Mort Lachman

Mame   1973
Produced by Robert Fryer and James Cresson
Directed by Gene Saks

Written by Paul Zandel, from the play by Jerome Lawrence and Robert E. Lee, and book by Patrick Dennis

TELEVISION

I Love Lucy   1950–
Here's Lucy   1960–
The Lucy Show   1967–8

BUSTER KEATON

In a way there could be said to be *two* Buster Keaton stories. One is of a high-flying star of silent films who ranks with Chaplin and Harold Lloyd as one of the great laughter-makers of the cinema. The second is of a vaudeville entertainer who graduated through the crudest kind of stage knockabout comedy to become a custard-pie comic in the bad old days of silent cinema: who married a wife who eventually stripped him of everything: money, property, and even his children; and who became an alcoholic, finishing his days as a gag-writer for MGM at 100 dollars a week, insulted by the comics he was writing jokes for ('Do you think that's *funny?*' he was asked by Groucho Marx on one occasion), an occasional guest on other people's TV shows, and front man in commercials for such products as Alka Seltzer and Seven Up. Both are true, and it's in the strange mixture of the man and his work that we find the puzzling story of Buster Keaton. A man with less talent would have gone under, a man more able to cope with life's vicissitudes would never have got into the situation in the first place.

He was born Joseph Frank Keaton on 4 October 1895 in the small Kansas town of Piqua. His mother, Myra, and father, Joe, were the mainstays of Myra's father's medicine show which moved around the corn-belt towns of the midwest dispensing their own brand of corn in the form of music, monologues, and playlets, and selling patent medicine.

Buster (named by Harry Houdini, the escape artist, who was touring with the Keatons, when their baby fell down a flight of stairs in the boarding house and came up smiling) had an early life fraught with accidents — fingers caught in a clothes wringer, fires in boarding houses, and even on one occasion being swept out of his bedroom by a cyclone and deposited unharmed in the middle of Main Street.

After that his parents thought it safer for the little lad to be on stage with them, and in 1898 Buster joined the act and The Two Keatons became The Three Keatons.

Myra played cornet and saxophone, Joe did comic monologues, first in blackface then as a comic Irishman. Buster was made up as a replica of his father — a 3-year-old with bald-pate wig, and a red fringe of beard. As Buster grew older and as the act developed the Keatons graduated from the medicine show to vaudeville where the act became a dazzling display of knockabout comedy: Buster would be hurled hither, thither, and yon and would get his revenge by breaking broom-handles over his father's head. According to Buster Keaton's own account he was never hurt by his father, who taught him how to take a fall, and, in fact, the whole family (another son and a daughter came along presently) had good relations until death separated them forever.

By the early years of the twentieth century The Three Keatons were doing well. So well, in fact, that they could rest up in the summer in a spot much frequented by vaudeville performers, the town of Muskegon near Lake Michigan.

By now Joe was drinking more than somewhat and in Los Angeles Myra and Buster had had enough. They grabbed their theatrical skips, left Joe to his fate, and headed east. Once his mother was safely ensconced in Detroit, Buster went on to New York alone. He planned on doing a solo act but the theatrical agent he saw got him a job in *The Passing Show* of 1917. *The Passing Show* was a revue in the manner of the *Ziegfeld Follies*. Buster was trying to put an act together for himself, but after a lifetime as one of The Three Keatons is wasn't easy for the 21-year-old to work out an act where there was no support. Roaming New York in despondent mood he ran into an old vaudeville friend, Lou Anger, who was now manager for Joseph Schenck, and who introduced him to 'the movies'. The Schenck studios were housed in an old Manhattan warehouse — the stars were Norma Talmadge, Schenck's wife, her sister Constance, and comedian Roscoe 'Fatty' Arbuckle. The Talmadge sisters were romantic leading ladies, or, at most, light comediennes. Fatty Arbuckle was a knockabout comic.

Today Arbuckle is remembered, if he is remembered at all, as the principal in a sensational murder trial in Hollywood in the twenties. In 1917 he was as popular as Chaplin in the field of comedy two-reelers, although Chaplin soon soared away to mega stardom and Arbuckle stumbled, fell from grace and popularity, and ended up forgotten and despised by all but a handful of friends, of whom Keaton was one of the staunchest. Keaton later claimed that Arbuckle taught him everything he knew about film-making, but on that fateful day at the Schenck studio Buster had not yet dipped a toe in the movies.

Arbuckle greeted him warmly (having admired the younger Keaton in vaudeville) and invited him to join them in the 'short' they were making, *The Butcher Boy*. Keaton became fascinated by the paraphernalia of film-making, took part in *The Butcher Boy*, forgot *The Passing Show*, and became a regular member of the Arbuckle team on a starting salary of 40 dollars a week.

Rudi Blesh in his biography of Keaton calls the early days of film-making 'almost unbelievably informal': 'Arbuckle never formally offered him [Keaton] a steady job on the payroll and Buster never asked for one. He simply went to work and was automatically paid.'

Keaton and Arbuckle became good friends and when the Company left New York for studios at Long Beach, California, they had already established a comedy rapport as good as any in the business at that time.

The day he joined the movies Buster also met the girl who was to become his first wife, Natalie Talmadge. Not an actress like her sisters, she was the production secretary/continuity girl on the Arbuckle pictures. Myra and Joe Keaton, now retired and together again, joined the Arbuckle film-makers in California. It was the high tide of film-making. From 1971 to 1972 when the first feature-length talking picure, *The Jazz Singer*, changed the movies forever, more money was made, more stars were born, more fan mail and hero and heroine worship generated than before or since. Salaries were astronomical — movies couldn't fail, and Buster Keaton rose on this wave of prosperity.

First, though, there was the little matter of the First World War to be contended with. In 1918 Buster Keaton was drafted into the Army. After training he went with his regiment, the 40th Infantry, to France, but luckily for him the war was over before he saw action and he returned to the USA in one piece in 1919 to rejoin Fatty Arbuckle and Al St John at Long Beach. His Army career had lasted less than a year but had given him a chance to broaden his experience, to see something of France, and to entertain his fellow infantrymen.

Soon after his return to the comparative calm of film-making, Buster Keaton married Natalie Talmadge. It was a marriage that was due to founder in acrimony, but, as with all marriages that break up, it's a question of, 'which came first, the chicken or the egg?' Natalie wanted the trappings of stardom: the big house, the limousines, the glittering parties where everybody *but* everybody was invited. Their two sons, Jimmy and Bobby, had governesses, and a butler to serve the food and drink at their parties.

Hollywood has always been a town full of snobs, the pecking order being dependent on the size of your salary and box-office appeal. In the twenties and thirties Buster Keaton had both a big income and a healthy popularity among the paying customers, and Natalie wanted, if only to keep up with her famous sisters, to show that she was on top of the Hollywood heap. Buster, on the other hand, only wanted to make pictures. In what leisure time he had he played bridge for high stakes and, like his father before him, began to drink heavily.

In 1932 affairs came to a head when he was found in bed on his yacht with a naked young woman. He was too drunk to know who she was or how she'd got there but Natalie, who'd been keeping tabs on him for some time, immediately sued for divorce and in the settlement cleaned Buster out.

From then on his drinking went from heavy to compulsive with DTs at the end of the line. During the binge years he married again — the nurse who'd been put in charge of him. He was later to describe this as 'a marriage of inconvenience' and it didn't last long.

By now he had left United Artists, where he ran his own company, and joined MGM. It was to prove a tragic mistake, for although the first two films he made for the company were profitable, gradually the quality deteriorated and Buster himself was in no great shape. In the end Louis B. Mayer sacked him.

Afterwards came a confused period when Buster tried to make films in Mexico, England and France — but they didn't work either. Buster Keaton drunk wasn't funny any more. In 1935 he underwent treatment for alcoholism and stayed on the wagon for five years. In 1940 he met and married his third wife, Eleanor, who cared for him, worked with him, and was a loyal and loving companion until Buster's death in 1966.

From 1917 until his death Buster Keaton appeared in over 120 films both short and long, silent and talkie. From the beginning as a small-part actor with Arbuckle in *The Butcher Boy*, Buster Keaton proved a most valuable, resourceful, and imaginative film-maker. Never content with anything less than perfection, a compulsively hard-working gag-writer and special effects inventor, he brought the skill of a vaudeville acrobat to the zany world of comedy movies.

As he matured and developed so his films became more sophisticated and technically brilliant. *Sherlock Junior*, made in 1924, had Buster as a cinema projectionist falling asleep and dreaming that he walks into the movie he is showing. Adjusting to one scene he finds himself in another, on the brink of a precipice one minute, in the jungle with a pride of lions the next. It was a *tour de force*.

The Navigator, also made in 1924, finds Buster and his girl, played by Kathryn McGuire, cast away in a deserted ship. Spies and cannibals come into the unlikely tale but it gave Keaton many opportunities for his own brand of knockabout comedy and was a great success.

Another big success of the twenties, a 'must' in every anthology of great silent films, was *The General*, a story of a railroad man caught up in the American Civil War.

His most famous film of that period is undoubtedly *Steamboat Bill Junior* where, as the wimpish son of a tough Mississippi steamboat captain, he endeavours to prove his manhood and win the girl. The climax comes as a cyclone hits town and the entire outside of a hospital — walls and ceiling — is blown away leaving Buster alarmed but unharmed in bed. Later, as he stands in the street contemplating what to do next, the entire front of a house crashes around him. By luck he is standing just where the upstairs window (no glass pane thanks to the cyclone) should have been. It was a brave stunt to pull as the house front was real and heavy, and had things gone wrong — had Keaton been standing just inches from the correct spot — it would have been 'bye 'bye Buster.

His two successes at MGM, *The Cameraman*, made in 1928, and *Spite Marriage*, his first talkie, made in 1929 (with sound added in 1930), were followed by some dismal romps. But in spite of his hard drinking and periods of irresponsibility, Buster Keaton was never out of work and rarely out of money. There was always a production company prepared to take a chance on the inherent genius of 'Stoneface'. Throughout his professional career Buster Keaton never smiled, and at times in his private affairs he had little to smile about. He was, however, never on Skid Row, and even towards the end of his life when his income was not as high as it had been, Paramount decided to make the story of his life, starring Donald O'Connor, and the fee he received for that enabled him to fulfil a lifetime's ambition — to own a small farm in the San Fernando Valley.

Although committed to film for most of his working life, Buster Keaton did make personal appearances — notably at the Cirque Medrano in Paris where, it is said, he held the audience in the palm of his hand with his elegant tumbling pantomime.

Perhaps that stint in Paris in 1953 was what Buster Keaton would have done on stage in 1917 had he not run into Lou Anger and joined the movies.

Let me quote Kevin Brownlow, the film historian, who wrote in his chapter on Keaton in *The Parade's Gone By*:

> To become a great comedian was never a conscious ambition of Buster Keaton. He made pictures the best way he knew how. He had a unique screen personality. He had real acting skill, with the sense of timing and of movement that this implies. He was a film director of brilliance, who knew exactly where to put the camera. He also had an intuitive sense of cutting, he was mechanically very ingenious, he had qualities of resourcefulness, authority and foresight. And he had a degree of personal courage ... But greatness would still be lacking were it not for one added quality; a capacity for tremendous hard work, a complete dedication to motion pictures which, fused with the other remarkable elements made Buster Keaton a master film maker.

The quality I most respect in Keaton is his humility in his professional approach. No job was beneath his dignity and he gave his utmost whether in front of or behind the camera. In spite of his drunken lapses, his bursts of anger, his momentary lack of charm, the qualities one most associates with this gifted little man are humility and dignity. And he was tough too. After all, he survived Hollywood.

FILMS

The Butcher Boy   1917
A Reckless Romeo   1917
The Rough House   1917
His Wedding Night   1917
Oh Doctor   1917
Fatty at Coney Island   1917
A Country Hero   1917
Out West   1918
The Bell Boy   1918
Moonshine   1918

Good Night, Nurse 1918
The Cook 1918
A Desert Hero 1919
Back Stage 1919
The Hayseed 1919
The Garage 1920

All the above produced by Comique Film Corporation/Paramount and directed by Fatty Arbuckle.

The Round-Up 1920
Produced by Famous Players–Lasky/Paramount
Directed by George Melford

One Week 1920
Buster Keaton Production/Metro
Directed by Buster Keaton and Eddie Cline

The Saphead 1920
Produced by John L. Golden and Winchell Smith/Metro
Directed by Herbert Blanche

Convict 13 1920
Buster Keaton Production/Metro
Directed by Buster Keaton and Eddie Cline

The Scarecrow 1920
Buster Keaton Production/Metro
Directed by Buster Keaton and Eddie Cline

Neighbors 1920
Buster Keaton Production/Metro
Directed by Buster Keaton and Eddie Cline

The Haunted House 1921
Buster Keaton Production/Metro
Directed by Buster Keaton and Eddie Cline

Hard Luck 1921
Buster Keaton Production/Metro
Directed by Buster Keaton and Eddie Cline

The High Sign 1921
Buster Keaton Production/Metro
Directed by Buster Keaton and Eddie Cline

The Goat   1921
Buster Keaton Production/Metro
Directed by Buster Keaton and Mal St Clair

The Play House   1921
Produced by Joseph M. Schenck/First National
Directed by Buster Keaton and Eddie Cline

The Boat   1921
Produced by Comique Film Corporation/First National
Directed by Buster Keaton and Eddie Cline

The Paleface   1921
Produced by Comique Film Corporation/First National
Directed by Buster Keaton and Eddie Cline

Cops   1922
Produced by Comique Film Corporation/First National
Directed by Buster Keaton and Eddie Cline

My Wife's Relations   1922
Produced by Comique Film Corporation/First National
Directed by Buster Keaton and Eddie Cline

Screen Snapshots   1922
Pathé Exchange
Produced by Jack and Louis Lewyn

The Blacksmith   1922
Produced by Comique Film Corporation/First National
Directed by Buster Keaton and Mal St Clair

The Frozen North   1922
Buster Keaton Production/First National
Directed by Buster Keaton and Eddie Cline

Day Dreams   1922
Buster Keaton Production/First National
Directed by Buster Keaton and Eddie Cline

The Electric House   1922
Buster Keaton Production/Associated–First National
Directed by Buster Keaton and Eddie Cline

The Balloonatic   1923
Buster Keaton Production/Associated–First National
Directed by Buster Keaton and Eddie Cline

The Love Nest   1923
Buster Keaton Production/Associated–First National
Directed by Buster Keaton

Three Ages   1923
Buster Keaton Production/Metro
Directed by Buster Keaton and Eddie Cline

Our Hospitality   1923
Buster Keaton Production/Metro
Directed by Buster Keaton and Jack Blystone

Sherlock Junior   1924
Buster Keaton Production/Metro
Directed by Buster Keaton

The Navigator   1924
Buster Keaton Production/Metro-Goldwyn
Directed by Buster Keaton and Donald Crisp

Seven Changes   1925
Buster Keaton Production/Metro-Goldwyn
Directed by Buster Keaton

Go West   1925
Buster Keaton Production/Metro-Goldwyn
Directed by Buster Keaton

Battling Butler   1926
Buster Keaton Production/MGM
Directed by Buster Keaton

The General   1926
Buster Keaton Production/United Artists
Directed by Buster Keaton and Clyde Bruckman

College   1927
Buster Keaton Production/United Artists
Directed by James W. Horne

Steamboat Bill Junior   1928
Buster Keaton Production/United Artists
Directed by Charles Reisner

The Cameraman   1928
MGM
Directed by Edward Sedgwick

Spite Marriage   1929
Produced by Edward Sedgwick/MGM
Directed by Edward Sedgwick

The Hollywood Revue of 1929   1929
Produced by Harry Rapf/MGM
Directed by Charles Reisner

Free and Easy 1930
Produced by Edward Sedgwick/MGM
Directed by Edward Sedgwick

Estrellados 1930
(Spanish version of *Free and Easy*)

Voice of Hollywood 1930
Produced by Louis Lewyn/Tiffany
Directed by Louis Lewyn

Doughboys 1930
Produced by Buster Keaton/MGM
Directed by Edward Sedgwick

De Fronte, Marchen 1930
(Spanish version of *Doughboys*)

Wir Schalten um auf Hollywood 1931
(German version of *The Hollywood Revue of 1929*)
Directed by Frank Reicher

The Stolen Jools 1931
Produced by Pat Casey/Paramount and National Screen Service
Directed by William McGann
(Released in England in 1932 as *The Slippery Pearls*)

Parlor, Bedroom and Bath 1931
MGM
Directed by Edward Sedgwick

Buster se Márie 1931
(French version of *Parlor, Bedroom and Bath*)
Directed by Claude Autant-Lara

Casanova Wider Willen 1931
(German version of *Parlor, Bedroom and Bath*)
Directed by Edward Brophy

The Sidewalks of New York 1931
Produced by Buster Keaton/MGM
Directed by Jules White and Zion Myers

The Passionate Plumber 1932
Produced by Buster Keaton/MGM
Directed by Edward Sedgwick

Le Plombier Amoureux 1932
(French version of *The Passionate Plumber*)
Directed by Claude Autant-Lara

Speak Easily   1932
MGM
Directed by Edward Sedgwick

Hollywood on Parade   1933
Produced by Louis Lewyn/Paramount
Directed by Louis Lewyn

What! No Beer?   1933
MGM
Directed by Edward Sedgwick

Le Roi de Champs-Elysees   1934
Produced by Nero Film/Paramount
Directed by Max Nosseck
(Released in France)

The Gold Ghost   1934
Produced by Educational/Twentieth Century Fox
Directed by Charles Lamont

Allez Oop   1934
Produced by Educational/Twentieth Century Fox
Directed by Charles Lamont

Palooka from Paducah   1935
Produced by Educational/Twentieth Century Fox
Directed by Charles Lamont

One Run Elmer   1935
Produced by Educational/Twentieth Century Fox
Directed by Charles Lamont

Hayseed Romance   1935
Produced by Educational/Twentieth Century Fox
Directed by Charles Lamont

Tars and Stripes   1935
Produced by Educational/Twentieth Century Fox
Directed by Charles Lamont

The E-Flat Man   1935
Produced by Educational/Twentieth Century Fox
Directed by Charles Lamont

The Timid Young Man   1935
Produced by Educational/Twentieth Century Fox
Directed by Mack Sennett

La Fiesta de Santa Barbara   1935
Produced by Louis Lewyn/MGM

Directed by Louis Lewyn

The Invader   1936
(Released in the US as *An Old Spanish Custom*)
Produced by British & Continental/MGM
Directed by Adrian Brunel

Three on a Limb   1936
Produced by Educational/Twentieth Century Fox
Directed by Charles Lamont

Grand Slam Opera   1936
Produced by Educational/Twentieth Century Fox
Directed by Charles Lamont

Blue Blazes   1936
Produced by Educational/Twentieth Century Fox
Directed by Raymond Kane

The Chemist   1936
Produced by Educational/Twentieth Century Fox
Directed by Al Christie

Mixed Magic   1936
Produced by Educational/Twentieth Century Fox
Directed by Raymond Kane

Jail Bait   1937
Produced by Educational/Twentieth Century Fox
Directed by Charles Lamont

Ditto   1937
Produced by Educational/Twentieth Century Fox
Directed by Charles Lamont

Love Nest on Wheels   1937
Produced by Educational/Twentieth Century Fox
Directed by Charles Lamont

Pest from the West   1939
Produced by Columbia
Directed by Del Lord

Mooching Through Georgia   1939
Produced by Columbia
Directed by Jules White

Hollywood Cavalcade   1939
Produced by Darryl Zanuck/Twentieth Century Fox
Directed by Irving Cummings

Nothing But Pleasure   1940
Produced by Columbia
Directed by Jules White

Pardon My Berth Marks   1940
Produced by Columbia
Directed by Jules White

The Taming of the Snood   1940
Produced by Columbia
Directed by Jules White

New Moon   1940
Produced by Robert Z. Leonard
Directed by Robert Z. Leonard

The Spook Speaks   1940
Produced by Columbia
Directed by Jules White

The Villain Still Pursued Her   1940
Produced by Franklin-Blank Productions/RKO
Directed by Eddie Cline

Li'l Abner   1940
Produced by Vogue/RKO
Directed by Albert S. Rogell

His Ex Marks the Spot   1940
Produced by Columbia
Directed by Jules White

So You Won't Squawk   1941
Produced by Columbia
Directed by Del Lord

General Nuisance   1941
Produced by Columbia
Directed by Jules White

She's Oil Mine   1941
Produced by Columbia
Directed by Jules White

Forever and a Day   1943
Produced by Anglo-American Productions/RKO
Produced and directed by Rene Clair, Edmund Goulding, Cedric Hardwicke,
Frank Lloyd, Victor Saville, Robert Stevenson, and Herbert Wilcox

San Diego, I Love You   1944
Produced by Universal

100

Directed by Reginald Le Borg

That's the Spirit   1945
Produced by Universal
Directed by Charles Lamont

That Night With You   1945
Produced by Universal
Directed by William A. Seiter

God's Country   1946
Produced by Action Pictures/Screen Guild Productions
Directed by Robert Tansey

El Moderno Barba Azul   1946
Produced by Alsa Films (Mexico)
(never released in the US)
Directed by Jaime Salvador

The Lovable Cheat   1949
Skyline Pictures/Film Classics, Inc.
Directed by Richard Oswald

In the Good Old Summertime   1949
Produced by MGM
Directed by Robert Z. Leonard

You're My Everything   1949
Produced by Twentieth Century Fox
Directed by Walter Lang

Sunset Boulevard   1950
Produced by Paramount
Directed by Billy Wilder
Written by Charles Bracket, Billy Wilder, and D. M. Marshman Jr

Un Duel à Mort   1950
Produced by Films Azur (France)
(never released in US)
Directed by Pierre Blondy

Screen Snapshots: Memories of Famous Hollywood Comedians   1951
Produced by Columbia
Directed and compiled by Ralph Staub

Paradise for Buster   1952
Produced by Wilding Pictures for Deere & Co. (shot in 16 mm private
company film)
Directed by Del Lord

Limelight   1952
Produced by Charles Chaplin

Directed by Charles Chaplin
Written by Charles Chaplin

L'Incantevole Nemica   1953
Produced by Orso Film (Italy)
(not released in US)
Directed by Claudio Gora

Around the World in 80 Days   1956
Produced by Michael Todd/United Artists
Directed by Michael Anderson and Kevin McClory
Written by James Poe, John Farrow, and S. J. Perelman, from the novel by
Jules Verne

It's a Mad, Mad, Mad, Mad World   1963
Produced by Stanley Kramer/United Artists
Directed by Stanley Kramer
Written by William and Tania Rose

A Funny Thing Happened on the Way to the Forum   1966
Produced by United Artists/Quadrangle
Directed by Richard Lester
Written by Melvin Frank and Michael Pertwee

W. C. FIELDS

W illiam Claude Dukenfield, better known as W. C. Fields, is possibly the oddest personality of all in the gallery of comedy greats.

Born in January 1880 in Philadelphia, he inherited, or at any rate learned, a love of things theatrical from his father, James, who was no mean singer, and his mother, Kate, who, it is said, had a lively sense of humour. W. C. Fields's description of his family was: 'Poor but dishonest', which is doubtless entirely untrue, but for the young William Claude brought up in a lively atmosphere, a career in vaudeville must have seemed enticing.

There are many stories, legends perhaps, of childhood poverty, running away from home, and odd jobs in circuses before Fields graduated to the professional theatre; doubtless times were tough in the USA in the eighties and nineties, but from an early age Fields had taught himself to be a proficient juggler and by the early 1900s he was an established performer earning good money worldwide with his act as a tramp juggler. He married Harriet (Hattie) Hughes in San Francisco in 1900 and she joined him in his act.

With the arrival of W. C. Junior in July 1904 Harriet quit show business and W. C. proceeded round the world on his own. It must have been difficult for the Fieldses to keep their affection intact throughout so much separation and, indeed, in the correspondence quoted in *W.C. Fields by Himself* — a compilation of press cuttings, letters, and autobiographical notes assembled by Ronald J. Fields, the great man's grandson — there appears a constant bickering about money that continued up until W. C.'s death on Christmas Day 1946. Typical is this one written in January 1944, which I quote in part.

Dear Harriet,

... can you imagine my surprise when I read your letter and you said we had gone through life doing nothing for each other.

Sixty smackers a week, year in and year out for forty years ($124,800.00) you consider nothing?

Hey-ho-lackaday.

Surprises never cease.

Fields's mistress for many years, Carlotta Monti, gets the same treatment. In June 1946 Fields wrote:

> Dear Carlotta,
>
> Since the other day when you chose to call me a stingy bastard because I would not raise your salary I have mulled the thing over and decided that you should get another position ...

From 1909 until 1914 he worked hard developing his vaudeville act, and, bit by bit, emerging from his out-and-out hobo outfit to a sort of seedy gentility in his presentation. By 1914 he had added a comedy billiards routine to his repertoire and was about to make the jump from endless tours to the more stable world of Broadway.

In 1915 he became a semi-fixture in the *Ziegfeld Follies* with a variety of routines which clearly delighted New Yorkers. In 1924 he was starring in the musical *Poppy*, but by 1926 he was back in the *Follies*, more outrageous and funnier than ever.

Soon after came Hollywood, but Fields's film career had begun in 1915 with a short based on one of his vaudeville routines — *Pool Sharks*, made by Gaumont in Flushing, New York. His first starring role, *Sally of the Sawdust*, was a 1925 adaptation of *Poppy*. Directed by the great D. W. Griffith, it allowed Fields the chance to air some of his routines, but the comedy was intercut with a rather heavy plot concerning the adventures of Sally, played by Carol Dempster, and didn't allow Fields the full flow of his comic invention. It does, however, give him one of the first of a gallery of comic names that marked his subsequent movies — Eustace McGargle.

From 1926 to 1929 W. C. Fields made several films at the Paramount Long Island studios, but none of them have survived and it's therefore difficult to assess how good they were. One thing is certain and that is that they included in one way or another the routines that Fields used, with small variations, in all his subsequent movies.

When talkies came, the big comedians of the day, with the exception of Chaplin who ignored the new phenomenon, had to rethink their approach to films and many went under. The talkies, however, enhanced Fields's work, for, although his international standing came from the fact that his act didn't need words, his muttered asides and astute use of sound effects added considerably to his comic range.

By and large his early films — particularly the four short films he made for Mack Sennett in 1932: *The Dentist* (must of which was devoted to a golf routine), *The Fatal Glass of Beer* (a cautionary tale set in the Yukon), *The Pharmacist*, and *The Barber Shop* — were combinations of routines developed elsewhere. These shorts, which undoubtedly put the Fields brand of comedy on the map, were preceded, however, by two films for Paramount. The first, *Million Dollar Legs*, was set in the fictitious European country of Klopstokia of which Fields is President, and concerned with winning medals and thus prestige at the Olympic Games held in the USA that year (1932). Although William K. Everson in his book, *The Art of W. C. Fields*, describes *Million Dollar Legs* as 'a somewhat disorganised mixture of farce, satire and imitation Sennett Slapstick', critics of the day loved it, and when I first saw it in the British Film Institute celebration of Fields's work at the National Film Theatre some years ago I enjoyed it immensely. The story seemed coherent, the idea (for 1932) topical, and it was well shot and edited.

Fields's next movie venture (also for Paramount, for whom he worked for 12 years) was a segment in the all-star *If I Had a Million*, a collection of stories, some grim, others comic, based on the premise that a multi-millionaire gives a million dollars to several people picked at random. The most famous sequence has Charles Laughton as a downtrodden clerk seeing in his million dollars an escape from the slavery of the office and giving his boss a raspberry. Fields's contribution was as an anti-road-hog motorist who gets his revenge on bad drivers by having them rammed by hired accomplices. The idea sounds unpromising today and wasn't of great moment when it was made, but it allowed Fields to give yet another example of his ability to be unlovable, a quality that today we find most endearing.

In 1933–4 Fields appeared in eight films, mostly in cameo roles. One was the musical *International House*, then came *Tillie and Gus* in which he co-starred with Alison Skipworth and Baby Leroy. His next role was Humpty Dumpty in *Alice in Wonderland*; then he had another chance to show his pool-room sketch in *Six of a Kind*. Then came *You're Telling Me*, a remake of the silent *So's Your Old Man*, in which Fields is an inventor of puncture-proof tyres (in the original it was shatterproof windscreens) and indulges (again) in a golf routine. *Mrs Wiggs of the Cabbage Patch* came next, with a part that did not require him to juggle, play pool or golf, or indeed to do much more than woo and win Zasu Pitts.

After *The Old Fashioned Way*, which Fields wrote under the pseudonym of Charles Bogle, came *It's a Gift*. It can be argued that *It's a Gift* is Fields's finest comedy, although I am a great fan of his 1940 film *The Bank Dick*. In *It's a Gift*, Fields plays Harold Bissonette, the somewhat downtrodden owner of a small-town corner store, whose one ambition is to move to California. It has that staple of Fields's films, a bad-tempered, malicious, selfish family, and in his working life Bissonette is plagued by awkward customers. The worst is Mr Muckle, the blind man, who wreaks havoc in the store, breaking the store windows, putting his foot into a basket of light bulbs, etc. He then purchases a stick of gum which he insists on having delivered and then taps his way safely across Main Street through a maelstrom of traffic.

Baby Leroy is another hazard and opens the tap on a tub of molasses which spreads a sticky sea across the store floor. Fields, returning to find this mayhem, puts up a sign which reads: 'Closed on account of Molasses'.

There is no doubt that Fields's heavy drinking prevented him from making the most of his amazing talent. His deeply suspicious nature, his catalogue of arbitrary likes and dislikes, and his estrangement from his wife also help to underline his misanthropic tendencies, but in more than one film the Fields theme seems to be that in a world of selfish fools the only alternatives are to be more dishonest and devious than others or to lie low and accept the slings and arrows of outrageous fortune until something turns up.

Both are to be seen in his career in the cinema, the most telling example in the adaptation of Dickens's *David Copperfield* where Fields played the engaging, optimistic mountebank, Wilkins Micawber, forever 'waiting for something to turn up'. It was Fields's only straight role and it fitted him like a glove, he being in real life something of a Dickensian character himself.

His delight in the use of strange names both for characters and on-screen credits (A. Pismo Clam, Otis J. Criblecoblis, Mahatma Kane Jeeves, Larsen E. Whipsnade, Egbert Sousé, Eustace McGargle, and Elmer Prettywilly being just some of them), his expletives — 'Mother of Pearl' and 'Godfrey Daniel' — his liking for strange get-ups, awful false moustaches, and extraordinary clothing, show him to have an unusual mixture of intellect, vulgarity, and eccentricity. Most of his films have happy endings, for it's a Fields theme that money brings contentment and that financial security solves all problems. That surely dates back to his earliest years of struggle and deprivation.

His cantankerousness may have been inborn. It certainly reaches a vivid, almost lethal, level when he engages in a battle of words with ventriloquist Edgar Bergen's dummy, Charlie McCarthy, in Bergen's long-running radio series. Here he has yet another run in with the aggressive dummy —

CHARLIE: What makes your nose so red?
FIELDS: That's a very good question, Charles. My scarlet proboscis is a result of an unfortunate accident in my youth.
CHARLIE: What did you do? Fall off the wagon?
FIELDS: Very funny, very funny — tell me, Charles, is it true that your father was a gate leg table?
CHARLIE: If it is — your father was under it.
FIELDS: Why you stunted spruce — I'll throw a Japanese beetle on you.
CHARLIE: Why you bar fly — I'll stick a wick in your mouth and use you for an alcohol lamp.
BERGEN: Charlie — apologise to Mr Fields this minute.
FIELDS: Don't waste your breath, Edgar. Everything you tell that kid goes in one knot hole — and out the other.

Romance came to Fields but fleetingly both on- and off-screen. In Mae West, in the film *My Little Chickadee*, he found an artiste of equal calibre and a similar attitude towards life, but sex never really came into the W. C. Fields equation. The best he could hope for on-screen was a loving teenage daughter. Off-screen he had the patient devotion of Carlotta Monti, but even that brought no lasting satisfaction and domestic peace as Chaplin's and Keaton's last marriages did.

When he died in 1946 one of the most exasperating, awkward, uncompromisingly original comedians of this or any other age had left the scene. The man who claimed, 'I've never struck a woman — not even my own mother' and 'I don't drink water, fishes f*** in it', who said 'No one who dislikes children and animals can be all bad', and whose epitaph was 'On the whole, I'd rather be in Philadelphia' was one of a kind. He was what many comedians are in their private lives — a monster of selfishness and ingratitude — but W. C. Fields gave the world, in his professional life, a great deal of laughter, and for those of us who only saw him from afar, up there on the screen he was, when he chose to be, as great a comedian as any we are ever likely to see.

FILMS

Pool Sharks 1915
Produced by Gaumont Company

Janice Meredith 1924
Produced by Cosmopolitan Pictures
Directed by E. Mason Hopper
Written by Lilly Hayward

Sally of the Sawdust 1925
Produced by Paramount
Directed by D. W. Griffith
Written by Forrest Halsey, from the stage play *Poppy* by Dorothy Donnelly

That Royle Girl 1926
Produced by D. W. Griffith
Directed by D. W. Griffith
Written by Paul Scholfield

It's the Old Army Game 1926
Produced by Adolph Zukor and Jessie L. Lasky
Directed by Edward Sutherland
Written by Thomas J. Geraghty

So's Your Old Man 1926
Produced by Famous Players–Lasky Corporation
Directed by Gregory La Cava
Written by J. Clarkson Miller

The Potters 1927
Produced by Famous Players–Lasky Corporation

Directed by Fred Newmeyer
Written by J. Clarkson Miller

Running Wild   1927
Produced by Paramount
Directed by Gregory La Cava
Written by Gregory La Cava and Roy Briant

Two Flaming Youths   1927
Produced by John Waters
Directed by John Waters
Written by Percy Heath and Donald Davis

Tillie's Punctured Romance   1928
Produced by the Christie Studio
Directed by Edward Sutherland
Written by Monte Brice and Keene Thompson

Fools for Luck   1928
Produced by Paramount
Directed by Charles F. Reisner
Written by J. Walter Ruben

The Golf Specialist   1930
Produced by Louis Brock
Directed by Monte Brice

Her Majesty Love   1931
Produced by Warners
Directed by William Dieterle
Written by Robert Lord and Arthur Caesar

Million Dollar Legs   1932
Produced by Paramount
Directed by Edward Cline
Written by Henry Myers and Nick Barrows, from a story by Joseph L. Mankiewicz

If I Had a Million   1932
Produced by Paramount
Directed by Ernst Lubitsch, Norman Taurog, Stephen Roberts, Norman McLeod, James Cruze, William A. Seiter, and H. Bruce Humberstone
Written by Claude Binyon, Whitney Bolton, Malcolm Stuart Boylan, John Bright, Sidney Buchman, Lester Cole, Isabel Dawn, Boyce DeGaw, Walter de Leon, Oliver H. P. Garrett, Harvey Gates, Grover Jones, Ernst Lubitsch,

Lawton Mackaill, Joseph L. Mankiewicz, William Slavens McNutt, Seton I.
Miller, and Tiffany Thayer, from a story by Robert D. Andrews

The Dentist   1932
Produced by Mack Sennett
Directed by Leslie Pierce
Written by W. C. Fields

The Fatal Glass of Beer   1933
Produced by Mack Sennett
Directed by Clyde Bruckman
Written by W. C. Fields

The Pharmacist   1933
Produced by Mack Sennett
Directed by Arthur Ripley
Written by W. C. Fields

The Barber Shop   1933
Produced by Mack Sennett
Directed by Arthur Ripley
Written by W. C. Fields

International House   1933
Produced by Paramount
Directed by Edward Sutherland
Written by Francis Martin and Walter de Leon

Tillie and Gus   1933
Produced by Douglas MacLean
Directed by Francis Martin

Alice in Wonderland   1933
Produced by Paramount
Directed by Norman McLeod
Written by Joseph L. Mankiewicz and William Cameron Menzies, from original
material by Lewis Carroll

Six of a Kind   1934
Produced by Paramount
Directed by Leo McCarey
Written by Walter de Leon and Harry Ruskin

You're Telling Me   1934
Produced by Paramount

Directed by Earle Kenton
Written by Walter de Leon and Paul M. Jones

Mrs Wiggs of the Cabbage Patch 1934
Produced by Douglas MacLean
Directed by Norman Taurog
Written by William Slavens McNutt and Jane Storm

The Old Fashioned Way 1934
Produced by William LeBaron
Directed by William Beaudine
Written by Garnett Weston and Jack Cunningham, from an original story by
Charles Bogle (W. C. Fields)

It's a Gift 1934
Produced by William LeBaron
Directed by Norman McLeod
Written by Jack Cunningham

David Copperfield 1935
Produced by David O. Selznick
Directed by George Cukor
Written by Howard Estabrook, from the novel by Charles Dickens

Mississippi 1935
Produced by Arthur Hornblow Jr
Directed by Edward A. Sutherland
Written by Francis Martin and Jack Cunningham

The Man on the Flying Trapeze 1935
Produced by William LeBaron
Directed by Clyde Bruckman
Written by Ray Harris, Sam Hardy, Jack Cunningham, and Bobby Vernon

Poppy 1936
Produced by William LeBaron
Directed by A. Edward Sutherland
Written by Waldemar Young and Virginia Van Upp

The Big Broadcast of 1938
Produced by Harlan Thompson
Directed by Mitchell Leisen
Written by Walter de Leon, Francis Martin, and Ken Englund

You Can't Cheat an Honest Man   1939
Produced by Lester Cowan
Directed by George Marshall
Written by George Marion Jr, Rick Mack, and Everett Freeman

My Little Chickadee   1940
Produced by Lester Cowan
Directed by Edward Cline
Written by Mae West and W. C. Fields

The Bank Dick   1940
Produced by Universal
Directed by Edward Cline
Written by Mahatma Kane Jeeves (W. C. Fields), from his original story

Never Give a Sucker an Even Break   1941
Produced by Universal
Directed by Edward Cline
Written by John T. Neville and Prescott Chaplin, from an original story by Otis J. Criblecoblis (W. C. Fields)

Tales of Manhattan   1942
Produced by Boris Morros and S. P. Eagle (Sam Spiegel)
Directed by Julien Duvivier
Written by Ben Hecht, Ferenc Molnar, Donald Ogden Stewart, Samuel Hoffenstein, Alan Campbell, Ladislas Fodor, L. Vadnai, L. Georog, Lamar Trotti, and Henry Blankfort

Follow the Boys   1944
Produced by Albert Rockett
Directed by Eddie Sutherland
Written by Lou Breslow and Gertrude Purcell

Song of the Open Road   1944
Produced by Charles R. Rogers
Directed by S. Sylvan Simon
Written by Albert Mannheimer

Sensations of 1945   1944
Produced by Andrew L. Stone
Directed by Andrew L. Stone
Written by Dorothy Bennett

LAUREL AND HARDY

I n many ways Laurel and Hardy are the most difficult of all the comedy greats to write about. It's not that they did so much that it's hard to cram it all in — although a film-by-film description of their monumental movie career would take a whole book — but there is so little that is dramatic in their careers.

They were, by all accounts, both sweet-tempered men who never fought, who liked and admired each other, but never had much personal contact until in the twilight of their career they toured Great Britain together, to a rapturous reception it must be said, and presently died, loved by all, with their films an almost permanent fixture on television screens the world over.

Stan Laurel was born on 16 June 1895. His real name was Arthur Stanley Jefferson, and he first saw the light of day in the industrial town of Ulverston in Lancashire. Perhaps 'seeing the light of day' is stretching it a bit as back in the 1890s, and indeed from the time of the Industrial Revolution until the 1960s, that part of the north of England was dark with smoke and fog tempered by rain, and in the brief summers the sun shone on grimy, soot-encrusted houses, cobbled streets, spouting factory chimneys, and the occasional brightly lit public house or theatre. Both of the latter were places to escape to, the sole palliatives to the gloom of the environment, and both were well patronized — as an escape from the realities of life into the amnesia of drunkenness or the fantasies of the theatre.

Stanley Jefferson came from a theatrical family. His father, Arthur 'A. J.' Jefferson was a theatre manager and occasionally a writer of sketches, and performer too. From his earliest days Stan wanted to be a music-hall comedian, and, after the almost traditional dropping out of school, he achieved his ambition at the age of 16. Like many other comedians, natural wit had to take the place of formal education (Buster Keaton claimed to have attended school for only one day in his entire life) and in young Stanley Jefferson the wit blossomed early, helped by the fact that the family was constantly on the move. From Ulverston to Gainford, Bishop Auckland and Tynemouth in the north-east of England, and finally to Glasgow, in Scotland, where 'A. J.' settled long enough for young Stan to develop his 'act'. His debut was at Pickards Museum, an amusement arcade which included a tiny theatre.

115

The audience liked him, and from this humble start Stanley Jefferson was on his way. His way led him through pantomime, understudying in touring shows, and a comedy character part in a play called *Alone in the World*. When that closed Stan joined the Fred Karno set-up, literally in the footsteps of Charlie Chaplin whom he understudied in the 'Mumming Birds' sketch called in the USA 'A Night in an English Music-Hall'. When Chaplin left the company in 1913 Stan took over briefly, but such was the pull of Chaplin's popularity that, in spite of another comedian being brought out from England, the Karno troupe was never a success without him, and Stan found himself at a loose end again.

On a previous tour Stan had walked out on Karno to start his own act. He found himself a partner in the person of Arthur Dandoe, another ex-Karno comedian, and devised a sketch called 'The Rum 'Uns from Rome'. When Dandoe left the act he was replaced by another out-of-work comic, Ted Leo.

The act had a mixed reception and Stan was pleased to return to the Karno fold in 1913. When that collapsed Stan formed a three-handed act with another ex-Karno trouper, Edgar Hurley, and his wife. They called themselves 'The Three Comiques', then changed it to Hurley, Stan, and Wren, and finally to The Keystone Trio, in which Stan did an impersonation of Chaplin, Hurley one of Chester Conklin, and Wren became Mabel Normand. With a change of cast it then became The Stan Jefferson Trio. Shortly after this in 1915 he changed his name to Stan Laurel on the grounds that 'it just sounded good' and teamed up with an Australian girl in an act called Stan and Mae Laurel. I'm indebted to John McCabe for this and much other information about Stan Laurel's early days, embodied in his book *Mr Laurel and Mr Hardy*.

In 1917 Stan Laurel made his first film, *Nuts in May*, which was sufficiently successful to get him a contract at Universal. When this ended Stan went back to vaudeville, was spotted by the producer Hal Roach, and used as a supporting comedian and gag writer until in 1926 Laurel came together with Hardy and a legend was born.

Oliver Norvell Hardy was born on 18 January 1892 in Harlem, Georgia. He was a member of a large family much given to singing, and it was from these parochial beginnings that 'Babe', as Oliver Hardy was affectionately known, acquired his urge to go into show business.

He joined a company called Coburn's Minstrels when he was 8, but was soon back at home studying at the Georgia Military College and subsequently the University of Georgia where he read Law.

In 1910 he retired from higher education and opened a movie theatre in Milledgeville, Georgia where his mother had moved from the previous family home in Madison. Running a movie house meant seeing the one- and two-reel comedies of the day several times, and after a while Oliver Hardy thought, 'I'm sure I can do as well or *better* than these so-called comedians', moved to Jacksonville, Florida, and got a job with Lubin Motion Pictures. At first he played 'the heavy', which with his massive build was appropriate. He graduated from playing villains to comedy in 1915 in a film called *The Paperhanger's Helper*.

In December 1918 he moved to Hollywood and worked with comedians Jimmy Aubrey, Earl Williams, and Larry Semon. Then came a time with Hal Roach and the two halves of the world's best-known double act finally drifted together.

There was no set plan to their coming together, it just emerged, and like all great double acts it was the coming together of people with similar backgrounds but different personalities. Both Stan and Ollie had, by 1926, a vast amount of experience of working in movies, but while Stan was the inventor, the gag man, the instigator of many of their comedy ideas, Oliver Hardy was content to be a comedian, adding his personal touches to the work in hand, but leaving the creative side of the partnership to the 'workaholic' Stan Laurel. When a picture was finished Babe would rather play golf.

There is another man as important to Laurel and Hardy as Stan and Ollie themselves and that is Hal E. Roach, the producer. The 'E.' stands for 'Eugene', and the man was born in Elmira, New York, only four days before Babe Hardy. It is said that Roach was very much like Hardy, sharing his 'take life as it comes and enjoy it' philosophy. His success as a producer stemmed from the fact that he was a great spotter of talent and subsequently let that talent develop in its own way.

According to John McCabe he was a good ideas man, but 'when it actually came to getting on to film he'd say "That's the idea, boys. Work it out. Know what I mean?" Then he'd walk away without people knowing what he meant'. His success was considerable, for not only did he make many successful silent comedies, including some with Harold Lloyd, but also the very popular *Our Gang* series of films, almost all of the Laurel and Hardy films, comedies such as *Topper*, and dramas of the calibre of *Of Mice and Men*. That he was a shrewd businessman there is no doubt, and he was a knowing and able showman too. Stan and Ollie made films for Roach for over 20 years and when the partnership ended in 1940 with the completion of *Saps at Sea* their remaining films, though peppered with reworking of old routines, were tired and fairly uninspired. The sadness is that, unlike Harold Lloyd or Chaplin, Laurel and Hardy never owned their films, and when the bonanza of TV re-runs came they couldn't capitalize on the work of their peak years.

Their appeal was mainly due to their childlike approach to life and their amiable foolishness. Two elements in their comedy are constantly repeated — one, the mutual destruction of property; the second, the presence of nagging wives. Disasters centred on the home, and often featured Laurel and Hardy as delivery men, as in *Hats Off*, where they have to deliver a washing machine, and their later sound film, *The Music Box*, where they have to deliver a piano to a house at the top of an enormous flight of steps. Moving a piano also features in *Swiss Miss* — this time complicated by a gorilla. Fights that develop into mass brawls are also a feature of their two-reelers, such as *You're Darn Tootin'*, *Should Married Men Go Home?*, which combines a nagging wife (as usual she's Hardy's) and a mass mudslinging fight as a finale.

Laurel and Hardy, now mainly remembered for their protrayal of bowler-hatted, middle-class, mid-Americans, frequently played sailors — *Two Tars*,

Sailors Beware, Why Girls Love Sailors, Men o' War, and *Any Old Port* being some of the films in which they assumed nautical roles. The fact of the matter is that Laurel and Hardy made so many films of two and three reels, *and* full-length features, they covered more comic ground than any other pair of film-makers in the twenties and thirties. Their best? Well, that's very much a matter of opinion, but there's little doubt that among their best features is *Way Out West*, which contains a dainty soft-shoe shuffle executed by Stan and Ollie for no apparent reason and the singing of 'In the Blue Ridge Mountains of Virginia', with Stan switching from his normal voice to bass and then to treble when hit on the head. It also contains the scenes where, when they are fording a river, Stan makes it easily, but on each crossing Ollie disappears into a pothole.

Blockheads was another winner. Starting off in the First World War with Hardy going over the top with the infantry regiment and Laurel left to guard the trench, we dissolve to 20 years later. Laurel hasn't been relieved but still stalwartly marches to and fro on guard. A mountain of empty baked-bean cans demonstrate how he's kept going throughout the period. Discovered by accident he returns to the States a hero and recuperates in a veterans' hospital. Hardy, now married, goes to see him and misunderstands Laurel's comfortable sitting position with one leg tucked under him and supposes that he's lost it in battle. It's a delightful, silly scene and shows Laurel and Hardy at their innocent best. All too soon their other standard routines — the nagging wife, the blonde next door, the mayhem as Laurel creates havoc with Hardy's home and property — make an appearance.

Laurel and Hardy's comedy style was a strange blend of sadism, vandalism, naïveté, chauvinism, and a sort of divine acceptance of what the universe could throw at them. At the peak of their careers they were popular all over the world as, whether silent or in talkies, their comedy appealed to many people.

In their lifetimes they never achieved the cult following of Chaplin or the Marx Brothers, but to the social historian they tell as much about middle-class America in the thirties as Chaplin does about the working classes in the teens and twenties of the twentieth century.

Since their demise (Oliver Hardy died on 7 August 1957 and Stan Laurel passed away on 23 February 1965), a semi-official fan club has sprung up called 'The Sons of the Desert', based on the 1934 feature in which Stan and Ollie escape from their wives(!) and go to a convention of the semi-secret society called — for no discernible reason — 'Sons of the Desert' (a variation of the Amos 'n' Andy 'Mystic Knights of the Sea') and which, one can assume, is based on the Elks, the Oddfellows, the Masons, and the other fraternities that flourished in the 1930s.

Today's Sons of the Desert, all fans of Laurel and Hardy films, and including many show-business folk in both the UK and USA, have regular meetings to honour their heroes, during which a good time is had by all.

Comedians, as I think this book has helped to show, come in all shapes and sizes, with personalities as various as in any other trade. I hazard a guess that none were sweeter than the simple, funny, delightful Laurel and Hardy. In their lives they made over 100 films together and added something special to the comedy of the twentieth century. Much imitated but inimitable, their ability to make people laugh will survive as long as there are copies of their films to be seen and people to see them. Like all comedy greats they are irreplaceable, but while they lived they made the world a happier place, and that is no mean achievement.

FILMS

Duck Soup   1926

Slipping Wives   1927
Directed by Fred Guiol

Love 'Em and Weep   1927
Directed by Fred Guiol

Why Girls Love Sailors   1927
Directed by Fred Guiol

With Love and Hisses   1927
Directed by Fred Guiol

Sailors Beware   1927
Directed by Fred Guiol

Do Detectives Think?   1927
Directed by Fred Guiol

Flying Elephants   1927
Directed by Frank Butler

All the above produced by Hal Roach – Pathé

Sugar Daddies   1927
Directed by Fred Guiol

Call of the Cuckoo   1927
Directed by Clyde Bruckman

The Second Hundred Years   1927
Directed by Fred Guiol

Hats Off   1927
Directed by Hal Yates

Putting Pants on Philip   1927
Directed by Clyde Bruckman

The Battle of the Century   1927
Directed by Clyde Bruckman

Leave 'Em Laughing   1928
Directed by Clyde Bruckman

The Finishing Touch   1928
Directed by Clyde Bruckman

From Soup to Nuts   1928
Directed by E. Livingston Kennedy

You're Darn Tootin'   1928
Directed by Edgar Kennedy

Their Purple Moment   1928
Directed by James Parrott

Should Married Men Go Home?   1928
Directed by James Parrott

Early to Bed   1928
Directed by Emmett Flynn

Two Tars   1928
Directed by James Parrott

Habeas Corpus   1928
Directed by Leo McCarey

We Faw Down   1928
Directed by Leo McCarey

Liberty   1929
Directed by Leo McCarey

Wrong Again   1929
Directed by Leo McCarey

That's My Wife   1929
Directed by Lloyd French

Big Business   1929
Directed by James Horne

Double Whoopee   1929
Directed by Lewis Foster
Written by Leo McCarey

Berth Marks   1929
Directed by Lewis Foster
Written by Leo McCarey

Men o' War   1929
Directed by Lewis Foster
Written by Leo McCarey

A Perfect Day   1929
Directed by James Parrott
Written by Leo McCarey

They Go Boom   1929
Directed by James Parrott
Written by Leo McCarey

Bacon Grabbers   1929
Directed by Lewis Foster
Written by Leo McCarey

Angora Love   1929
Directed by Lewis Foster
Written by Leo McCarey

Unaccustomed As We Are   1929
Directed by Lewis Foster
Written by Leo McCarey

Hollywood Review   1929
Produced by MGM

Hoosegow   1929
Directed by James Parrott
Written by Leo McCarey

Night Owls   1930
Directed by James Parrott
Written by Leo McCarey

Blotto   1930
Directed by James Parrott
Written by Leo McCarey

Rogue Song   1930
Produced by MGM
Directed by Lionel Barrymore
Written by Frances Marion and John Cotton, from Franz Lehar's operetta
Gypsy Love

Be Big   1930
Directed by James Parrott

Brats   1939
Directed by James Parrott
Written by Leo McCarey

Below Zero   1930
Directed by James Parrott
Written by Leo McCarey

The Laurel and Hardy Murder Case   1930
Directed by James Parrott

Hog Wild   1930
Directed by James Parrott
Written by Leo McCarey

Another Fine Mess   1930
Directed by James Parrott

Chickens Come Home   1931
Directed by James Horne

Laughing Gravy   1931
Directed by James Horne

Our Wife   1931
Directed by James Horne

Come Clean   1931
Directed by James Horne

Pardon Us   1931
(released in Europe as *Gaol Birds*)
Directed by James Parrott
Written by H. M. Walker

One Good Turn   1931
Directed by James Horne

Beau Hunks   1931
(released in Europe as *Beau Chumps*)
Directed by James Horne

Helpmates   1931
Directed by James Parrott

Any Old Port   1932
Directed by James Horne

The Music Box   1932
Directed by James Parrott

The Chimp   1932
Directed by James Parrott

County Hospital   1932
Directed by James Parrott

Scram   1932
Directed by Raymond McCarey

Pack Up Your Troubles 1932
Directed by George Marshall and Raymond McCarey
Written by H. M. Walker

Their First Mistake 1932
Directed by George Marshall

Towed in a Hole 1933
Directed by George Marshall

Twice Two 1933
Directed by James Parrott

Me and My Pal 1933
Directed by Charles Rogers and Lloyd French

Fra Diavolo (The Devil's Brother) 1933
Directed by Hal Roach and Charles Rogers
Written by Jeannie McPherson

The Midnight Patrol 1933
Directed by Lloyd French

Busy Bodies 1933
Directed by Lloyd French

Dirty Work 1933
Directed by Lloyd French

Sons of the Desert 1934
(released in Europe as *Fraternally Yours*)
Directed by William A. Seiter
Written by Frank Craven and Byron Morgan

The Private Life of Oliver the Eighth 1934
Directed by Lloyd French

All the above produced by Hal Roach – MGM

Hollywood Party 1934
Produced by MGM
Directed by Richard Boleslawski
Written by Howard Dietz and Arthur Kober
Music and lyrics by Rodgers and Hart, Arthur Freed, and Gus Kahn

Going Bye Bye 1934
Directed by Charles Rogers

Them Thar Hills 1934
Directed by Charles Rogers

Babes in Toyland 1934
(Reissued under title of *March of the Wooden Soldiers*), based on the operetta by
Victor Herbert
Book and lyrics by Glen MacDonough
Directed by Gus Meins and Charles Rogers
Screenplay by Nick Grinde and Frank Butler

The Live Ghost 1934
Directed by Charles Rogers

Tit for Tat 1935
Directed by Charles Rogers

The Fixer Uppers 1935
Directed by Charles Rogers

Thicker Than Water 1935
Directed by James Horne

Bonnie Scotland 1935
Directed by James Horne
Written by Frank Butler and Jeff Moffitt

The Bohemian Girl 1936
Directed by James Horne and Charles Rogers
Scenario by Alfred Bunn, from the opera by William Balfe

Our Relations 1936
Stan Laurel Productions for Hal Roach–MGM
Directed by Harry Lachman
Written by Richard Connell, Felix Adler, Charles Rogers, and Jack Jevne, from the
story 'The Money Box' by W. W. Jacobs

Way Out West 1937
Stan Laurel Productions for Hal Roach–MGM
Directed by James Horne
Written by Jack Jevne, Charles Rogers, James Parrott, and Felix Adler

Pick a Star 1937
Produced and directed by Edward Sedgwick
Written by Richard Flournoy, Arthur Vernon Jones, and Thomas J. Dougan

Swiss Miss 1938
Directed by John G. Blystone
Written by James Parrott, Felix Adler, and Charles Nelson, from an original story
by Jean Negulesco and Charles Rogers

Blockheads 1938
Stan Laurel Productions for Hal Roach–MGM
Directed by John G. Blystone

Written by James Parrott, Harry Langdon, Felix Adler, Charles Rogers, and Arnold Belgard

The Flying Deuces   1939
RKO Radio
Produced by Boris Morros
Directed by Edward Sutherland
Written by Ralph Spence

A Chump at Oxford   1940
Hal Roach–United Artists
Directed by Alfred Goulding
Written by Charles Rogers, Harry Langdon, and Felix Adler

Saps at Sea   1940
Hal Roach–United Artists
Directed by Gordon Douglas
Written by Charles Rogers, Harry Langdon, Gil Pratt, and Felix Adler

Great Guns   1941
Twentieth Century Fox
Produced by Sol M. Wurtzel
Directed by Monty Banks
Written by Lou Breslow

A-Haunting We Will Go   1942
Twentieth Century Fox
Produced by Sol M. Wurtzel
Directed by Alfred Werker
Written by Lou Breslow

Air Raid Wardens   1943
MGM
Produced by B. F. Zeidman
Directed by Edward Sedgwick
Written by Martin Rackin, Jack Jevne, Charles Rogers, and Harry Crane

Jitterbugs   1943
Twentieth Century Fox
Produced by Sol M. Wurtzel
Directed by Malcolm St Clair
Written by Scott Darling

The Dancing Masters   1943
Twentieth Century Fox
Produced by Lee Marcus
Directed by Malcolm St Clair
Written by Scott Darling and George Bucker

The Big Noise   1944
Twentieth Century Fox
Produced by Sol M. Wurtzel
Directed by Malcolm St Clair
Written by Scott Darling

Nothing But Trouble   1944
MGM
Produced by B. F. Zeidman
Directed by Sam Taylor
Written by Russell Rouse and Roy Golden

The Bullfighters   1945
Twentieth Century Fox
Produced by William Girard
Directed by Malcolm St Clair
Written by Scott Darling

Atoll K   1952
Fortezza Films and Les Films Sirius, France
Produced by R. Elger
Directed by John Berry and Leo Joannon

WOODY ALLEN

W hen I first became aware of Woody Allen, back in the mid sixties, I thought of him as a sort of American Marty Feldman: small, Jewish, sad-faced, and very, very clever. All of that was true as far as it went, but I didn't really suspect the comic genius that lay somewhere inside the man, and which today, a dozen or more films later, is obvious to all.

I first saw Woody Allen in a film produced by another Feldman, Charles K. Feldman, a man known as 'The Caliph of Camp' who had a string of hits to his credit, including *The Seven Year Itch* and *A Streetcar Named Desire*. The new film was called *What's New, Pussycat?* In it Allen co-starred with Peter Sellers, Peter O'Toole, Ursula Andress, Capucine, Paula Prentiss, and Romy Schneider. Woody Allen also wrote a screenplay for the film. It wasn't *the* screenplay because he wasn't the only writer, or the first. I. A. L. Diamond was one of several who'd had a crack at it, but Allen brought most to the picture and then had the misery of seeing that 'most' largely re-written out of existence, by the cast and the ubiquitous Charles K. Feldman.

When the film was released in 1965 it received rotten notices, 'unwholesome' being a typical comment, but in spite of that (or maybe because of it) it made a profit of over 17 million dollars. Woody Allen was to say later of *Pussycat*, 'If they had let me make it I could have made it twice as funny and half as successful', and of Charles Feldman, 'He had no regard for writers, absolutely none whatsoever'. But then, not many film producers do, and that, in the long run, is what drove Woody Allen to make his own films; to write, star and direct, to choose the cast and to have a say in every aspect of the work in hand. As time has gone on the films have got better and the genius that lurked in the man has surfaced to bring us such delights as *Play it Again, Sam, Love and Death, Sleeper, Annie Hall, Manhattan, Purple Rose of Cairo, Hannah and her Sisters, Radio Days*, and the rest. But even before his film-making career took off Allen was a great laughter-maker in cabaret, on record, and as a writer for other comedians.

Born Alan Stewart Konigsberg in Flatbush, New York, on 1 December 1935, Woody Allen followed a path almost traditional among comedy writers. A dropout at school where the only subject to interest him was English and where, thanks to an endless stream of adolescent funnies, he was nicknamed Korny

129

Konigsberg, he frequently absented himself to haunt the cinemas and magic shops of downtown New York.

By the age of 15 he had an encyclopaedic knowledge of radio and movie comedians, and by the time he was 16 he was writing 50 jokes a day for 25 dollars a week for a public relations company. That went up to 40 dollars a week when he went to New York University to study motion picture production — a course that he failed. Then came a job at 175 dollars a week writing for NBC on the ailing Colgate Comedy Hour in Hollywood. The show foundered but Woody formed a useful association with Danny Simon, playwright Neil Simon's brother, who helped to shape the talented joke-maker into an efficient and disciplined screenwriter.

In his private life Allen married his boyhood sweetheart, the 16-year-old Harlene, in 1954 — and divorced her in 1960. After that came a series of romances with arty New York girls, which fired Woody Allen's urge to pick up the education he'd missed out on in school and college. Now back in New York writing TV material for Kay Ballard, Carol Channing, Stubby Kaye, and others, Woody read avidly — Plato, Aristotle, Dante, James Joyce, and many more. In his excellent biography Eric Lax says: 'Woody's pursuit of culture was typical of the way he treats new interests. Initial enthusiasm is followed by learning all he can on the subject and pursuing it until it stops being fun. But only philosophy, magic and the clarinet have become constant avocations.' I have a lot of respect for a man who'd rather play jazz clarinet in a New York bar than be in Hollywood collecting an Oscar — which was what happened in 1987 when *Hannah and her Sisters* hit the jackpot in film awards.

By the early sixties Woody was earning in the region of 1700 dollars a week, but dropped out of scriptwriting to perform in clubs for around 75 dollars. His managers, Jack Rollins and Charles H. Joffe, looked after him and made sure that his apprenticeship as a performer was as untraumatic as possible. After a two-year period of small clubs and even smaller audiences, Woody's intimate and entirely original style clicked, and he became a regular entertainer in Las Vegas.

In an interview subsequently, Woody Allen expressed great respect for Bob Hope, claiming to admire and emulate his 'one-liner' style and delivery, and there's no doubt he can do it. But whereas Bob Hope is always upbeat — a winner every time, a travelling salesman among joke-tellers — Allen, even in his early days as a stand-up comedian, had more to say than the joke he was telling. His anecdotes, his routines of those days, combine the embroidered story of his childhood and upbringing, his failed marriage, and his bad luck in social encounters with fantastic extensions of those semi-realities.

Typical is the story of Allen shooting a moose. But the bullet had just creased its scalp — so the moose wakes up as he's driving home. The moose is strapped to the fender (to the British the bumper) of his car,

> and there's a law in New York State against driving with a conscious moose on your fender, Tuesdays, Thursdays and Saturdays, and I'm

very panicky, then, it hits me. Some friends of mine are having a costume party. I'll go, I'll take the moose, I'll ditch him at the party — it wouldn't be my responsibility.

So he does, and the moose is a great success except that when the time comes to judge the best costume,

> First prize goes to the Berkowitzes, a married couple dressed as a moose. The moose comes in second. The moose is furious! He and the Berkowitzes lock antlers in the living room. They knock each other unconscious. Now, I figure, here's my chance. I grab the moose, strap him on my fender, shoot back to the woods. But! I've got the Berkowitzes ...

A wonderfully inventive piece of surreal humour where fantasy and reality mix to extraordinary comic effect. As his career has progressed, much of the fantasy has dropped away and more and more of the real Woody Allen has come through. And it must be said that in revealing himself he has revealed a great deal about ourselves to those of us who sit in the dark cinemas worldwide and nod wisely or shake with laughter at his beautiful inventions.

Of his movies Woody Allen says, 'Serious directors have the most fun', and he quotes Bergman, Antonioni, and Bertolucci both in discussion of his work and in the films themselves. His one entirely serious film, *Interiors*, is very much in the manner of Bergman and there are moments of what could be called 'Homage to the masters' in many of his pictures — Bertolucci in *Everything You Always Wanted to Know About Sex (But Were Afraid to Ask)*, Bergman again in *Love and Death*, and some wonderful imagery in everything he does. 'But', says Allen, 'when it comes down to survival it's laughs that a comedy has to have ... laughs are hard to get ... but ... laughs are the heart and blood of a comedy.'

How does Woody Allen get his laughs? Well, it's not that easy to define. He makes use of the device that all the good joke-makers have in their repertoire — surprise. He leads you down one line of thought and then suddenly switches direction. For instance, in *Sleeper*, when being questioned about his past life, he says,

> My wife divorced me. She said I was a pervert ... because I drank the water bed.

In *Annie Hall* when Diane Keaton, as Annie, mentions that Hollywood is cleaner than New York, she gets the answer:

> Sure Hollywood is clean. They don't throw their garbage away here — they turn it into television shows.

He frequently uses the rhetorical question, such as 'Do I believe in God?' and then embroiders a surreal answer:

> Do I believe in God? I did until Mother's accident. She fell on some
> meatloaf and it penetrated her spleen. She lay in a coma for months
> unable to do anything but sing 'Granada' to an imaginary herring.

Allen can be direct in the style of the more traditional stand-up comic:

> Back in the fifties I was dating this girl. I was doing to her what
> Eisenhower was doing to the country.

But again and again he forms his jokes as questions. In *Love and Death*, a film full
of visual delights, the hero asks:

> If Jesus was a carpenter I wonder how much he charged for bookshelves?

In a piece written for the *New York Times* in 1972, 'A Brief, Yet Helpful, Guide to
Civil Disobedience', Allen offers the following advice:

> When demonstrating it is good to carry a placard stating one's position.
> Some suggested positions are (1) lower taxes, (2) raise taxes, and (3) stop
> grinning at Persians.

In a piece he wrote for the *New Yorker* in 1973, 'Examining Psychic Phenomena',
there's the following:

> The most astonishing case of transubstantiation was that of Sir Arthur
> Murray who vanished with an audible pop while he was taking a bath and
> suddenly appeared in the String section of the Vienna Symphony
> Orchestra.
>   He stayed on as first violinist for twenty-seven years, although he
> could only play 'Three Blind Mice', and vanished abruptly one day dur-
> ing Mozart's Jupiter Symphony, turning up in bed with Winston Chur-
> chill.

His essay 'Fabulous Tales and Mythical Beasts' first appeared in the *New Republic*
magazine. The mythical beasts include the flying snoll:

> A lizard with four hundred eyes, two hundred for distance, two hundred
> for reading. According to legend, if a man gazes directly into the face of
> the snoll he immediately loses his right to drive in New Jersey.

Then there's the frean:

> The frean is a sea monster with the body of a crab and the head of a cer-
> tified public accountant.

And the weal:

> A large white mouse with the lyrics to 'Am I Blue?' printed on its stomach.

> The weal is unique amongst rodents in that it can be picked up and played like an accordion. Similar to the weal is the lunette, a small squirrel that can whistle and knows the mayor of Detroit personally.

So many times in his written work and his screenplays we get this exotic combination of the mundane and the bizarre, and one giggles at the constant surprises that pop out from Woody Allen's dialogue like rabbits from a magician's hat.

Zelig is, I suppose, the visual limit (so far) of this trick of juxtaposition in Allen's work. This short film has as its theme the chameleon-like figure of the eponymous Zelig turning up in all kinds of historic situations — for instance, waving and smiling at the camera from behind Hitler as he makes a speech filmed in Munich in 1937.

But in all his work, whether the artistic and deeply felt *Interiors*, or the knockabout sex comedy of *Annie Hall*, the mingling of fantasy and the mundane in *The Purple Rose of Cairo*, or the 'times remembered' quality of *Manhattan* and *Radio Days*, Woody Allen shows us a depth of insight and an intellectual understanding of the world he inhabits that is so rare as to be almost unique.

How much 30-odd years of psychoanalysis have helped in the personal mind-stretching of the kid from Flatbush, or how much the Jewish family background and the adventure of growing up in the forties and fifties in an America bursting with vitality, optimism, and ideas have sharpened his responses to what he sees it's hard to say, but Woody Allen's vision is one to cherish.

There are many Americans I know and like, and many American artsists and authors I admire. The late S. J. Perelman, whom I knew slightly and whose work I love, is one, Kurt Vonnegut is another, and Mel Brooks fills me with admiration at his mischievous and fearless iconoclasm. But high on my list of US all-time greats is the wispy, red-headed, bespectacled genius who, as they say, is the sort of man who only happens once in a lifetime. I feel lucky, delighted, and profoundly grateful that Woody Allen happened in mine.

FILMS

These include:

What's New, Pussycat? 1965
Produced by Charles K. Feldman
Directed by Clive Donner
Written by Woody Allen

Casino Royale 1967
Produced by Charles K. Feldman
Directed by John Huston, Kenneth Hughes, Val Guest, Robert Parrish, and Joseph McGrath

Written by Wolf Mankowitz, John Law, and Michael Sayers, from the novel by Ian Fleming

Don't Drink the Water 1969
Produced by Charles Joffe
Directed by Howard Morris
Written by R. S. Allen and Harvey Bullock, from the stage play by Woody Allen

Take the Money and Run 1969
Produced by Charles H. Joffe for Palomar Pictures
Directed by Woody Allen
Written by Woody Allen and Mickey Rose

Bananas 1971
Produced by Jack Grossberg
Directed by Woody Allen
Written by Woody Allen and Mickey Rose

Play it Again, Sam 1972
Produced by Arthur P. Jacobs
Directed by Herbert Ross
Written by Woody Allen

Everything You Always Wanted to Know About Sex (But Were Afraid to Ask) 1972
Produced by Charles H. Joffe
Directed by Woody Allen
Written by Woody Allen, from the book by David Reuben

Sleeper 1973
Produced by Jack Grossberg
Directed by Woody Allen
Written by Woody Allen and Marshall Brickman

Love and Death 1975
Produced by Charles H. Joffe
Directed by Woody Allen
Written by Woody Allen

The Front 1976
Produced by Martin Ritt–Jack Rollins–Charles H. Joffe Productions
Directed by Martin Ritt
Written by Walter Bernstein

Annie Hall 1977
Produced by Charles H. Joffe
Directed by Woody Allen
Written by Woody Allen and Marshall Brickman

Interiors 1978
Produced by Charles H. Joffe
Directed by Woody Allen
Written by Woody Allen

Manhattan 1979
Produced by Charles H. Joffe
Directed by Woody Allen
Written by Woody Allen and Marshall Brickman

Stardust Memories 1980
Produced by Robert Greenhut
Directed by Woody Allen
Written by Woody Allen

A Midsummer Night's Sex Comedy 1982
Produced by Robert Greenhut
Directed by Woody Allen
Written by Woody Allen

Zelig 1983
Produced by Robert Greenhut
Directed by Woody Allen
Written by Woody Allen

Broadway Danny Rose 1984
Produced by Robert Greenhut
Directed by Woody Allen
Written by Woody Allen

The Purple Rose of Cairo 1985
Produced by Robert Greenhut
Directed by Woody Allen
Written by Woody Allen

Hannah and her Sisters 1986
Produced by Robert Greenhut
Directed by Woody Allen
Written by Woody Allen

Radio Days 1987
Produced by Robert Greenhut
Directed by Woody Allen
Written by Woody Allen

September 1988
Produced by Robert Greenhut
Directed by Woody Allen
Written by Woody Allen

JOHN CLEESE

I t's more difficult to write about John Cleese than many other comedy greats because, for one thing, I know him quite well: I have worked with him, eaten at his table, been on terms of affectionate mockery with him, and find him both wildly funny and, in his more serious moments, just a little naïve. Furthermore, he's still alive and, I should imagine, his best work is yet to come.

In most of his working life John Marwood Cleese (born 27 October 1939 in Weston-Super-Mare) has been part of a team — with David Frost in *The Frost Report* television series, with Marty Feldman, Tim Brooke-Taylor, and Graham Chapman in *At Last the 1948 Show*, a mould-breaking television series of the 1960s, and the iconoclastic, runaway success of *Monty Python's Flying Circus*. But in spite of this teamwork John has always been a loner, an individual within the group, never sacrificing his own individuality for the greater glory of the whole but making the whole more glorious by his unique contribution. Even his most successful TV series, *Fawlty Towers*, which he co-wrote with Connie Booth (who was at that time his wife), was a team effort that gave Prunella Scales, as his no-nonsense wife Sybil, and Andrew Sachs, as the cute but incompetent Spanish waiter Manuel, starring parts. Even so it was Cleese who actually and metaphorically towered over everyone and gave the doings at a fourth-rate hotel in a mediocre seaside resort a comic madness that defied the mundane plots and became, understandably, one of the hottest properties ever produced by the comedy department of the BBC.

Simultaneously, Cleese as part of the video production company Video Arts (and needless to say the most important part) made a number of training films of the 'how to – how not to' variety which have become extremely popular with businesses — small, medium and multinational — which feel that a little humour with their staff training is no bad thing.

In repose Cleese looks the epitome of the tall, good-looking, Anglo-Saxon, middle-class hero; the sort who built the Empire but lost the colonies, a banker perhaps, or an upper-echelon civil servant, as traditionally British as roast beef and Windsor Castle. He has none of what are regarded as the assets of major comedians. He's not short, or Jewish, or black, or winsome. He has none of the acrobatic prowess of Buster Keaton or the physical ingenuity of Chaplin; he hasn't the vulgar audacity of Mel Brooks or the repose of Jack Benny. And yet in his work he can produce most of those effects. In one *Monty Python* sketch, as a merchant banker unable to understand that in giving to charity you receive nothing in return, he is all silky urbanity until the full horror of not making a profit on his investment of a shilling in the collecting tin dawns on him.

The 'Ministry of Silly Walks' sketch shows him as a towering grotesque, and as the irate purchaser of a theoretically live parrot that turns out to be dead, he handles the verbal cascades of sub-genteel abuse and thesaurus-like descriptions on the parrot's lack of animation, with a skill that transcends mere comic acting.

CLEESE: Look, my lad — that parrot is definitely deceased! And when I bought it not half an hour ago, you assured me that its lack of movement was due to it being tired and shagged out after a long squawk.

PALIN: It's probably pining for the fiords.

CLEESE: Pining for the fiords — what kind of talk is that? Look, why did it fall flat on its back the moment I got it home?

PALIN: The Norwegian Blue prefers kipping on its back. It's a beautiful bird — lovely plumage.

CLEESE: Look, I took the liberty of examining that parrot, and I discovered that the only reason it had been sitting on its perch in the first place was that it had been nailed there.

PALIN: 'Course it was nailed there, otherwise it would have muscled up to those bars and voom!

CLEESE: Look, matey, this parrot wouldn't 'voom' if I put four thousand volts through it. It's bleeding demised.

PALIN: It's not — it's pining!

CLEESE: It's *not* pining — it's passed on! This parrot is no more! It has ceased to be! It's expired and gone to meet its maker! This is a late parrot! It's a stiff! Bereft of life it rests in peace — if you hadn't nailed it to the perch it would be pushing up the daisies! It's rung down the curtain and joined the choir invisible! THIS IS AN EX-PARROT!

PALIN: Well, I'd better replace it then.

CLEESE: (*To camera*) If you want to get anything done in this country you've got to complain until you're blue in the mouth.

PALIN: Sorry, guv, we're right out of parrots.

CLEESE: I see, I see — I get the picture.

PALIN: I've got a slug.

CLEESE: Does it talk?

PALIN: Not really, no.

CLEESE: Well it's scarcely a replacement, then, is it?

I suppose if one had to compare him with any of the *late* greats, the one who springs to my mind is W. C. Fields. There is in Cleese an assumption of the worthlessness of mankind and a deep suspicion of people's motives that is evident in a great deal of Fields's work.

It's difficult for a tall comedian to get sympathy. Six-footer Jacques Tati had to resort to the incompetence and foolish lovableness of M. Hulot to do it; Carl Reiner has used his baldness to disarm the onlooker — his sketch as a toupee salesman in *Rowan and Martin's Laugh-In*, back in the seventies, was a classic of its kind. Both of them, like Cleese, also wrote. It's easier for a tall man to find an outlet for his comedy as a writer rather than as a performer and even though John Cleese, who became abnormally tall when in his early teens, must have used his height for laughs just as years later, in other circumstances, Marty Feldman used his strange, swivelling eyes, he was in his early days primarily a writer.

Like so many other British performers before and since, John Cleese has in his time been one of the stalwarts of the Cambridge Footlights revue. These annual university revues started life in the nineteenth century as smoking concerts (men only) and a chance for the young undergraduates to let off steam. The tradition flourished and at one time in Cambridge was as well known for its comedians as for its academics and scientists. Today, of course, it is notoriously the spawning ground of Britain's must successful post-war spies, Burgess, Maclean, Blunt, Philby, and others who cannot be named, but back in 1963 it was proving a vintage year for the Footlights.

Cleese, on course for a career in law, was sidetracked by BBC headhunters, and after graduation started work as a scriptwriter on radio. His first assignment was to write a Christmas 'special' called *Yule Be Surprised*. When he delivered the script he was told there were too many jokes in it! He persisted as a writer and at last found himself in company with a group of like-minded wits in a hit radio show of the late 1960s, *I'm Sorry I'll Read That Again*.

Many of the characters became 'regulars'. Two such were John and Mary, played by John Cleese and Jo Kendall, and written by John Cleese.

JOHN: Ah, how I love to be alone in the country.
MARY: John?
JOHN: Yes?
MARY: *I'm* with you.
JOHN: How I love to be alone in the country.
MARY: But John — *you* brought me with you!
JOHN: I didn't. You hid in the back.
MARY: But you must have noticed.
JOHN: Not at all — it's a very large tandem.
MARY: But John — when we fell off going down the stairs — you *must* have seen me.
JOHN: I thought you were a hitchhiker.
MARY: But I'm your wife. You must have recognized me.
JOHN: I didn't Mary.
MARY: Why not?
JOHN: Well, because you were disguised as a cactus.
MARY: Oh, John — why don't you admit it ? You don't love me any more.
        (*Pause*)
JOHN: All right. I admit it.

> MARY: John — once we had something that was pure, and wonderful, and — good ... what's happened to it?
>
> JOHN: You spent it all.

Before *I'm Sorry I'll Read That Again* the Footlights revue, *Cambridge Circus* had been revived by an enterprising entrepreneur who took the show to New Zealand and the USA.

When the rest of the cast returned to the UK (and they included Tim Brooke-Taylor and Graham Chapman with whom Cleese was to be reunited in *At Last the 1948 Show*), John stayed on in the States, appearing in the musical *Half a Sixpence*, working as a journalist on *Newsweek*, and subsequently performing in a touring version of *The Establishment Show*, where he met his first wife, Connie Booth.

On his return to England he joined the *I'm Sorry I'll Read That Again* company as writer and performer, and then crossed over to television at the request of David Frost, whose place in the sixties satire movement under the benign producership of Ned Sherrin had made him rich and famous both in the UK and the USA. In 1966 he'd won the Golden Rose of Montreux, the top prize in the annual international TV comedy festival, for his 'special' *Frost Over England*. When the BBC decided to spin this one off into a series called *The Frost Report*, John Cleese was recruited to write and perform. His height and manner were used to great effect in a sketch by John Law and Marty Feldman on class distinction. The point was rammed home by the fact that John Cleese, at six foot five inches, towered over Ronnie Barker's five foot nine inches, and Ronnie Corbett's five foot one inch.

> CLEESE: I look down on him (*indicating Barker*) because I am upper class.
>
> BARKER: I look up to him (*indicating Cleese*) because he is upper class; but I look down on him (*indicating Corbett*) because he is lower class. I am middle class.
>
> CORBETT: I know my place. I look up to them both. But I don't look up to him (*Barker*) as much as I look up to him (*Cleese*), because he has got innate breeding.
>
> CLEESE: I have got innate breeding, but I have not got any money. So sometimes I look up (*bending knees and doing so*) to him (*Barker*).
>
> BARKER: I still look up to him (*Cleese*) because although I have money, I am vulgar. But I am not as vulgar as him (*Corbett*), so I still look down on him (*Corbett*).
>
> CORBETT: I know my place. I look up to them both; but while I am poor, I am honest, industrious and trustworthy. Had I the inclination, I could look down on them. But I don't.
>
> BARKER: We all know our place, but what do we get out of it?
>
> CLEESE: I get a feeling of superiority over them.

BARKER: I get a feeling of inferiority from him (*Cleese*) but a feeling of superiority over him (*Corbett*).

CORBETT: I get a pain in the back of my neck.

The friendship that had developed over the years between Cleese and Chapman, Feldman and Brooke-Taylor grew in 1967 into a professional team with *At Last the 1948 Show*, written and performed by the quartet and made by the commercial television company Associated Rediffusion. In a shake-up in the Independent Television company structure, Associated Rediffusion amalgamated with ABC Television to form a new company called 'Thames Television', and another new company, headed by David Frost, called 'London Weekend Television', was created to split the lucrative franchise of the London area. There was no room in the new set-up for *At Last the 1948 Show*, and a planned third series was never made.

Marty Feldman and Tim Brooke-Taylor crossed over to the BBC to make a series called *Marty* (with contributions from Cleese and Chapman as well as other well-known comedy writers, although the major part of the writing was done by Marty Feldman and me).

Meanwhile, Michael Palin and Terry Jones, along with Eric Idle and Terry Gilliam the animator (who had also contributed to *Marty*) were making a series for the new Thames Television called *Do Not Adjust Your Set*, aimed at children, but attracting a wider audience. The series *had* survived from Associated Rediffusion where it had originated the year before. By 1969 the sextet of Cleese, Chapman, Palin, Jones, Idle, and Gilliam had come together to create the historic series *Monty Python's Flying Circus*. Cleese's contribution, especially when writing with Graham Chapman or appearing on screen with Michael Palin, was enormous.

Here's a typical piece of Cleese/Chapman writing:

CHAPMAN: Hullo, Mrs Premise.

CLEESE: Hullo, Mrs Conclusion.

CHAPMAN: Busy day?

CLEESE: Busy? I just spent four hours burying the cat.

CHAPMAN: *Four hours* to bury a cat?

CLEESE: Yes — it wouldn't keep still.

CHAPMAN: Oh — it wasn't dead, then?

CLEESE: No, no — but it's not at all well, so as we were going away for a fortnight's holiday I thought I'd better bury it to be on the safe side.

CHAPMAN: Quite right — you don't want to come back from Sorrento to a dead cat. It'd be so anticlimactic. Yes, kill it now, that's what I say. We're going to have our budgie put down.

CLEESE: Really — is it very old?

CHAPMAN: No, we just don't like it. We're going to take it to the vet tomorrow.

CLEESE: Tell me, how do they put budgies down, then?

CHAPMAN: Well, it's funny you should ask that, because I've just been reading a great big book about how to put your budgie down, and apparently, you can either hit them with the book, or you can shoot them just there, above the beak.

CLEESE: Just there? Well, well, well. 'Course, Mrs Essence flushed hers down the loo.

CHAPMAN: No, you shouldn't do that — no, that's dangerous. They *breed* in the sewers!

After three series John Cleese became frustrated by the constraints of working with a team and wanted to get away and work on his own. As he expressed it to me, 'I'm fed up with being told to turn up at 8 a.m. on Monday morning on Wakefield railway station dressed as a penguin.'

So the other five pressed on with series four, and John Cleese and Connie Booth sat down to devise a brand new series. What emerged was *Fawlty Towers*, and although only 12 episodes were ever made, the series set in a fourth-rate hotel reminiscent of one Cleese himself had stayed in while shooting film sequences for *Python*, was a huge success.

The stories — concerning a visitor found dead in bed, a pet rat loose in the restaurant, a confidence trickster bouncing dud cheques — were the mundane base on which was built a pyramid of humour, brilliant characterizations, and farce of a very high order. But although as a writing partnership Connie and John were a success, their private relationship deteriorated, and in 1976 they parted for good, their daughter Cynthia spending her time equally with her two parents.

In 1981 John married Barbara Trentham, whom he'd met during the Pythons' American tour in the mid seventies. She had a similar background to Connie, being multi-talented and American. She and John now live separately, their daughter Camilla (born 1984) spending time with both parents.

In the gap between marriages, John Cleese had suffered bouts of deep depression and had sought help in psychotherapy. It so intrigued him and he found it all so effective that in collaboration with psychiatrist, Robin Skynner, he wrote a book, *Families and How to Survive Them*, which has sold well and which I know has been a great help to people who lack the insight or the knowledge to cope with their emotional problems. The form is that of a conversation — mainly question and answer — between Cleese and Skynner, which covers almost every aspect of the emotional relationships, hidden and overt, that can occur in the family. Cleese's first impulse was to make it as a television series but he soon realized, as others have before him, that television tends to shy away from real emotion and true understanding and much prefers programmes (e.g. soap operas) that are predictable and therefore not uncomfortable or disturbing. Another Cleese/Skynner book is being written, developing themes touched on in *Families*.

It took a long time to persuade the BBC that *Monty Python's Flying Circus* was a good idea, just as in the USA *Rowan and Martin's Laugh-In* was felt to be a dangerous and radical concept; it was only kept on the screen because of its massive popular appeal and the ingenuity and skill of producer George Schlatter in persuading NBC that it really was innocuous.

Schlatter, incidentally, had great regard for Cleese although, to my knowledge, they worked together only once when John figured in the English segment of a TV 'special', *It's a Wacky World*, in 1972.

The success of the *Python* team on TV led to books, LPs and enormously profitable stage tours. Then came the movies. The first was *And Now For Something Completely Different*, which wasn't — different that is. It was a remake of some of the better *Python* sketches. The team's first original film was *Monty Python and the Holy Grail*, an Arthurian legend told in surreal terms, mainly on location in Scotland.

Cleese's major contributions to the movie were in the character of the Black Knight who, in an epic duel with King Arthur, has all his limbs hacked off, but is still game and shouts at the retreating figure of King Arthur, 'Come back here ... and I'll bite your legs off', and as an extremely bizarre Frenchman shouting eccentric abuse from a castle battlements.

The next *Python* film was *Monty Python's Life of Brian* — a story set in biblical times, with Brian having a parallel existence to Jesus. EMI, the entertainment conglomerate, were going to make it but pulled out at the eleventh hour because of its possible blasphemy and for fear of offending its more religious cinema ticket buyers. George Harrison, ex-Beatle and close friend of Eric Idle and Michael Palin, came to the rescue, formed a company called Handmade Films, and the project was off and running.

Life of Brian was patchy. One scene with the shepherds — the ones who 'watched their flocks by night' as the carol has it — comparing sheep with cats to the latter's detriment, was funny on paper but didn't raise much laughter when filmed, and was finally cut from the picture. John Cleese's major contribution was as an Israelite freedom fighter asking his comrades, apropos the Romans, 'What have they ever done for us?' and having reluctantly to admit the many blessings — water, roads, a police force, etc., that the Romans had brought with them. 'But apart from the roads, the wine, the aqueduct ... etc., etc., what have they done for us?' It was the speech of a fair-minded bigot and very funny.

Much of the film, however, isn't funny, but it caused a great deal of argument when it was released and, probably because of the furore, made a considerable profit.

John Cleese next played Petruchio in Jonathan Miller's TV production of *The Taming of the Shrew*, which was a beautifully staged version of the Shakespeare play. In it John showed an ability to play classical comedy with style and repose.

He then played a small part — that of Robin Hood — in Terry Gilliam's film *Time Bandits*.

The next *Python* film was *Monty Python's The Meaning of Life*, which started with a birth and climaxed with Terry Jones as an incredibly obese diner in a West End restaurant, suavely served by Cleese, exploding — one last gluttonous mouthful causing his disintegration.

John also played the part of a world-weary schoolmaster taking a sex education class in a private school in which the boys are as bored by the subject as he is.

John Cleese is quoted in George Perry's book *Life of Python*, which chronicles the careers of the six people chiefly involved, as saying of *The Meaning of Life* that 'the film was a tedious experience', a verdict with which I, as a viewer, can concur. However, like all *Python* films, it has moments to delight, and one scene, set in the trenches of the First World War, is one of the funniest I have encountered in the cinema for many years.

Cleese then spent some time in minor work, making 'How to' films, advertising in Britain and Australia, and then, surprisingly branched into politics, becoming a major force in the TV presentation of the new political party, the Social Democrats. Cleese's manic TV persona sat uneasily with this avowedly moderate party, which, in any case, disintegrated after the General Election of 1987.

My own feeling is that making as much money as he has, and being as successful in his profession as he undoubtedly is, has depressed Cleese. His uneasiness in social encounters, his need for the reassuring presence of psychiatrist, Robin Skynner, his *conscience*, which must be disturbed by the ease with which advertisers can be made to cough up large sums of money for what are, frankly, poor pieces of work on John's part, must be disturbing.

In October 1987 I was surprised and disturbed to read in the *Daily Mail* a story headlined:

CLEESE: I HAVE LOST MY COMIC POWERS.

It went on:

> Comedy king John Cleese has a problem ... he fears he is losing the power to make people laugh.
> ... the 48-year-old creator of Basil Fawlty and the Ministry of Silly Walks added: 'As I have got older I don't think I am quite in contact with audiences in the way I used to be.'

Certainly in the film *Clockwise*, Cleese, as a time-obsessed headmaster running his vast comprehensive school with split-second timing and then finding a series of frustrating obstacles in his path en route to a headmasters' conference, is far from funny. The frustrations in the film seem far too contrived and in many cases unreal, and Cleese's character never survives its inherent lack of sympathy.

Where Chaplin or Keaton or Tati could have added a personal, perhaps even sentimental, note to the proceedings, John Cleese keeps so rigidly in character that very little comedy escapes on to the screen.

I think John Cleese's problem can be solved in two words — Michael Palin. With Palin, Cleese is at his best, and the blend of the two personalities seems to enhance both individuals. I'd recommend a course of Palin, and if that fails Cleese has only one remedy — to go broke. Poverty, as this history of many comedians shows, is an amazingly useful spur to comic action.

AFTERTHOUGHT

When that was written I hadn't seen *A Fish Called Wanda* (indeed it hadn't been made) but in it Cleese is reunited with Palin and the film is as funny, inventive, and impressive as anything John Cleese had done. He wrote, co-produced, and co-directed the film and it shines with the sort of originality that all the 'greats' have brought to their work. I cannot see poverty, as I suggested in the previous paragraph, being even a remote possibility in John Cleese's future.

FILMS

These include:

Interlude   1968
Produced by David Deutsch and Jack Hanbury
Directed by Kevin Billington
Written by Lee Langley and Hugh Leonard

The Best House in London   1968
Produced by Carlo Ponti, Philip Breen, and Kurt Unger
Directed by Philip Savile
Written by Denis Norden

The Magic Christian   1969
Produced by Denis O'Dell
Directed by Joseph McGrath
Written by Terry Southern, Joseph McGrath, and Peter Sellers, from the novel by Terry Southern

The Rise and Rise of Michael Rimmer   1970
Produced by Harry Fine
Directed by Kevin Billington
Written by Peter Cook, John Cleese, Kevin Billington, and Graham Chapman

And Now For Something Completely Different   1971
Produced by Patricia Casey
Directed by Ian McNaughton
Written by John Cleese, Graham Chapman, Terry Gilliam, Eric Idle, Michael Palin, and Terry Jones

The Statue   1970
Produced by Anis Nohra

Directed by Rod Amateau
Written by Alec Coppel and Denis Norden

It's a 2' 6" Above the Ground World   1972
(also known as *The Love Ban*)
Produced by Betty Box and Ralph Thomas
Directed by Ralph Thomas
Written by Kevin Laffan, from his play

Monty Python and the Holy Grail   1975
Produced by Mark Forstater
Directed by Terry Gilliam and Terry Jones
Written by Graham Chapman, John Cleese, Terry Gilliam, Eric Idle, and Michael
Palin

Monty Python's Life of Brian   1979
Produced by John Goldstone
Directed by Terry Jones
Written by John Cleese, Graham Chapman, Eric Idle, Michael Palin, Terry Gilliam,
and Terry Jones

The Great Muppet Caper   1981
Produced by David Lazer and Frank Oz
Directed by Jim Henson
Written by Tom Patchett, Jay Tarses, Jerry Juhl, and Jack Rose

Time Bandits   1981
Produced by Terry Gilliam
Directed by Terry Gilliam
Written by Michael Palin and Terry Gilliam

Privates on Parade   1983
Produced by Simon Relph
Directed by Michael Blakemore
Written by Peter Nichols, from his play

Yellowbeard the Pirate   1983
Produced by Carter de Haven Jr
Directed by Mel Damski
Written by Graham Chapman, Peter Cook, and Bernard McKenna

Monty Python's The Meaning of Life   1983
Produced by John Goldstone
Directed by Terry Jones
Written by Graham Chapman, John Cleese, Terry Gilliam, Eric Idle, Michael Palin,
and Terry Jones

Silverado   1984
Produced by Lawrence Kasdan
Directed by Lawrence Kasdan

146

Written by Lawrence and Mark Kasdan

Clockwise   1985
Produced by Michael Codron
Directed by Christopher Morahan
Written by Michael Frayn

A Fish Called Wanda   1987
Produced by John Cleese and Michael Shamberg
Directed by John Cleese and Charles Crichton
Written by John Cleese

TELEVISION

including:

That Was the Week That Was   1962–3 BBC
writing contributions

The Frost Report   1966–7 BBC
writing contributions and performing

At Last the 1948 Show   1967 Rediffusion
co-writing and performing

Monty Python's Flying Circus   4 series 1969–74 BBC

Fawlty Towers   1975 and 1979 BBC
co-writing and performing

TONY HANCOCK

Tony Hancock was an enigma. There has never been a better comic actor on British television and radio, nor one who at his peak was surrounded by finer people, and yet he died a failure: bitter, drunk, and alone. His producers, Dennis Main Wilson on radio and Duncan Wood on television, were among the best of a very talented group working for the BBC in the fifties and sixties. His writers, Alan Simpson and Ray Galton, have never been surpassed. Their great creation, the TV series *Steptoe and Son*, which was adapted as *Sandford and Son* in the USA and translated into many languages worldwide, is still today regarded as one of the peaks of television situation comedy. Their writing for Tony Hancock was always good, and at times rose to unparalleled heights of invention.

Hancock's supporting cast were the best available too. South-African-born Sid James, subsequently the star of many TV series and films, was a brilliant foil; he played a smart-alec hanger-on, at once the butt of Hancock's barbed remarks and the scheming mountebank luring his partner into a series of dubious and unsuccessful ventures. Other great performers graced both the radio and, for a time, the TV shows: Hattie Jacques, whose bulk (circa 280 pounds) was belied by a dainty style of speech and mannerism, Kenneth Williams (112 pounds), himself a major comic figure in the English tradition of broad comedy and who appeared in the majority of the highly successful *Carry On* movies. Then there was the Australian, Bill Kerr, who is known internationally today for his fine character acting in such films as *Gallipoli*. These people, and many others too, surrounded Tony Hancock with a back-up few star performers have ever had, and yet one by one he shed them, sacked them, allowed them to leave, and finished up dispirited, deserted, and alone in the Australian hotel where he took his own life ... a flop.

Many other funny men before and since Hancock have trodden this path, and although the details vary the pattern is very much the same. But what *is* the pattern? What was the pattern of Tony Hancock's life?

He was born into a lower-middle-class family in the Midlands town of Birmingham in 1924. When he was 3 his family moved to the seaside town of Bournemouth, Dorset, which in the summer months hummed with show business — actors, singers, comedians, and jugglers imported to amuse the holidaymakers who thronged to this popular south-coast resort.

149

Tony's father, Jack, sold his laundry business to acquire a pub, The Railway Arms, which Tony's mother, Lily, ran while her husband was out and about — as a semi-professional entertainer. Though not amazingly affluent, the Hancocks weren't short of money through the depression years of the thirties and, in fact, when Tony's younger brother, Roger, appeared on the scene, young Tony, now aged 7, was sent to boarding school in nearby Swanage. When Tony was 11 his father died, and shortly afterwards Lily married again and became Mrs Robert Walker.

It's not difficult to see that the combination of losing his father when at an impressionable age and, because of his mother running the pub, having little traditional home life, left Tony feeling alone and neglected, and he claimed to have spent most of his formative years by himself in the local cinema. He left school for good — the school in question being Bradfield College in Berkshire — when he was 15.

After a series of jobs he started on the path that was to lead, in time, to great fame and a modest fortune as a comedian. But it was for a fee of 10 shillings a time at semi-professional concerts that he learned the awful truth — he was at that period of his life a very, very bad comedian indeed.

Even though it was wartime and audiences, particularly audiences of servicemen, would laugh at almost anything, however unsubtle, Tony Hancock flopped. But bit by bit, joke by joke, Tony improved both timing and material and by 1942 when he was called up he was quite a presentable stand-up comedian. Later in his RAF service he joined one of the Ralph Reader Gang Shows — groups of servicemen with show business experience who toured the various war zones entertaining the troops. Tony was a big success. Through the last years of the Second World War he travelled through North Africa and Italy and even reached Gibraltar entertaining troops. Towards the end of his service career Tony met and worked alongside Peter Sellers who, like Hancock, had made the grade as an entertainer at troop concerts. But then most of the British comedians who became stars in the post-war period had learned their basic training in show business while serving in either the Army, the Navy or the RAF. The truth of the matter is that although war is hell it actually consists of short periods of extreme terror which punctuate long periods of great boredom: of waiting for action. In these periods the entertainer, however raw and inexperienced, is a godsend — he helps to ease the boredom and to banish temporarily the pain of homesickness.

Civilian audiences, however, are more difficult to please, and it was some time before Tony Hancock (and the same applied to Peter Sellers and the rest) began to emerge as an original and funny comedian. He did what was at the time an almost obligatory apprenticeship, a season at the Windmill Theatre, a few scattered dates in provincial music-halls, pantomimes, summer seasons, and then co-starred with Jimmy Edwards in two West End revues. He made a television series for Associated Rediffusion, and a great many radio appearances of one kind and another, but the show that really brought him stardom was *Hancock's Half Hour*.

On radio *Hancock's Half Hour* was an attempt by Tony and his writers to break the mould of radio comedy. Up to then it had been a matter of brief sketches stitched together in a simple story line with each character having their own 'catchphrase', a line or word which, repeated every week, would cause the audience to laugh in anticipation of the jokes to come.

Galton and Simpson, having served their radio apprenticeship writing this type of material (mainly for Tony Hancock), wanted to write something more realistic. The producer chosen to push radio comedy into the future was Dennis Main Wilson, who had successfully piloted *The Goon Show* to success and was later to have great success on television with *Till Death Us Do Part*, and the Marty Feldman series, *Marty*. But high though the hopes of something completely different were, the addition of Kenneth Williams to the show with his so-called 'snide' character and his constantly repeated 'Stop messing about' soon put paid to the 'no catchphrase' ruling.

The shows were domestic comedies to the extent that Hancock was said to be living with two spongers, played by Bill Kerr and Sid James, and concerned Hancock's fictionalized attempts to create a successful show-business career. They were much superior shows to any of their contemporaries and can be heard today on LP or cassette with great pleasure.

The television *Hancock's Half Hour* programmes had a somewhat wider scope but of necessity were contained within the same parameters as the radio shows. Subsequently that was to change!

In the 10 years from 1952 to 1962 Tony Hancock was without doubt one of the most — if not *the* most—popular comedians in Britain. His solo performances were said to be a torture to him, as, being a sensitive man, he suffered horribly with pre-performance nerves. The fact is that his 'act' was one of enormous impudence: impersonations of forgotten stars, such as George Arliss, or hackneyed ones, such as Charles Laughton in *Mutiny on the Bounty* — 'Mr Christian ... I'll have you hanging from the highest yardarm in the British Navy' — and Long John Silver as portrayed by that eye-rolling giant of the cinema, Robert Newton. That plus mockery of a third-rate concert party made up the rest of his solo offering, and, seen at the time or remembered subsequently, doesn't explain Tony Hancock's popularity. But as eye witnesses aver it was what Tony didn't do that was so funny. His ability to communicate with the audience without words was unusually well developed and, as with Jack Benny, audiences read into those silent looks a wealth of detail of their own creation.

When it came to radio there wasn't much call for long, meaningful silences, but such was the skill of Ray Galton and Alan Simpson that the dialogue was, as it were, wrapped around these silences as when, in one episode, the action, or rather non-action, revolved around a wet Sunday afternoon when nothing (of interest or excitement) happened.

Looking back, it was non-happenings that made up most of the plots of Hancock's most successful radio and television shows. The army reunion where none of the wartime colleagues that Hancock remembered so vividly from the Second World War lived up to his expectations is typical. One is now a clergyman,

151

another, once a hell-raiser, is now a henpecked teetotaller; known only by his nickname, 'Smudger', in the Army, it turns out that his real name is Clarence.

After Tony's startled reaction to this piece of information, Smudger/ Clarence says:

> SMUDGER: I don't want the name 'Smudger' to get round, it might jeopardize my position at the bank. I've got my own window now you know.
>
> TONY: Oh, good. I always said you'd get on. What happened to the plans you had for when you got out — whale fishing, and lumberjacking and crocodile hunting in Australia.
>
> SMUDGER: Well, I thought it over and I decided the security at the bank was a better idea.
>
> TONY: What about that restless urge for adventure you always had? Surely a job like that can't satisfy a firebrand like you?
>
> SMUDGER: Oh well, it's quite exciting. Sometimes at the end of the day we're five shillings short. It's quite thrilling.

Thus are dreams turned to dust.

In 1959 Tony recorded the last of the radio *Hancock's Half Hour* programmes. There had been 102 altogether, plus a Christmas 'Special'. In 1960 the BBC recorded the last series of the television *Hancock's Half Hour* programmes, as by now Tony Hancock felt he was becoming stereotyped as half of a double act with Sid James who, with only two exceptions, had appeared in all episodes of all six series.

By the 1961 television series Sid James had gone. A great loss as an important part of the Hancock saga, but his going allowed Hancock more of the 'freedom' he so desperately desired. In *Hancock* as the new series was called, many of the old Hancock repertory company still carried on. Hugh Lloyd (the actor who played Smudger and who was in many of the television *Hancock's Half Hour* programmes) appeared in three of the six episodes in this series, in which Tony appeared solo in one and with three women only in another. Other actors who had been with Tony Hancock in his previous series included June Whitfield, Peggy Ann Clifford, Brian Oulton, Partrick Cargill, Alec Bregonzi, and John Le Mesurier, plus many more, but none of the radio stalwarts, Sid James, Kenneth Williams, Hattie Jacques, Bill Kerr, ever worked with Hancock again. At the end of this series Tony Hancock ended his association with the BBC, and, more importantly, with his producer, Duncan Wood, and his writers, Galton and Simpson.

From then on Tony Hancock's career went into a slow decline. He did a television series for ATV in 1963, written variously by Terry Nation, Godfrey Harrison, Richard Harris, and Dennis Spooner, compèred a series of variety shows in 1966 for ABC TV, and in 1967 made a series called *Hancock's*, also for ABC TV which, it must be said, was not a success.

By now Hancock was drinking heavily, his private life was in tatters, his occasional stage appearances were undisciplined and, frankly, unfunny. In 1968 he went to Australia to record a TV series in Melbourne and died before it could be completed.

In his all-too-short career (he was only 44 when he died) Tony Hancock probably made more people laugh than any other British comedian before or since. His film career was short and not successful and he only starred in two films, although he had appeared in minor roles in others.

The first of his starring roles was in *The Rebel* where, as an office worker with artistic aspirations, he gives up his mundane life in London for the exotic world of the artists' quarter of Paris. His paintings are rubbish but when a connoisseur (played by George Sanders) mistakes the work of a fellow artist for Hancock's, Tony finds himself lionized, and until the error is discovered becomes the 'in' person of the international art world, fawned on by the rich and famous. An ingenious ending whereby the really talented artist becomes the new celebrity and Hancock retreats to his old life and surroundings concludes what could have been a triumphant success. The trouble was that good though the screenplay was and no matter how accurately the world of pseud art-lovers was parodied, Hancock was diminished by the big screen.

His second 'big' film, *The Punch and Judy Man*, was smaller, more domestic and harked back to Hancock's memories of living at the seaside. It was written by Hancock and the novelist and poet, Philip Oakes. It also failed to grip audiences in the cinema, although when viewed on television, somewhat surprisingly, it comes to life and makes a pleasant 96 minutes' viewing.

The fact of the matter is that Tony Hancock was at his best in the intimate media of radio and television. His humour was that of the aside, the close-up — room-size, intimate, and just right for its time.

Looking back at old video tapes of his television work, one is often astounded at the crudeness of the production techniques, the primitive lighting, and the flapping scenery, but the writing of Ray Galton and Alan Simpson was taut and funny, and Tony Hancock's performances in the late fifties and early sixties, before booze and despair got him, were examples of fine comic acting. At that time, in his home near Lingfield in Surrey, where he spent what passed for a private life, Tony was fascinated by philosophy and read — patchily I suspect — the work of Plato, Wittgenstein, Kant, Hegel, Russell, Ayer, and Descartes. In one room in his house he had jotted down on the walls what could be described as the *bon mots* of the great thinkers of history. He rather hoped that when complete these gems from the philosophers would connect up, and that the riddle of the universe, 'Why are we born to suffer and die?', would at last be solved.

Tony's tragedy was that he aspired to too much and in consequence felt ashamed when he fell short of his own aspirations. He wasn't content to be the finest comic actor in the country, he wanted to be its finest thinker and intellectual too, and the task was too much for him.

It could be said that Tony was as vain and foolish as any number of other comedians, and I suppose that is true. But silly and flawed as he might have been, at his best he was a great original and as such earned our respect, admiration, and affection.

FILMS

Orders Are Orders   1954
Produced by Donald Taylor
Directed by David Paltenghi
Written by Donald Taylor and Geoffrey Orme, from the play by Ian Hay and Anthony Armstrong

The Rebel   1960
Produced by W. A. Whittaker
Directed by Robert Day
Written by Alan Simpson and Ray Galton

The Punch and Judy Man   1962
Produced by Gordon L. T. Scott
Directed by Jeremy Summers
Written by Philip Oakes and Tony Hancock

Those Magnificent Men in Their Flying Machines   1965
Produced by Stan Margulies
Directed by Ken Annakin
Written by Jack Davis and Ken Annakin

The Wrong Box   1966
Produced by Bryan Forbes
Written by Larry Gelbart and Burt Shevelove, from the novel by Robert Louis Stevenson and Lloyd Osborne

RADIO AND TELEVISION

Hancock's Half Hour   6 radio series 1954–9 BBC
Hancock's Half Hour   6 television series 1956–60 BBC
Hancock   1 television series of six 25-minute programmes 1961 BBC
The Tony Hancock Show   2 television series 1956–7
                          Associated Rediffusion
Hancock   1 television series 1963 ATV
The Blackpool Show   1 television series 1966 ABC
Hancock's   1 television series 1967 ABC

PETER SELLERS

Writing about Peter Sellers is like trying to describe a chameleon. All through his life he changed with each new environment in which he found himself, and always, it must be said, blended into that environment, just as a chameleon would, to perfection.

Most creatures who survive in the entertainment jungle do so because of clearly marked and unchanging characteristics. Even Woody Allen's insecurity is constant, and only Charlie Chaplin ever changed his working persona, and that with reluctance, as the medium of film and his own view of the world changed.

With Peter Sellers it was quite another case. He was infinitely versatile and worked as fluently and successfully in radio, when 'the wireless' was *the* medium in the UK, as in movies.

His film career was less a meteoric rise than a steady progress from occasional character roles in such films as *The Ladykillers*, with Alec Guinness in 1955, or as the aged cinema projectionist in *The Smallest Show on Earth* in 1957, to the box-office heights of the *Pink Panther* films, the emotional peaks of *Dr Strangelove* (1963), and the controlled characterization of the gardener who becomes the President's confidant in *Being There* (1980).

Born in 1925 into a theatrical family, Peter Sellers shared with many people of a similar background (the late Dick Emery, another versatile character actor, springs to mind) a frightening lack of confidence in his ability and a constant need for reassurance: the reassurance of a new car, or a new woman, a new hobby, or a new home. Something to prove that in spite of his private misgivings he was still rich, potent, fascinating, clever, and discerning.

Most of us want to feel that we are all those things but don't go to extreme lengths to prove that we are. We're content to accept the fact that we are some of them (potent, discerning, etc.) some of the time and that at others we're not. Peter Sellers, I suspect, felt that life was a race against being exposed as a charlatan who could only impersonate people but who had no *real* personality of his own.

The truth is that Sellers's talent was so huge that it was too big for him to see it. Consequently he must have thought that he would only find true happiness with the next woman, the next car, or the next role. It's sad to think that on

157

reaching each of those goals he must have felt, looking back, that it was the last woman, car, or part that had given him true happiness. This then led to dissatisfaction with the current state of affairs, and the search for something new began all over again. Not different, you understand, but new. A new version of the old lover. Sellers had many, but when you look at their photographs each one is very similar to the rest.

It was the same with motor cars. As someone once said, 'Every automobile is basically a Chevy', and whether it's a Rolls or a Mercedes or a Mini, a car is, after all, only a car. But cars and women were in a way Sellers's household gods — if his wishes weren't granted they were replaced.

Peter Sellers's formative years were spent with his parents touring the British music-halls of the thirties. His father was a pianist and, subsequently, a patter and ukelele man. His mother — the dominant partner — a soubrette who specialized in 'artistic poses'. His mother's performances are said to have fascinated him and the applause to have excited and delighted the small boy as much as the environment disgusted him. Having been in that same music-hall profession myself, I remember the atmosphere well — the smell of lysol and orange peel in the theatres, the grim backstages, and the awful lodging houses (the so-called) 'theatrical digs'), where the atmosphere was of decay tempered by the smell of overcooked cabbage and the perspiration of a thousand acrobats.

Sellers's own forays on to the variety stage in later life were far from successful, and I can remember vividly his telling me of an occasion (I believe in Coventry) where the reaction of the audience to his twice-nightly performance was so lukewarm that on Thursday he abandoned his regular act and took on to the stage a record player and a Jimmy Shand record. (Jimmy Shand was a popular Scottish bandleader whose musical ensemble of accordion, violin, and percussion were ideal for Scottish dancing.) Peter played the record of reels and strathspeys — and just sat there. Then, when the record ended, he took a bow and made his exit. 'And', he told me, 'I got more applause for that than when I did my act.'

He was often booked, with the other Goons, by Joe Collins, then a big-time variety agent (and, incidentally, father of Joan and Jackie Collins) as by the mid nineteen-fifties BBC Radio's *The Goon Show* was a huge nationwide hit, and people would go to the music-halls to see what their radio heroes actually looked like.

The Goon Show had fairly humble origins. Immediately after the Second World War, Jimmy Grafton, ex-Army captain, scriptwriter and pub-owner, had taken a number of aspiring comedians under his wing. They were all ex-servicemen, and among these hopefuls were Spike Milligan, Harry (now Sir Harry) Secombe, an old Etonian from Watford who claimed to be Peruvian, Michael Bentine, and Peter Sellers. Under Grafton's guidance the quartet wrote and performed what *they* called *The Goon Show* but which the BBC, for arcane reasons, called *Crazy People*.

It was a success right from the start being, for those days, fresh, iconoclastic, and, as hindsight shows, crammed with brilliant performers. None was more brilliant than Sellers, whose range of comic voices turned the characters he created into national heroes.

Simultaneously he was also appearing in another hit radio show, *Ray's a Laugh*, and those shows plus theatre appearances gave him modest stardom.

I remember one appearance at the London Palladium which I thought one of the funniest things I had ever seen. The act included a quick-change routine in which Sellers purported to make himself into a perfect replica of Queen Victoria 'when she was a lad'. Darting behind a screen he emerged some moments later in a wig, a large ginger beard, a corset, unlaced army boots, and carrying a stuffed crocodile. Stepping down to the footlights he said, with commendable honesty, 'I'd like to be the first to admit that I do not know what Queen Victoria looked like when she was a lad.' It was a marvellously surreal moment.

About this time Peter Sellers started making records — funny character pieces which still cause chuckles today — but most of all he wanted to be in pictures, and very soon he was; not as part of *The Goon Show* but as a character actor in his own right.

Before long he became the star of the films in which he appeared, even if he didn't have top billing. But first he had to go through the mill of small parts and doing 'voice overs' — on one occasion impersonating Winston Churchill, on another Humphrey Bogart, and on a third, it is said, a parrot.

In 1955 came his first decent role, as a shifty slob of a crook supporting Alec Guinness in the Ealing comedy, *The Ladykillers*. Shortly after came the aged projectionist suffering, he alleged, from 'creeping alopaecia', in *The Smallest Show on Earth*, a part in *Tom Thumb* with Terry Thomas, and several roles in *The Naked Truth*, a black comedy in which Terry Thomas and Dennis Price also starred.

In 1959 came his first major role in an important film. The picture was *I'm All Right, Jack*, a story about an industrial dispute in which Sellers played the part of the recalcitrant shop steward, Fred Kite. Haircut, moustache, clothes, and an accent that sounded like a sort of strangulated working-class pedant completed the character. It won him the British Academy Award.

In 1951 Peter had married Anne Hayes, an Australian actress who gave up her promising career to care for Peter, and subsequently their two children, Michael and Sarah. By the early sixties Peter Sellers's income was large enough for him to sell his comfortable home in the prosperous suburb of Whetstone in north London and move to an enormous manor house at Chipperfield in Hertfordshire.

It was a long way from the theatrical digs of his childhood and the small flats in the mean blocks of suburban London during the period when, living with his parents and newly married, his career was struggling towards the light of international stardom. But even now in 1961 he was only halfway there, a star of British films with over a dozen to his credit but little known to world audiences.

His obsessional need to find the way to play each character — the right voice, the right make-up — was causing both Sellers and those around him a great deal of stress. In fact his marriage was on the rocks, and it would only be a matter of time before the final parting. It is questionable whether Sellers's infatuation for Sophia Loren during the making of *The Millionairess* in 1961 caused the break-up, or whether the incipient break-up of the marriage caused Sellers to fall more heavily for the glamorous Italian star than he would have done in other circumstances.

But if Sellers's private life was in tatters his professional career was in full bloom. Between the making of *I'm All Right, Jack* in 1959 and *Dr Strangelove* in 1963, Sellers made 11 other movies, including *Two-Way Stretch, Only Two Can Play, Lolita, The Dock Brief,* and *Mr Topaze* (which he also directed).

The Pink Panther, which he took on late in 1963, almost as a lark, or an antidote to the seriousness and intensity of *Dr Strangelove*, gave him, ironically, in the part of the bungling detective Inspector Clouseau, the most prominent role of his career. *The Pink Panther* and its sequels — *A Shot in the Dark, The Return of the Pink Panther, The Pink Panther Strikes Again,* and *The Revenge of the Pink Panther* — made box-office music worldwide and in many ways show Peter Sellers at his best. The character changes little in any of the films, which, for the chameleon-like Sellers, is a rare achievement, and the humour shared with its creator, the producer Blake Edwards, is at times of epic proportions. The endless permutations of ineptness and near-lethal accidents were handled by both Edwards and Sellers with great skill, and the only possible flaw the movies can be accused of possessing is that the skill of the supporting players can only rarely live up to that of the star.

Soon after the first of the *Pink Panther* films opened — and by then Peter had divorced Anne and she had married the pleasant, undemanding architect/designer, Ted Levy — he met the lady who was to become his second wife, Britt Ekland. In the interim he'd been comforted by other companions, including the actress Janette Scott, who had left him abruptly after suffering his frequent mood changes and impossible temperament. He spotted Britt Ekland at the Dorchester Hotel where they were both staying, made himself known to her, made love to her, smoked pot with her, and very soon after married her.

Britt Ekland, on her way to a medium-sized film career of her own, was flattered and amused by a man she'd never heard of before they met. The marriage was short and traumatic. Only weeks after they were married, in February 1964, Peter Sellers, in the Cedars of Lebanon Hospital in Los Angeles where he'd gone for a check-up, had two massive heart attacks. It speaks volumes for the skill of the hospital staff that he survived that nearly fatal 6 April in 1964.

He came out of hospital a changed man. That experience plus his unhappiness with the atmosphere of Hollywood and his disagreements with Billy Wilder during the making of *Kiss Me, Stupid*, the film in progress when his coronaries occurred, seemed to make him harder, less responsible to outside influences, and even more engrossed with perfecting his technique.

In other areas his technique was in no need of perfecting — Britt was pregnant, and in the following January their daughter, Victoria, was born.

Peter's next film was *What's New, Pussycat?* (I have written more about this production in the chapter on Woody Allen in this book.) After that came *After the Fox*, a film which cinema historian Leslie Halliwell called 'Unlikeable and unfunny farce'. Still, Britt Ekland was in it so Peter must have been fairly happy even if no one else was.

But if *After the Fox* was bad, *Casino Royale*, another Charles K. Feldman picture, based on the first and arguably the best of Ian Fleming's James Bond stories, was worse. Poorly directed, with a screenplay monstrously written and rewritten until no trace of humour or style was left in the film, it was disgraceful. Halliwell called it: 'One of the most shameless wastes of time and talent in screen history.' Peter Sellers was having a bad time. His next film, *The Bobo*, about a timid bullfighter, wasn't much better. Halliwell describes it as 'silly and boring'. It really looked as if Sellers had lost his grip. Peter Evans in his biography of Peter Sellers, *The Mask Behind the Mask*, recalls that at that time (1967) the star was obsessed with the notion of protecting himself from the mediocre, and quotes him as saying: 'You must be ruthless to survive.' Unfortunately, mediocrity was what dominated that time of his life. One of Peter Sellers's problems was that for all his superficial hardness (and he could be as ruthless as any comedy star — a breed noted for their toughness) he was deeply insecure and unsure of his talent. Constant introspection often enabled him to create wonderful characters, deeply felt and brilliantly portrayed, but it also led him down blind alleys and into roles in which he was neither funny nor moving.

My own encounters with Peter Sellers were few. We knew each other slightly from our early days in radio, but we hadn't seen each other for years. One night in the late sixties he phoned me in a panic. He was flying to Dublin the next day to appear on an Irish chat show hosted by the excellent Gay Byrne, and asked if I knew any Irish jokes he could tell. I couldn't help him myself but phoned a Dublin acquaintance of mine, explained the problem, and he gave me some suitable stories which I then relayed to Peter. I'm not sure if he used them or not — my guess is that he didn't. He'd just panicked at the thought that he'd have nothing to say.

Some time later we met in Eire, where he was in temporary residence, for tax reasons, in the salubrious neighbourhood of Maynooth. Actually he'd rented half a castle and I was there, with a BBC producer, to interview him for a radio series about celebrated British comedians. We'd flown over from London that morning and would return on the late afternoon plane with the interview safely on tape. Well, that was the idea! John Browell, the producer, had also been responsible for producing many episodes of *The Goon Show* and Peter knew and liked him. When we arrived at 'the castle' we found Peter alone — I think he was between wives at the time. He greeted us warmly enough, showed us round the estate and, proudly flinging open the doors of a barn, revealed his latest acquisition — a gleaming white Aston Martin. We were suitably impressed. I asked him how he found driving it on the narrow, twisting Irish roads. He looked at me as if I was mad. 'Drive it? Here? Have you seen the way they drive? I wouldn't dream of driving it in Ireland.' I choked back the question, 'Then why on earth did you buy it?' and we walked down the road to a local pub for a drink and a sandwich. Then he said, 'I've decided not to do the interview. I just can't face it.'

Browell went white, then red, and then, poor man, was struck by a savage attack of migraine. We go him back to Sellers's castle, and laid him out gently to give him a chance to recover. As the poor man lay there groaning quietly, Peter took over. 'I'll work the tape recorder, you hold the mike', he instructed. I said, 'You mean you'll do the interview after all?' 'Yes,' he said, 'I can't let poor old John down.' And do the interview we did, with reminiscences of his music-hall days, the story of how he got into BBC Radio by phoning a senior producer and giving a brilliant impersonation of one of the stars of the day, Kenneth Horne, lauding the unknown Sellers to the skies.

He talked with affection of *The Goon Shows*, and giggled at the memory of his appearance at the Aldwych Theatre in a farce called *Brouhaha* when, on one occasion, he got so drunk he informed the audience that he was too plastered to continue, and on another he waltzed his leading lady so energetically round the stage that they tripped and fell into the orchestra pit.

Eventually we ran out of tape, the chauffeur-driven car arrived to take us back to Dublin and we helped John Browell, still feeling not too good, on to the back seat where he could stretch out. Peter was charming and concerned. He'd given a splendid interview (much of which was used again, years later when he died, as part of an obituary tribute) and smiled cheerfully as he waved us goodbye.

When we got on the plane John Browell felt much better but was extremely gloomy. 'All that way and no interview', he kept saying. I told him, 'You wait till you get back to London and listen to the tape.'

My only other encounter with Peter Sellers was during the making of an LP called *He's Innocent of Watergate*, which purported to be extracts from President Nixon's missing tapes. I'd been approached by *another* ex-*Goon-Show* producer, Peter Eton, who had the idea to do the missing Nixon tapes and asked me to put together a writing team who could deliver good, original material fast. He would arrange things with Spike Milligan and Peter Sellers and book a cast to go with them. In the event, much of the material from first-class established writers, N. F. Simpson, Alan Coren, and Richard Ingrams among them, in the raw state — that's to say unsullied by actors — was excellent, but was bowdlerized by Milligan and Sellers. The result was a mess and Peter Eton retreated behind his preferred pseudonym, borrowed from W. C. Fields, J. Pismo Clam.

I don't think the LP sold many copies, or indeed *any*, as after he'd completed the recording Sellers asked for the record not to be issued. He said he 'felt it was unfair to Nixon'. But it's possible that having heard it, he felt it was unfair to himself.

This all happened in 1974, when another batch of poor movies had depressed Peter Sellers. Their titles and Leslie Halliwell's comments provide what criticism is necessary:

Hoffman (1970) 'Tasteless and boring.'
A Day at the Beach (1970) 'Not released.'
Where Does it Hurt? (1972) 'Dislikeable plodding smut,'
The Blockhouse (1973) 'Not released.'
The Optimists of Nine Elms (1973) 'Well observed wistful melancholia falsified by its star performance.'
Soft Beds and Hard Battles (1973) 'Ragbag of poor sketches and dirty jokes.'
The Great McGonagall (1974) 'No comment.'

Fortunately the next film that Peter Sellers made was *The Return of the Pink Panther* ('not bad in parts', commented Halliwell).

By the end of 1968 Sellers's marriage to Britt Ekland had ended in divorce. She is quoted as saying of him: 'He is a genius. Impossible, moody, temperamental, jealous ... but life with him was extraordinary, stimulating, memorable.' There is no record of what Sellers said about life with her.

In August 1970 he was married again — this time to Amanda Quarry, the daughter of Lord Mancroft, an amiable and witty Tory peer. That ended in 1974, and in 1976 he married for the last time. His new wife was the young actress Lynne Frederick, who starred with him in an undistinguished production of *The Prisoner of Zenda*. He was to make two more films before his death in 1980. One was *The Fiendish Plot of Dr Fu Manchu*, the other *Being There*, in which all the layers of his outrageous personality have been stripped away and the character of the simple gardener, Chance, seems to resemble the true Peter Sellers. His personality was laid bare, the canvas on which he had painted so many characters — the childish bluebottle, the self-righteous Fred Kite, the evil Dr Strangelove, the dignified idiot Clouseau — was empty. The party was over.

Peter Sellers was a difficult man to live with, to be a friend to, to work with as either employee or employer. His tantrums became legendary in the film industry, his affairs notorious, his eccentricity almost impossible to bear. But — and it's one of the biggest buts in the world — he had the magic gift of making people laugh. At that, when he chose, he was a genius, and when the rest is forgotten it will be Peter Sellers's God-given ability to raise a smile that will be remembered.

FILMS

Penny Points to Paradise 1951
Produced by Advance/Adelphi Production
Directed by Tony Young
Written by John Ormonde

Down Among the Z Men 1952
Produced by E. J. Faucey
Directed by Maclean Rogers
Written by Jimmy Grafton and Francis Charles

Orders Are Orders 1954
Produced by Donald Taylor
Directed by David Paltenghi
Written by Donald Taylor and Geoffrey Orme, from the play by Ian Hay and Anthony Armstrong

John and Julie 1955
Produced by Herbert Mason
Directed by William Fairchild
Written by William Fairchild

The Ladykillers 1955
Produced by Seth Holt
Directed by Alexander Mackendrick
Written by William Rose

The Smallest Show on Earth 1957
Produced by Michael Relph
Directed by Basil Deardon
Written by William Rose and John Eldridge

The Naked Truth 1958
Produced by Mario Zampi
Directed by Mario Zampi
Written by Michael Pertwee

Tom Thumb 1958
Produced by George Pal
Directed by George Pal
Written by Ladislas Fodor

Up the Creek 1958
Produced by Henry Halsted
Directed by Val Guest
Written by Val Guest

Carlton Browne of the F.O. 1958
Produced by John Boulting
Directed by Jeffrey Dell and Roy Boulting
Written by Jeffrey Dell and Roy Boulting

The Mouse That Roared 1959
Produced by Carl Foreman
Directed by Jack Arnold
Written by Roger Macdougall and Stanley Mann, from the novel by Leonard Wibberley

I'm All Right, Jack 1959
Produced by Roy Boulting
Directed by John Boulting

Written by Frank Harvey and John Boulting, from the novel *Private Life* by Alan Hackney

The Battle of the Sexes   1960
Produced by Monja Danischewsky
Directed by Charles Chrichton
Written by Monja Danischewsky, from James Thurber's story 'The Catbird Seat'

Two-Way Stretch   1960
Produced by M. Smedley Aston
Directed by Robert Day
Written by John Warren and Len Heath

Never Let Go   1961
Produced by Peter de Sarigny
Directed by John Guillermin
Written by Alun Falconer

The Millionairess   1961
Produced by Pierre Rouve
Directed by Anthony Asquith
Written by Wolf Mankowitz, from the play by Bernard Shaw

Mr Topaze   1961
Produced by Pierre Rouve
Directed by Peter Sellers
Written by Pierre Rouve, from the play *Topaze* by Marcel Pagnol

Only Two Can Play   1962
Produced by Launder and Gilliat
Directed by Sidney Gilliat
Written by Bryan Forbes, from the novel *That Uncertain Feeling* by Kingsley Amis

Lolita   1962
Produced by James B. Harris
Directed by Stanley Kubrick
Written by Vladimir Nabokov, from his novel

The Waltz of the Toreadors   1962
Produced by Peter de Sarigny
Directed by John Guillermin
Written by Wolf Mankowitz, from the play by Jean Anouilh

The Dock Brief   1963
Produced by Dimitri de Grunwald
Directed by James Hill
Written by John Mortimer and Pierre Rouve

Heavens Above 1963
Produced by Roy Boulting
Directed by John Boulting
Written by Frank Harvey and John Boulting

The Wrong Arm of the Law 1963
Produced by Aubrey Baring and E. M. Smedley Aston
Directed by Cliff Owen
Written by John Warren and Len Heath

The Pink Panther 1963
Produced by Martin Jurow
Directed by Blake Edwards
Written by Maurice Richlin and Blake Edwards

Dr Strangelove; Or How I Learned to Stop Worrying and Love the Bomb 1963
Produced by Stanley Kubrick and Victor Lyndon
Directed by Stanley Kubrick
Written by Stanley Kubrick, Terry Southern, and Peter George, from the novel
Red Alert by Peter George

The World of Henry Orient 1964
Produced by Jerome Hellman
Directed by George Roy Hill
Written by Nora and Nunnally Johnson, from the novel by Nora Johnson

A Shot in the Dark 1964
Produced by Blake Edwards
Directed by Blake Edwards
Written by Blake Edwards and William Peter Blatty

What's New, Pussycat? 1965
Produced by Charles K. Feldman
Directed by Clive Donner
Written by Woody Allen

The Wrong Box 1966
Produced by Bryan Forbes
Directed by Bryan Forbes
Written by Larry Gelbart and Burt Shevelove, from the novel by Robert Louis
Stevenson and Lloyd Osborne

After the Fox 1966
Produced by John Bryen
Directed by Vittorio de Sica
Written by Neil Simon and Cesare Zavattini

Casino Royale 1967
Produced by Charles K. Feldman

Directed by John Huston, Kenneth Hughes, Val Guest, Robert Parrish, and Joseph McGrath
Written by Wolf Mankowitz, John Law, and Michael Sayers, from the novel by Ian Fleming

The Bobo 1967
Produced by Elliot Kastner, Jerry Gershwin, and David R. Schwarz
Directed by Robert Parrish
Written by David R. Schwarz, from his play, and the novel by Burt Cole

Woman Times Seven 1967
Produced by Arthur Cohn
Directed by Vittorio de Sica
Written by Cesare Zavattini

The Party 1968
Produced by Blake Edwards
Directed by Blake Edwards
Written by Blake Edwards, and Tom and Frank Waldman

I Love You Alice B. Toklas 1968
Produced by Paul Mazursky and Larry Tucker
Directed by Hy Averback
Written by Paul Mazursky and Larry Tucker

The Magic Christian 1969
Produced by Dennis O'Dell
Directed by Joseph McGrath
Written by Terry Southern, Joseph McGrath, and Peter Sellers, from the novel by Terry Southern

Hoffman 1970
Produced by Ben Arbeid
Directed by Alvin Rakoff
Written by Ernest Gebler, from his novel

There's a Girl in My Soup 1970
Produced by John Boulting
Directed by Roy Boulting
Written by Terence Frisby, from his play

Where Does it Hurt? 1972
Produced by Rod Amateau and William Schwarz
Directed by Rod Amateau
Written by Rod Amateau, from the novel *The Operator* by Budd Robinson and Rod Amateau

Alice's Adventures in Wonderland 1972
Produced by Derek Horne

Directed by William Sterling
Written by William Sterling

The Optimists of Nine Elms   1973
Produced by Adrian Gaye and Victor Lyndon
Directed by Anthony Simmons
Written by Anthony Simmons, from his novel
Co-writer Tudor Gates

Soft Beds and Hard Battles   1973
Produced by John Boulting
Directed by Roy Boulting
Written by Leo Marks and Roy Boulting

The Great McGonagall   1974
Produced by David Grant
Directed by Joseph McGrath
Written by Joseph McGrath and Spike Milligan

The Return of the Pink Panther   1975
Produced by Blake Edwards
Directed by Blake Edwards
Written by Frank Waldman and Blake Edwards

Murder By Death   1976
Produced by Ray Stark
Directed by Robert Moore
Written by Neil Simon

The Pink Panther Strikes Again   1977
Produced by Blake Edwards
Directed by Blake Edwards
Written by Frank Waldman and Blake Edwards

The Revenge of the Pink Panther   1978
Produced by Blake Edwards
Directed by Blake Edwards
Written by Frank Waldman, Ron Clarke, and Blake Edwards

The Prisoner of Zenda   1979
Produced by Walter Mirisch
Directed by Richard Quine
Written by Dick Clement and Ian La Frenais

Being There   1979
Produced by Andrew Braunsberg
Directed by Hal Ashby
Written by Jerzy Kosinski, from his novel

The Fiendish Plot of Dr Fu Manchu   1980
Produced by Hugh Hefner
Directed by Piers Haggard
Written by Jim Moloney and Rudy Dochtermann

JACQUES TATI

I 'm still not sure why Jacques Tati didn't like me. I suspect it was because I was wearing a grey suit and looked like an accountant.

It was in Paris in the spring of 1971, and a time when people are supposed to fall in love, but on that occasion Jacques Tati and I stood nose to nose in the bar at the France Film Studio and argued, while the crowd in the bar (including Jean Paul Belmondo and Omar Sharif) looked on open-mouthed as these tall, grey-haired men carried on a heated discussion about comedy. Not that I was arguing about Tati's talent, which I thought then, and still do today, to be exquisite and superb but ... well, let me start at the beginning of what for me was many years of admiration for this great French comic actor, writer, and film director.

My first sight of Jacques Tati (born Jacques Tatischeff in 1908) in action was in the film *Jour de Fête* where, as the provincial postman imbued with the ambition to emulate the efficiency of the American post office, he executes prodigies of postal delivery, racing from customer to customer on an ancient bicycle distributing letters and parcels at breakneck speed.

The film itself, though scattered with frantic action, is a leisurely evocation of a day when the travelling fair arrives in a Normandy village, and reflects with accuracy and affection provincial France in 1949 — the year it was made. Like all Tati films it has long moments when nothing appears to happen and then, like a clap of thunder on a humid summer's day, come jokes of such originality and flair you forget the longueurs and laugh aloud with delight.

It's difficult to describe jokes without destroying them, which is why there are few comedy films of any note that have not been controlled by the star or stars who are also the authors — or at least who have what William Goldman describes in his book about Broadway as the 'muscle'. That is Goldman's description of the person who is the most important, i.e. powerful, in any production. Charlie Chaplin had it and so did Noel Coward. Mel Brooks has it and Woody Allen has it too. In fact there are few people whose careers are outlined in this book who did not play the key role in any production they starred in. Jacques Tati was one of this illustrious band.

In *Jour de Fête*, Tati's tall, bony figure in its ill-fitting postman's uniform, his dignity and pride, not to mention his clumsiness, all contribute to what could be described as 'all the fun of the fair'. There's a hilarious sequence in which he directs a group of ill-starred rustics in the gentle art of erecting a flag pole, and a high-speed cycling sequence which culminates in both Tati and bike careering off the road and disappearing in a graceful arc into the river.

The eminent film historian, Leslie Halliwell, describes Tati's films as 'little more than strings of sight gags on a theme', and while it's true that they are not thematically complex, the end result of a Jacques Tati movie is a heightened awareness of the themes he chooses whether those themes are to do with problems of holidaymaking, modern culture, or the increasing mechanization of our lives.

His next film, made in 1952, was *M. Hulot's Holiday*. It's Tati's first appearance as the accident-prone innocent, M. Hulot, whose aspirations to social grace are frustrated by his own inability to cope with the task he has set himself.

Driving an incredibly antique and underpowered car, M. Hulot sets off on holiday. When he is mending a puncture, the inner tube rolls towards a cemetery gathering fallen leaves as it goes. M. Hulot retrieves it only to find himself in the line of wreath-bearing mourners queueing to pay their respects to the widow.

On arriving at a small hotel in Brittany, mayhem soon takes over as M. Hulot directly or indirectly affects the lives and holidays of all the other guests.

His attempt to play tennis produces an automaton-like service action undreamt of by John McEnroe or Ivan Lendl, and a foray into horse riding produces a scene where Tati, waiting in an elegant salon, fully dressed and equipped for the ride, manages accidentally to dislodge every picture on the wall with the tip of his riding crop and get his spurs entangled with a fox-fur rug.

His attempts to paint a canoe whilst sitting in it in the shallows are no more successful. The climax of the film comes when M. Hulot accidentally sets off the fireworks stored in a shed prior to that evening's pyrotechnic display, and he exits fast into the night pursued by an angry, yapping dog.

Jacques Tati's powers of observation of people faced with the sheer cussedness of life and of the malevolence of inanimate objects is unequalled.

His next film, *Mon Oncle* (1958), again starred the ill-fated M. Hulot, faced this time with the new affluence of the French middle classes. M. Hulot is fascinated and bewildered by electrically operated garage doors, the latest in domestic appliances and plastics. In *Mon Oncle*, Tati is recording with nostalgic regret the passing of the old France and the emergence of modernity. The 'modernity' of the late fifties in France mercifully is being replaced today by more traditional and discreet styles in cars, furniture, and houses but *Mon Oncle* is there on film to remind us of the crassness that came with the return of prosperity after the degradation, poverty, and powerlessness of France in the years from 1940 to 1944.

If you are unfortunate enough to obtain a video of *Mon Oncle* with a sound-track adapted for non-French speakers let me advise you that it is unspeakable. The original version, while not Tati's best, is an interesting example of his developing powers as a film-maker, and his ability to create comedy by combining the characteristics and behaviour of a number of people.

By the time Jacques Tati came to make *Playtime* (1968) he'd had 10 years to digest what had gone before and evolve his philosophy. *Playtime* has a broader view than *Mon Oncle* but the obsession that new is worse than old is still there, and that modernity is sterile is as much in evidence as in *Mon Oncle*, where M. Hulot's sister, living in the ultimate suburban modernity, gives her son his supper using serving tongs while wearing rubber gloves. It's in stark contrast to the boy's outing with Hulot earlier that day when the lad consumes a vast sort of doughnut bought from a fly-blown street vendor.

Playtime begins in an anonymous modern building which could be a hospital, an airline terminal, or an office building. It turns out to be the latter and, as in Tati's previous movie, he's trying to get a job and failing miserably to cope with '*le système*'.

Later he observes people buying a hurried meal in '*le drugstore*'. When taken from the quick-service counter to the eating area, neon-lit in a sickly green (a colour traditionally associated with French pharmacies), the hamburgers and croques-monsieur turn an unpleasant colour, which causes a consequent loss of appetite in the consumers. The climax of the film concerns the opening of a new night club where nothing is actually ready and where, not surprisingly, chaos ensues.

Slowly throughout this sequence a waiter is divested of his outer garments to provide other members of the restaurant staff with pristine jackets, shirts, trousers, etc., as they meet with accidents caused by flying food.

The dance floor is laid with large plastic tiles glued to a concrete base. Alas the glue hasn't been applied efficiently or dried completely, and one dancer finds himself dancing with a tile fixed firmly to one foot.

One of the better jokes concerns the plate-glass door of the establishment. It boasts a large gold handle and M. Hulot, as doorman, shows great panache as he opens the door and ushers the guests into the night club. In one of the innumerable disasters that plague this opening night, the plate glass of the door is shattered but Tati, with the same panache as before, sweeps the gold handle back and forth as if the door still exists — and for a moment such is the skill of the mime that you believe the door is still there.

The last shots of the film illustrate an idea that Jacques Tati touched on in *Mon Oncle* and returned to in his last film, *Traffic*. This is the thought that sooner or later the motor car would be self-destroying, or, in any event, a useless artefact actually contradicting the idea of 'going places'. In *Playtime* cars converge on a roundabout and, because once they are in the stream they can't get out again, they finish up all going round and round; as the camera pulls up and away we seem to see them transformed into a funfair roundabout.

The film *Traffic* is a simple tale of a man taking a car-cum-caravan from Paris to Holland for the Dutch Motor Show. The hero is again M. Hulot, and inevitably

173

there are distractions and side issues, and a multiple car crash in which, incidentally, no one gets hurt. In Tati's films everyone is frustrated but no one ever comes to harm physically.

At one point M. Hulot runs out of gas and, walking along an empty country road, petrol can in hand, sees coming towards him another car driver also carrying a petrol can and obviously in the same plight. Their anguish when they see each other and realize that there is no garage for miles *either* direction is a joy to behold. It goes almost without saying that M. Hulot arrives at the Motor Show after it has closed. Like all Jacques Tati's films it is long and full of longueurs. Like most actors who control every aspect of their productions, self-indulgence can creep in among the moments of brilliance and so it was with *Traffic*.

At the time it was showing in a cinema on the Champs-Elysées the management decreed it was too long by four minutes. Tati protested but the four minutes were removed by the distributors. Curiously though, when the film was next shown its running time was exactly the same as before the cut had been made. Enquiries were made and it turned out that Tati had prevailed upon the projectionist to put back the offending four minutes. He was sternly ordered to remove them and for a few days all was well. Then, mysteriously, the film was back at its pre-cut length. Tati had again persuaded the projectionist to reinstate the offending scene.

This was happening at a time when I was in Paris with an American production team making a segment of a TV special to be called *It's a Wacky World*. It was planned to be a round-up of world humour, and we had shot scenes in London with John Cleese and Tony Curtis, and in Sussex with a Swedish team of comedy acrobats called The Stupids. Jacques Tati was essential to the project; without him it would be like the Royal Family without the Queen or Dallas without JR. So, to Paris we went: the producer George Schlatter, his assistant, and me. There we met the German director, Michael Pfleger, who was to shoot both the French and German sequences, and waited for Jacques Tati to arrive at the rendezvous.

The previous week I'd read an article in a magazine in which Tati had gone on at some length about the crassness of American television, and I was slightly apprehensive as to his attitude towards our motley team. But George Schlatter, who had recently completed a run of the immensely successful *Rowan and Martin's Laugh-In*, while enthusing over Tati's comic genius admitted that he'd never actually seen any of his films. I was able to fill him in on the main points and when at last Tati arrived (he seemed always to be late for appointments) George was able to convince him that he was among friends and, more than that, amongst people who also revered Tati's heroes Laurel and Hardy, and W. C. Fields.

It was arranged that we would film in one week's time ('I must go to Trouville for a few days to improve my complexion') at a café on the boulevard St Germain in Paris, and subsequently on an open-air lot at Francefilms. Tati was to star in a series of cameos in which he would play a variety of waiters and customers in a typical Parisian café/restaurant. A week later we were in position — the American production team, the German film unit, a second film unit recruited from a German news crew who happened to be in town covering a sports story, the extras in the scene, and me.

By 9 a.m. there was no sign of Tati and people were beginning to get restive. By 10 a.m. panic was starting to set in when suddenly a small car drew up, Tati got out, and with sighs of relief the producer and his assistants surrounded him and bade him welcome.

I was some distance off chatting to the German assistant director when one of the group with Tati disengaged herself and walked across to me. Somewhat surprisingly she asked, 'What's five million lire in dollars?' I asked why she wanted to know. 'That's what Tati's asking for the day's filming.' In the euphoria of getting him to agree to film they'd forgotten to negotiate the fee, and Tati had decided, presumably during his week in Trouville, that five million lire was a nice round sum. The point was that, owing to the cost of making *Traffic*, he was bankrupt in France and would have to be paid in Italy.

Neither I nor my German companions could find a piece of paper, so I worked out the sum on the bark of a convenient plane tree; lire into pounds and then pounds into dollars. In fact it was a very reasonable fee for a star of Jacques Tati's eminence. So, the deal was struck and filming commenced. Later that day, in a break in the filming, we were standing in the bar of the studio and I happened to mention to Jacques Tati that some years before I had met the great French mime Marcel Marceau, who had offered me a job with his company in France. I was then a fresh-faced young actor and Marceau and I had met during one of his London seasons. For some reason Jacques Tati came to the conclusion that I was *comparing* him with Marcel Marceau and grew quite angry. 'He is always the same,' he said dismissively, 'I am different.' I defended Marceau, because in my view his 'sameness' is the sameness of perfection in what he does. Tati painted on a broader canvas, I argued, but surely both in their own ways were great.

By this time we were getting quite heated, and the crowd in the bar was deeply interested in our 'discussion'. Tati ended it by declaring roundly, 'Besides, what do you know — you're only an accountant.' I protested my innocence. 'But you *are*,' he said, 'and there is a tree in the boulevard St Germain to prove it.' I was never able to convince him otherwise, or even explain that the grey suit I was wearing was for an interview I was to have later that day at the BBC in London.

In spite of our differences (and I can quite see that a man to whom talent meant much more than money, would abhor anyone he thought held the purse strings), I regard Jacques Tati as one of the most creative comic actors of the twentieth century, fit to walk the Elysian Fields with those other comic greats, Jack Benny, Harpo Marx, Stan Laurel, and W. C. Fields.

The comedian who came up from the French music-halls and night clubs, through small parts in films, to become the creator of comic masterpieces such as *M. Hulot's Holiday*, *Playtime*, and *Traffic* deserves his place among the immortals.

JACQUES TATI

FILMS

Sylvia et la Fantôme   1944
Produced by Andre Paulve
Directed by Claude Autant-Lara
Written by Jean Aurenche, from the play by Alfred Adam

Le Diable au Corps   1947
Produced by Transcontinental
Directed by Claude Autant-Lara
Written by Jean Aurenche, and Pierre Bost, from the novel by Raymond Radiguet

Jour de Fête   1952
Produced by Fred Orain
Directed by Jacques Tati
Written by Jacques Tati and Henri Marquet

M. Hulot's Holiday   1954
Produced by Fred Orain
Directed by Jacques Tati
Written by Jacques Tati and Henri Marquet

Mon Oncle   1958
Produced by Louis Dolivet
Directed by Jacques Tati
Written by Jacques Tati and Jacques Lagrange

Playtime   1968
Produced by Rene Silvera
Directed by Jacques Tati
Written by Jacques Tati and Jacques Lagrange

Traffic   1972
Produced by Robert Dorfman
Directed by Jacques Tati
Written by Jacques Tati and Jacques Lagrange

THE MARX BROTHERS

It's possible that there have been more books, articles, retrospectives, discussions about and analyses of the Marx Brothers than any other comic figures of the twentieth century, except perhaps Charlie Chaplin and Buster Keaton.

Their films embodied a spirit of anarchy which delighted sophisticated cinemagoers of the day, but in their early productions the mass audience found the plots confusing and the ad lib mayhem of the Brothers hard to relate to. In fact by 1933 they were something of a flop. A change of studio and writers helped to put them back on top, but at the end of their screen careers their work deteriorated to a point where one was grateful when they'd stopped making movies.

At their peak, however, they were indeed comedy greats and had earned their right to stardom.

Like Keaton and Chaplin, W. C. Fields and Jack Benny, the Marx Brothers come from the background of American vaudeville, a similar institution to the British music-halls which flourished in the early years of the twentieth century, where a number of specialist acts — singers, dancers, wire-walkers, jugglers, magicians, trained animals, and many other strange and exotic performers — combined to entertain the populations of towns and cities large and small the length and breadth of the land.

It was a style of entertainment that was popular from the 1890s until the early 1930s, when talking pictures and radio changed the habits of both Britain and the USA. Vaudevillians spent their working lives moving from town to town across the country. They endured long hours in railway journeys at weekends and lived in inexpensive boarding houses during their engagements, which rarely lasted more than one week and could, if the act was not to the liking of the local audience or theatre proprietor, be terminated abruptly.

Although vaudeville was fairly well down the social scale of public entertainment it was superior to burlesque where rough-and-tumble comics raced through routines in questionable taste between strip-tease and fan dancers who disrobed more or less discreetly and more or less explicitly for the delectation of their (mainly) male audiences.

In the UK this form of entertainment was known as the 'Strip Show' and bloomed briefly in the forties and fifties, vanishing as abruptly as did variety when the cathode-ray tube made home viewing a preferable alternative to two hours in a crumbling theatre, watching shows that only with luck brought any display of real talent. At the time when the Marx Brothers were touring the USA there was no better light entertainment available, and if through the very nature of their calling the vaudevillians were little more than vagrants, at least some of the glamour of thespian and gypsy clung to them.

The respectable elements of society would have nothing to do with the coarse-textured vaudeville, and the travelling actors had to make their fun as and when they could. According to Groucho Marx, quoted in Charlotte Chandler's record of his last years, *Hello I Must Be Going*, acts were often invited to local brothels, where they entertained and were entertained by the girls who manned these early twentieth-century comfort stations, learning in the process a lot about love life and about the social diseases that all too often accompanied promiscuous liaisons.

It was not this side of the life of the touring entertainer which had attracted the Marx Brothers' mother, Minnie. She had emigrated to New York from Germany with her family in 1880 when she was 15. Her husband-to-be, Sam, had come to the USA by the same route four years earlier from Alsace-Lorraine, and they met and married in 1884 when Sam was 23 and Minnie 19. Their first son, Manfred, died young but in 1887 Chico (Leonard) was born — followed in 1888 by Harpo (Adolph), in 1890 by Groucho (Julius), 1897 by Gummo (Milton), and in 1901 by Zeppo (Herbert).

Minnie Marx was always ambitious for her boys and, having a younger brother, Al Shean, already in the business and doing well in a comedy partnership with Eddie Gallagher, she felt, 'Why not my brood in that set-up too?' After all, it was better than scrambling for a living in Yorkville, NY. Added to that, Minnie was no *Hausfrau*, preferring to leave the cooking to husband Sam, nicknamed 'Frenchie', and who, though calling himself a tailor, was in fact more at home at the stove than at the cutter's bench or Hoffman presser. So she pursued the bookers and got her sons work, and badgered Al Shean to write them some material; piece by piece the act came together.

The first piece was when in 1905 Groucho, a boy soprano and at that time still called Julius, joined an act called The Leroy Trio as a female impersonator. A year later Groucho had his first dramatic role in a play called *The Man of My Choice*. He then teamed up briefly in a double act with Harpo. In 1909 Groucho was teamed with the 13-year-old Gummo in a singing act which, with the addition of 'a crossed eyed girl' named Mabel O'Hara, became The Three Nightingales. Then Minnie Marx joined the act herself and soon after added Harpo and her sister, Hannah, and the name was changed to The Six Mascots.

In 1910 the family moved to Chicago and The Six Mascots tried the midwest vaudeville circuit, and then the deep south. Their success was moderate, but at Nacoqdoches, Texas, came the turning point. According to Charlotte Chandler's account, The Mascots were in mid-act when a mule tethered outside the theatre got loose and ran away. The audience, who clearly knew their priorities, left the theatre to give chase, returning when the unruly beast had been captured.

The Mascots were incensed by this slight on their abilities, and shouted insults at the audience such as 'The jackass is the finest flower of Texas', and 'Nocoqdoches is full of roaches'. Instead of being offended the audience laughed, and the Marx Brothers' brand of entertainment was born — music interspersed with comedy.

Soon the comedy took over as The Mascots put together a sketch called 'Fun in Hi Skule', with Groucho as the teacher, Harpo as the dumb student, and the rest of The Mascots in various roles. Later Chico, who had been working as a song-plugger in and around Chicago with the Shapiro Bernstein Company, joined the 'Hi Skule' act as the comic Italian, which character he kept both on stage and in films to the end of his career.

The act developed a larger and more ambitious formula, still keeping the schoolroom as the basis but using more music, with Chico playing piano and Harpo playing the harp (playing it 'all wrong' as it happened, having taught himself, and inventing his own technique but still making an extremely popular contribution to the act).

It was in 1914 that the Marx Brothers were given the nicknames that were to stick to them for the rest of their lives. The 'namer' was a vaudeville comedian by the name of Art Fisher. Julius became Groucho, Adolph became Harpo, Leonard became Chico because he was always chasing young women, or 'chicks', and Milton became Gummo because he wore rubber overshoes at all times. The other Marx Brother, Herbert, was 13 at the time and only became Zeppo when Gummo joined the Army in 1918 and Herbert replaced him in the act.

By now Minnie Marx had given up touring and was established as a theatrical agent in Chicago, representing her sons, and other small-time acts. She persuaded her brother, Al Shean, to write the boys a better act and he did so, calling the piece 'Home Again'. It's significant that in the Marx Brothers' history it was the first time the characters that later became world famous in the cinema were established. Groucho became the wise-cracking talker, Chico the cocky but dumb — that's to say, stupid — straight man, and Harpo became literally dumb. Before 'Home Again' he'd had quite a lot of dialogue and sang. Afterwards, his contribution was pantomime and harping, and in consequence he became the most loved (and in reality probably the most lovable) of the Brothers.

Gummo was the straight man and romantic lead, and Zeppo made such a successful replacement that when Gummo came out of the Army he never returned to performing, but became a theatrical agent in New York. Zeppo was never really happy as a straight man, wanting to get the same sort of laughs as his brothers; on one occasion, when Groucho developed appendicitis, Zeppo covered for him so successfully that even Groucho's friends mistook Zeppo for the older brother.

181

Eventually 'Home Again' made the vaudeville big time when it was booked at the Palace Theatre, New York. The Brothers were a great hit and subsequently made frequent appearances at the Palace, the New York equivalent of the London Palladium.

Tiring of 'Home Again' they put together another concoction of music and jokes called 'On the Mezzanine Floor', subsequently incorporating some of this material into *I'll Say She Is*, the production which finally catapulted them to fame and fortune. The story was slight — a millionairess looking for thrills — and was a rehash of a musical comedy called, at one time or another, *Love For Sale* and *Gimme a Thrill*, but with the injection of the Marx Brothers and some new dialogue and music *I'll Say She Is* became a hit.

On 19 May 1924 *I'll Say She Is* opened at the Casino Theatre in New York. The critics, and in particular the influential Alexander Woollcott, raved about the show, or rather the Brothers' contribution to it, and from then on, for a few years at any rate, it was roses all the way.

Harpo was taken up by the Algonquin set of which Woollcott was the ringmaster, and which included Robert Benchley, Dorothy Parker, and many contributors to the *New Yorker* magazine. It would not be too far-fetched to call him the darling of the intellectuals of the period, and looking back at his movie appearances I think that one can see why. Harpo's comedy was a strange mixture of cruelty, sentiment, and surrealism — all the things that were enjoyed by the serious minds of the early twentieth century. By his silence Harpo spoke for everyone, because everyone could interpret his work in the way *they* wished. He symbolized anything that anyone wished or believed that he symbolized, and he made few enemies and many friends.

Chico was a compuslive gambler and, it seems, a compulsive loser, as all through his life he was constantly in debt to bookmakers, casinos, and any cardplayer who held four kings to his three aces.

Zeppo and Harpo, it must be said, shared Chico's weakness for gambling, inherited from their mother, who was never happier than when playing poker. They, however, were less compulsive than Chico and tended to win more than they lost, and when Zeppo quit performing for business he was a success in whatever he attempted whether as an agent, a factory-owner, or in real estate.

Groucho was at that time happily married to his first wife, Ruth, and lived quietly at Great Neck, where their daughter, Miriam, was born in 1927. He spent his spare time playing tennis, golf, and writing articles for the *New Yorker*. On stage he ad libbed a lot, and acquired a reputation as a man quick on the draw when it came to wise-cracking repartee.

One of the great impresarios of the American theatre was a man by the name of Sam Harris, and he staged the Marx Brothers' next production. Called *The Coconuts* and set in a resort hotel in Florida, it was written by George S. Kaufman and Morrie Ryskind — and rewritten by the Marx Brothers!

It opened in 1925 and ran for three years, and is notable for the fact that it marked Margaret Dumont's first appearance with the Brothers. Margaret Dumont played a range of stylized upper-crust dowagers over the years and became a vital element in the Marx Brothers' films. It was said that she never understood the jokes, but the fact that she played everything straight and for real made her impact even greater.

The next success was also written by Kaufman and Ryskind and was *Animal Crackers*. Irving Berlin had written the music for *The Coconuts*, but Bert Kalman and Harry Ruby were brought in to write the music for *Animal Crackers* and contributed, among other items, Groucho's 'Captain Spaulding' song, the one which starts:

> Three cheers for Captain Spaulding
> The African Explorer
> Did someone call me Schnorrer?
> Hooray! Hooray! Hooray!

and is, unsurprisingly, almost totally forgotten today. *Animal Crackers* also contained Groucho's second most memorable line: 'One morning I shot an elephant in my pyjamas. How he got into my pyjamas I don't know.' (Groucho's most famous line was, of course: 'I wouldn't join a club that would have me as a member.')

In 1929 the stage hit *The Coconuts* was made into a film at the Paramount studios at Astoria, Long Island, and was directed by Robert Florey. It was as good as sound films could be in those early talkie days, when microphones were not as technically sophisticated as they became later, and picked up *every* sound in the vicinity, including the whirring of the camera motor. To solve this particular problem the camera and cameraman were put into an insulated, soundproof box, where the cameraman was often nearly asphyxiated as the air supply diminished. The cast tended to cluster round the mike, and movement was thus limited. Surprisingly, given the handicaps that *The Coconuts* had to contend with — not least of which was the Marx Brothers' lack of discipline — the film is amusing, and some critics think it better than many of their subsequent Hollywood efforts.

Animal Crackers was made on Long Island in 1930 also for Paramount, and was followed, at yearly intervals, by *Monkey Business, Horse Feathers*, and *Duck Soup*, by which time the centre of production had moved to Hollywood. In 1933 the Marx Brothers' popularity was slipping. In spite of some distinguished writers, including S. J. Perelman, and some great jokes, a lack of realism in the plots and a good deal of self-indulgence by the Brothers had diminished their box-office appeal. Zeppo left the team to become a theatrical agent like his brother Gummo, and things were at a low ebb for Groucho, Chico, and Harpo. Fortunately, the legendary Irving Thalberg came to the rescue and gave them a contract at MGM. The result was probably the best of all the Marx Brothers' films, *A Night at the Opera*, where the Brothers first sabotage and then help an opera company to triumph.

Margaret Dumont, who had joined the team again in *Duck Soup*, also appeared in *A Night at the Opera*, and the script is credited to George S. Kaufman and Morrie Ryskind. Allan Jones replaced Zeppo as the romantic lead and the film contains the scene in which a tiny cabin on an ocean liner fills up with an assortment of characters, including chambermaids, a manicurist, waiters, and the Brothers themselves, who, at the climax of the scene, explode into the corridor like a set of human champagne corks.

This film was followed in 1937 by *A Day at the Races*, which combined fun in a hospital with sequences on a racetrack, was written by Robert Pirosh, George Seaton, and George Oppenheimer, and brought together the same team as *Opera* — Margaret Dumont, Allan Jones, Sig Rumann, plus the young Maureen O'Sullivan.

It could be argued that the rest of the Marx Brothers' film career was a downhill slide. Morrie Ryskind's *Room Service* (1938) received poor reviews. *At the Circus*, made in 1939, fared little better, and *Go West* was described by one reviewer as 'pretty soggy'. *The Big Store* (1941) was nothing to rave about, and after it the Marx Brothers announced their retirement. They came together again in *A Night in Casablanca* in 1946. This had some vintage Marx Brothers routines with Groucho as a harassed hotel manager trying to keep a grip on things, but in the last analysis the qualities that had made the Marx Brothers the epitome of eccentric inventiveness in *The Coconuts*, *Duck Soup*, and *A Night at the Opera* had degenerated into routine gag-making.

At the time that *A Night in Casablanca* was due to go into production, Warner Brothers threatened legal action on the grounds that it in some way infringed the copyright of their film, *Casablanca*, which starred Humphrey Bogart and Ingrid Bergman and which had been made five years before. Groucho replied to the Warner Brothers, in part, as follows:

> Up to the time we contemplated making this picture I had no idea that the city of Casablanca belonged exclusively to Warner Brothers.
> ... I just don't understand your attitude. Even if you plan on re-releasing your picture, I am sure that the average movie fan could learn in time to distinguish between Ingrid Bergman and Harpo. I don't know whether I could, but I certainly would like to try.

More correspondence followed and Groucho responded:

> I have a hunch that this attempt to prevent us from using the title is the brainchild of some ferret-faced shyster serving a brief apprenticeship in your legal department.

After further exchanges in which Groucho outlined various bizarre story outlines for the forthcoming movie, Warner Brothers capitulated.

Chico died aged 74 in 1961. Harpo died in 1964 aged 75, and Groucho survived until the late seventies when, after a court battle about who should care for the senile 86-year-old he finally threw in the towel and departed this life on 19 August 1977.

At their best, on stage or screen, the Marx Brothers had been great stars. They'd earned their fame and the money that went with it, even if in Chico's case he threw his millions away gambling. They were great womanizers and great practical jokers, and totally self-indulgent. Harpo became the darling of the New York intellectuals and Groucho the epitome of the wise-cracking American comedian. Gummo and Zeppo both played their parts too in the Marx Brothers' story. Their upbringing in vaudeville helped to toughen them up and always working together gave them strength and a feeling of solidarity. They were, after all, a family. As long as film lasts people will be able to look and marvel at these extraordinary men who by entertaining themselves managed also to entertain the world.

FILMS

The Coconuts   1929
Produced by Walter Wanger and James R. Cown
Directed by Robert Florey
Written by George S. Kaufman and Morrie Ryskind

Animal Crackers   1930
Produced by Paramount
Directed by Victor Heerman
Written by Morrie Ryskind, from a musical play by Morrie Ryskind and George S. Kaufman

Monkey Business   1931
Produced by Paramount
Directed by Norman Z. McLeod
Written by S. J. Perelman, Will B. Johnstone, and Arthur Sheekman

Horse Feathers   1932
Produced by Paramount
Directed by Norman Z. McLeod
Written by Bert Kalmar, Harry Ruby, S. J. Perelman, and Will B. Johnstone

Duck Soup   1933
Produced by Paramount
Directed by Leo McCarey
Written by Bert Kalmar, Harry Ruby, Arthur Sheekman, and Nat Perrin

A Night at the Opera   1935
Produced by Irving Thalberg

Directed by Sam Wood
Written by George S. Kaufman and Morrie Ryskind

A Day at the Races   1937
Produced by Max Siegel
Directed by Sam Wood
Written by Robert Pirosh, George Seaton, and George Oppenheimer

Room Service   1938
Produced by Pandro S. Berman
Directed by William A. Seiter
Written by Morrie Ryskind, from a play by John Murray and Allen Boretz

At the Circus   1939
Produced by Mervyn Le Roy
Directed by Edward Buzzell
Written by Irving Brecher

Go West   1940
Produced by Jack Cummings
Directed by Edward Buzzell
Written by Irving Brecher

The Big Store   1941
Produced by Louis K. Sidney
Directed by Charles Reisner
Written by Sid Kuller, Hal Fimberg, and Ray Golden

A Night in Casablanca   1946
Produced by David L. Loew
Directed by Archie Mayo
Written by Joseph Fields, Roland Kibbee, and Frank Tashlin

Love Happy   1949
Produced by Lester Cowan and Mark Pickford
Directed by David Miller
Written by Ben Hecht, Frank Tashlin, and Mac Benoff

BILL COSBY

Bill Cosby is not so much a comedian as a phenomenon. Born in Philadelphia in 1937 he was, like so many other comedians, one of a large family whose father drank and eventually walked away from his brood, leaving them to survive on 'Relief' and what his wife and Bill, the oldest son, aged 11, could earn.

He started his education, or at least was enrolled in a 'ghetto school', in north Philadelphia, and he found it a puzzling mixture of tough kids and middle-class teachers, each group having a quite separate and distinct way of expressing itself. Children in poor neighbourhoods everywhere, from Rio de Janeiro to Toxteth and from Bangladesh to Soweto, live in a world where survival is the only goal and where the dream of escape is made real only to a blessed few. The rest? Well, they stay poor and beget another generation a fraction less prosperous and even less in touch with couth middle-class people, who not only aspire but achieve. To come out of this milieu and not only survive but prosper is given to only a few — the entrepreneurs, the prize fighters, and in Britain and the USA and among poor Jews everywhere, the comedians.

Woody Allen, Mel Brooks, Harpo Marx, W. C. Fields, Charlie Chaplin, Buster Keaton, George Burns — meet Bill Cosby. He, like you, fought his way out of poverty and despair by means of humour. He couldn't hope to cope with the heavies. Nicknamed 'Shorty', his only way to gain acceptance in his peer group was by making them laugh. But where did that humour spring from?

It seems unlikely that it came from his heavy-drinking, violent father but, says his biographer, Ronald L. Smith, his mother, Anna Cosby, would read extracts from Mark Twain's *Tom Sawyer*, *Huckleberry Finn*, and *Pudd'nhead Wilson*, and Twain became a model and a hero to the young Cosby. From these slender literary beginnings he found such delight in language and the whole elaborate paraphernalia of communication that he progressed through college and postgraduation studies to become, at the age of 39, a Doctor of Education at the University of Massachusetts. Before that he had become a major star of TV, a cabaret entertainer in constant demand, and a recording artist whose LPs sold in millions.

The joke-telling, wise-cracking 'Shorty' didn't do well at school, too often preferring to read comic books than work for exams, but he developed into a first-class sportsman. With the help of one teacher, a Miss Forchic, he overcame his natural abhorrence of learning and received her accolade on leaving the 6th Grade: 'He would rather be a clown than a student ... [but] he should grow up to do great things.'

His alternatives on leaving high school seemed to be low-paid menial work or the high-reward, high-risk life of a petty thief. Many of Bill Cosby's contemporaries chose the latter, others the drudgery of the former. He took a right turn, and in 1956 joined the Navy. Bill Cosby as a medical orderly didn't see action, but his athletic prowess grew and he represented his naval base in track and field events, running the 100 yards in 10.2 seconds, and reaching six foot five inches in the high jump — no mean feat for the ex-'Shorty', who was now a lean six-footer.

When his spell in the Navy was over Bill Cosby, now nearly 23 years old, went to Temple University on an athletic scholarship and, incidentally, had the chance to earn real money cracking jokes. Cosby's natural wit and quick mind were absolutely attuned to the America of the late fifties. It was a period of quite extraordinary development in American comedy, especially for monologists. Shelly Berman, Mort Sahl, and Bob Newhart were wildly popular in clubs and on records, as were Mike Nichols and Elaine May. And then there were a number of black comedians making a big impression and a lot of money in cabaret. Among them were veteran Nipsy Russell, Pigmeat Markham, Redd Foxx, Flip Wilson, and possibly the most successful of all, Dick Gregory.

So Cosby went to Greenwich Village in New York and joined the crowd of entertainers making towards the big time — Woody Allen, Barbra Streisand, Simon and Garfunkel, Joan Rivers — and, to the surprise of nobody who saw him then, quickly became a success.

By 1962 he had created routines that were all his own, like the one in which a puzzled Noah is asking God why he must build an ark.

> Noah hears a voice —
> 'NOAH.'
> 'Who is that?'
> 'It's the Lord, Noah.'
> 'Right!'

When Noah finally believes that he's actually talking to the Lord, he wonders why:

> 'I want you to build an ark.'
> 'Ri-ight. What's an ark?'
> 'Get some wood. Build it 300 cubits by 80 cubits by 40 cubits.'
> 'Right. What's a cubit?'

When the Lord tells him he plans to destroy the world, Noah can't believe it:

> 'Am I on *Candid Camera*?'

'I'm gonna make it rain 4000 days and drown them right out!'
'Ri-ight. Listen, do this and you'll save water. Let it rain for 40 days and 40
nights and wait for the sewers to back up.'
'RIGHT!'

Apart from his set piece routines Cosby had a good line in racial and political
jokes, but as he progressed he realized that he was in danger of becoming another
stereotype, the black comedian. He started to feel that as a second Dick Gregory
he was going to wind up second-best, and began to drop the specifically 'black'
references in his act. His comments and quips became those of an American, not a
negro American, but *any* American concerned with the way things were in
society.

In 1963 he met the girl he was to marry, Camille Hanks. She was 19 and the
daughter of a medical research worker. The other big event of the year was that
Bill Cosby made it on to *The Tonight Show, the* big television showcase of the day.
It was thanks to Alan Sherman, who was deputizing for Johnny Carson and who
liked Cosby's work, that Bill got on the show with a routine about karate — and
the audience loved it. Then came a recording contract with Warner Brothers, and
really big money in cabaret.

In 1964 Bill and Camille were married and at the start of a long and fulfilling
family life together. Bill's material became more family-orientated too, with anecdotes of his childhood: playing street football, sleeping in the same bed as his
bedwetting brother, and so on.

Also in 1964 he was invited by Sheldon Leonard to co-star in an espionage
series with Robert Culp. It was called *I Spy*, and in it Culp and Cosby were US
agents masquerading, respectively, as a tennis star and his trainer. It was one of a
number of spy series current at the time, including *The Man from U.N.C.L.E.*, and
the Don Addams spoof, *Get Smart*.

It seems strange from the vantage point of the late 1980s to look back and
find that the TV network worried because Bill Cosby, a black man, had a 'buddy'
relationship with a white man. As Bill Cosby said at the time, 'My people would
just like to enjoy an hour of TV where a negro isn't a problem. People can see I'm
a negro; we don't need to say anything else'.

As it turned out the business did the talking: *I Spy* quickly went into the US
National Top 20, and Cosby won the prestigious Emmy Award as Best Dramatic
Actor in a Series. *I Spy* ran for three years and Bill Cosby won three Emmys.

So, stardom came to Bill Cosby, and he enjoyed the trappings of success in
his California home with his wife, his mother, and two daughters. He also enjoyed
driving, and had much the same sort of car bug as Peter Sellers, of whom at that
time it was said 'he changed his cars more often than he changed his underwear'.
Bill Cosby, however, liked to keep *his* cars and just added another one to the
garage — a Mercedes, a Cadillac, a Ferrari, a Rolls-Royce, and so on.

From the late sixties Bill Cosby's rise has been steady and spectacular. TV
variety 'specials', guest host of *The Tonight Show*, concerts, LPs, a cartoon series

based on the characters of his anecdotes, and a sitcom in which he played a teacher added millions to his fan club and billions to his bank account. He's been criticized for not joining in 'the black struggle' or helping to solve 'the black problem', but by keeping cool on screen and working out the mundane humours of middle-class life he has come to symbolize what most Americans aspire to — a rich, comfortable lifestyle with few worries and a couple of laughs along the way.

Moving from California to Massachusetts, his family growing up and increasing in numbers (Bill and Camille Cosby now have five children), making occasional forays to New York or California to work on TV programmes such as *The Electric Company* (an educational series designed to help 7- to 10-year-olds improve their reading and writing) — and working for his Master's Degree — for Bill Cosby the seventies were a busy and fulfilling time. But what about movies?

Well, in the seventies Bill made movies too. The first, *Man and Boy* (1972), was a somewhat sentimental 'family' Western about a father and son tracking down a horse thief. Also in 1972 he made *Hickey and Boggs* with Robert Culp — but this time the *I Spy* team were shabby detectives. In 1974 came *Uptown Saturday Night*, co-starring and directed by Sidney Poitier. It was a story about a stolen lottery ticket. In 1975 another Poitier picture, *Let's Do it Again*, was followed in 1976 by *Mother, Jugs, and Speed*, with Raquel Welch and Harvey Keitel as a crazy ambulance crew — a film which has been described as 'M.A.S.H. on wheels'. Then came another Poitier picture, *A Piece of the Action*, made in 1977, and *California Suite* (1978), in which Bill Cosby teamed up with Richard Pryor in a segment of an episodic film written by Neil Simon and directed by Herbert Ross. Finally, in 1981 came *The Devil and Max Devlin*, an updated twist on the Faust story.

On stage he teamed up with Sammy Davis Junior for a Broadway run — *Sammy and Cos* — but unfortunately the run was extremely short as few people bothered to come to see those two talented men. After all, why pay 50 dollars when you can see them on TV for nothing? But on TV things hadn't been going too well either. *The New Bill Cosby Show* had a shortish run from September 1972 to May 1973, and three years later *Cos*, a mish-mash of music, interviews, and monologues ran for only seven weeks in September–October 1976 before it was dropped.

But, although his shows didn't do much for his prestige, his selling power in TV commercials was, and is, enormous, as from Pan Am to Coca Cola many sponsors sought to use his image to sell their product.

In 1984 came the cherry on the cake — *The Cosby Show*. It quickly became the hit of the season, and the next, and the next, and in 1988 a syndication deal made Bill Cosby the highest-paid performer in American history.

The Cosby Show, for those who *don't* watch sitcom on TV, is a domestic comedy about a middle-class black family where the father is a gynaecologist and the mother is a lawyer. The children are as believably lovable or awful as the script wills them to be, and its success is amazing. That is to say, it's amazingly popular in the USA. In Britain it has to struggle for an audience on the minority Channel 4, and has never been given much in the way of critical acclaim.

192

None the less, black *and* white Americans love it, and its success proves yet again that you don't have to shout to get attention — a touch of folk wisdom in a believable setting, with a family *being* a family is all you need ... oh, and a touch of wit helps too, and that's where Bill Cosby comes in, for Bill Cosby, Master of Education, is also master of comedy.

FILMS

Man and Boy   1972
Produced by Marvin Miller
Directed by E. W. Swackhamer
Written by Harry Essen and Oscar Saul

Hickey and Boggs   1972
Produced by P. Fouad Said
Directed by Robert Culp
Written by Walter Hill

Uptown Saturday Night   1974
Produced by Melville Tucker
Directed by Sidney Poitier
Written by Richard Wesley

Let's Do it Again   1975
Produced by Melville Tucker and Pembroke J. Herring
Directed by Sidney Poitier
Written by Richard Wesley

Mother, Jugs, and Speed   1976
Produced by Joseph R. Barbera
Directed by Peter Yates
Written by Tom Mankiewicz

A Piece of the Action   1977
Produced by Melville Tucker
Directed by Sidney Poitier
Written by Charles Blackwell

California Suite   1978
Produced by Ray Stark
Directed by Herbert Ross
Written by Neil Simon

The Devil and Max Devlin   1981
Produced by Jerome Courtland
Directed by Steven Hilliard Stern
Written by Mary Rodgers

TELEVISION

I Spy   1965–8 NBC
The Bill Cosby Show   1969–71 NBC
The Electric Company   1971–6 PBS
Fat Albert and the Cosby Kids   1972 CBS
The New Bill Cosby Show   1972–3 CBS
Cos   1976 ABC
The Cosby Show   1984– NBC

JACK BENNY

It is night. The scene is a suburban street. A pedestrian walks his solitary way homewards. From out of the shadows steps a hold-up man, gun pointed at his victim. 'Your money or your life,' croaks the gunman. There is a long pause as the victim considers the option. Then — 'I'm thinking it over.' It is perhaps the best-known of all the 'stingy' jokes perpetrated by that incomparable master of timing, Jack Benny.

Miserliness, misanthropy, vanity, and uncompromising selfishness, characteristics that were Jack Benny's stock in trade, would hardly seem appropriate to a comedian. Indeed, meeting them in real life would be positively repellent, but with Benny they added piquancy and flavour to a comedy style that was at bottom gentle, sardonic, observant, and deeply amusing. Even Jack Benny's violin playing, which never rose above the mediocre, gave him a basis for humour that took him from entertaining his fellow sailors in the US Navy in 1918 to the great concert-halls of the world in the sixties, seventies, and eighties, when Jack Benny was the acknowledged master comedian of the English-speaking world.

No comic who knew Jack Benny had anything other than reverence for the man, or would consider themselves his superior as a laughter-maker. No one copied his style, or if they did that copy was never recognizable. Benny was charmingly, engagingly unique.

Away from the stage, or TV screen, radio, or the movie set, he was generous in praise and help to others in his profession, an indefatigable giver to charity and an enthusiast for show business, who hated any time when he wasn't working at being funny or encouraging others to give of their best. The legend is that it was his silences that produced the laughter he generated rather than the things he said, but there are other comedians whose timing was as good (and after all, 'timing' is only a word to describe the rhythm of what is being said and the pauses between words and phrases), and there are comic actors who never utter a word at all, Marcel Marceau being the most obvious example. Jack Benny's special flair was to use silence to underline the significance of what was said, never using two words when one would do.

Jack Benny had the insight to see that, vain and miserly as he was supposed to be, it was the fact that *we* saw him as a simpleton imposed upon by all around

197

him that made us love him; and no comedian was more loved or more genuinely lovable than Jack Benny.

Jack Benny was born Benjamin Kubelsky on 14 February 1894 in Chicago, a city which his mother thought would look better on his birth certificate than Waukegan, a small town on the Lake Michigan shore, where his father, Meyer Kubelsky, ran a saloon. Both his father and mother were immigrants from Lithuania who had met and married in the USA through the good offices of a Chicago marriage-broker.

Later, at Mrs Kubelsky's insistence, her husband gave up the saloon and went into the haberdashery business. It was hoped by his loving parents that young Benny Kubelsky would become a concert violinist, for he wasn't a particularly great scholar. He left school early and only belatedly picked up knowledge and information through voracious reading.

As a violinist he was adequate rather than scintillating, and he had his first brush with show business when he got a job in the pit band at the Waukegan Barrison Theatre in 1911. There he played for the vaudevillians of the day, including the young Marx Brothers, whose mother, the redoubtable Minnie Marx, suggested that young Kubelsky should tour with the act adding special effects on violin to her sons' onstage antics.

By 1912 Benny had become a fully fledged performer in his own right as part of a piano and violin duo, Salisbury and Kubelsky, whose billing was 'From Grand Opera to Ragtime'. The Salisbury of the act was Cora Salisbury, a 'brilliant' pianist in the rhinestone and candelabra style later made popular by Liberace. Cora was much older than the 18-year-old and looked after him in a motherly way on their exhausting tours of the midwest in 1912–14. During this time young Kubelsky changed his name to Ben K. Benny and when Cora Salisbury gave up the business to care for her ailing mother, Benny became Bennie, and the owner of this new, more 'up-market' name teamed up with Lyman Woods, a young pianist without Cora Salisbury's scholarly musicianship but with a natural flair for the instrument. Bennie and Woods became a moderately successful vaudeville act, although the big time eluded them.

In 1917 two events of major importance to the 23-year-old Benny Kubelsky occurred. Sadly, his mother became ill and died, and the USA entered the war. Benjamin joined the Navy, but the amount of action seen by the US Navy on the Great Lakes in 1917–18 was, to put it mildly, minimal, and Kubelsky/Benny/Bennie was in demand as an entertainer, for a time partnering Zez Confrey, the man who subsequently gave the world that minor piano classic 'Kitten on the Keys'.

By 1921, in another and final name change, Jack Benny was born. Billed in theatre programmes and on billboards as 'The Aristocrat of Humour', his mixture of dry wit and violin playing quickly established him as a first-rate monologist, and practice and experience ensured that he was constantly in work and frequently topped the bill.

In 1927 he met and married Sadie Marks, who was working at the time as a sales assistant behind the hosiery counter at the May Company in Los Angeles. She joined him in his act and after herself having a name change or two (Marie Marsh was one) eventually settled for Mary Livingstone. Jack and Mary were married for 48 years and although they never had children of their own they adopted a girl, christened her Joan Naomi, called her Joanie, and lavished on her everything that doting parents could give a child. In return she gave them love and four grandchildren.

Meanwhile Jack Benny's professional star was rising. New York stage hits and Hollywood movies came his way, but most important was radio. Jack Benny made his first broadcast in March 1932 on *The Ed Sullivan Show*. His often quoted first line was: 'Ladies and gentlemen this is Jack Benny talking. There will be a slight pause while you say "who cares?" '

By May 1932 Jack Benny had his own series, sponsored by the Canada Dry Ginger Ale Company. He did 78 programmes for Canada Dry, but the sponsors didn't care for the cavalier way they thought Jack treated the product. For instance, one ad was supposed to be a telegram from a Canada Dry salesman who had found eight tourists stranded in the Sahara Desert. They'd been without water for 40 days and the wire read: 'I came to their rescue, giving each of them a glass of Canada Dry. Not one of them said they didn't like it.'

Humour and advertising have always been uneasy bedfellows, and case histories of people remembering the commercials but being unable to remember the name of the product are legion. Looking back it seems that Jack Benny's gentle spoofing of the product was harmless and, in fact, beneficial, but Canada Dry withdrew their sponsorship and the Chevrolet division of General Motors took over. In time they were replaced by General Tire, and then General Goods with the product Jello. Jello, a gelatine dessert 'in six delicious flavours', although virtually unknown in Britain became, partly thanks to *The Jack Benny Show*, a household word in the States.

The laws governing broadcasting in the UK in the thirties did not allow commercial sponsorship and at the time of writing (1988) still don't, but the continental stations Radio Normandie and Radio Luxembourg, which vied with the BBC for audiences, encouraged sponsorship. Before the Second World War, Ovaltine, Oxydol soap powder, and Betox, a meat extract, not to mention Bird's custard, Kraft cheese, and many other products, became well known to those listeners who tuned in to Radio Luxembourg and Radio Normandie. In the USA almost all radio programmes were sponsored, and sponsors competed for the most successful entertainers.

In 1934 Jack Benny was voted radio's favourite comedian. Other favourites in other categories included Bing Crosby (male singer), Leopold Stowkowski (symphonic conductor), and the Boswell Sisters (harmony team).

From a simple formula of monologues, sketches, and songs Jack Benny and his writers evolved a concept new to radio variety shows then and rarely, if ever, improved upon since. The basic idea was to build the programme around the preparations leading up to the recording of that week's show. Characters played variously by Mary Livingstone, bandleader Phil Harris, and announcer Don

Wilson would wander in and out of the central situation, putting Jack down, commenting on his miserliness or vanity, and with the addition of Eddie 'Rochester' Anderson in 1937 and singer Dennis Day in 1939, the team was finally complete. Eddie Anderson had been a big hit as Noah in the 1935 all-black production *Green Pastures*, and in 1937 he auditioned for and got the part as a train porter in one programme. The Bennys are on their way from New York to Hollywood. Here's a sample of the dialogue.

> (*Sound effect of train in motion*)
>
> MARY LIVINGSTONE: Say, Jack, look out the window ... they sure dress funny here in Hollywood.
>
> JACK: Those are Indians. This is New Mexico.
>
> MARY: Oh.
>
> JACK: Hey, porter. Porter.
>
> ROCHESTER: Yes-suh.
>
> JACK: What time do we get to Albuquerque?
>
> ROCHESTER: What?
>
> JACK: Albuquerque.
>
> ROCHESTER: I dunno. Do we stop there?
>
> JACK: Certainly we stop there.
>
> ROCHESTER: My my!
>
> JACK: Hm.
>
> ROCHESTER: I better go up and tell the engineer about that.
>
> JACK: Yes — do.
>
> ROCHESTER: What's the name of that town again?
>
> JACK: Albuquerque.
>
> ROCHESTER: Albuquerque. What they gonna think up next.
>
> JACK: Albuquerque is a town.
>
> ROCHESTER: You better check on that.
>
> JACK: I know what I'm talking about ... Now, how long do we stop there?
>
> ROCHESTER: How long do we stop where?
>
> JACK: In Albuquerque.
>
> ROCHESTER: (*Laughs*) There you go again.

From the beginning a long-running relationship emerged, with Rochester as a cynical and disbelieving manservant, that was one of the highlights of Jack Benny's radio and television shows.

Dennis Day was the last in the line of boyish tenors who gave the audience a breather from the quickfire jokes and commercials that dominated the shows. His predecessors had been Kenny Baker, Frank Parker, and Mike Bartlett, and Day was originally signed on a two-week contract. It eventually became a 35-year connection! Dennis had a high tenor voice and an engagingly gauche manner. The show's writers seized on this and gave him a dominating 'mother' played by Verna Felton who, when Jack said, 'Sing, Dennis', would shout, 'Not now, Dennis. *I'll* tell you when to sing.' When Day, on his debut, was asked his age he answered, '59 including mother.' The mother was a successful running character for several seasons and was only dropped when it was felt that Dennis Day could stay naïve for only just *so* long.

In the mid fifties Jack Benny swapped radio for television and his stardom continued undiminished. The formula developed more into situation comedy, with the by now obligatory injection of guest stars, and in the late sixties Jack, now in his seventies, gave up the regular 30-minute slot in favour of one-hour 'specials'. These had a similar formula, with sketches, monologues, and guest stars, and were as popular as ever.

By quitting the weekly grind Jack Benny found that he too could guest for other people's 'specials', and whether as a guest of Bob Hope, George Burns, or Rowan and Martin he was accommodating and unfailingly amusing. I have a particular fondness for one sketch from one of his own 'specials' made in 1969 where the guest star was Gregory Peck. The point of the sketch was that Jack was organizing a charity show and needed Peck as the main attraction. Jack duly paid a visit to Gregory Peck's home and after skirting the question for some time Jack blurted out, 'Now — look, Greg — what fee would you ask for appearing at this function?' Peck's immediate response was, 'Jack, I'll do it for nothing.' There was a long pause while Jack considered this. His expectation of having to haggle was so strong that he couldn't choke back his prepared reply. Eventually he blurted out: 'We weren't thinking of going that high.' Like most of Jack Benny's lines it doesn't seem much written down, but the way it was delivered turned it, for me anyway, into a minor comic masterpiece.

I'd first heard Jack Benny on the wireless when the BBC, to pep up its flagging wartime output, started airing American radio shows. Of them all Jack Benny's was the best. I'd also seen him in movies such as *Charley's Aunt*, and *To Be or Not to Be*, an Ernst Lubitsch film about a troupe of Polish actors in Warsaw at the outbreak of the Second World War. It was a fairly controversial film at the time as it satirized the Nazis, but did it in a way that left the audience feeling uncomfortable.

Jack Benny, masquerading as a Gestapo officer, was neither outrageous enough nor was the satire pungent enough to dispel the uneasiness that hung over the film. Seeing it recently on television, time had not treated it kindly, and Mel Brooks's eighties remake didn't do much to improve matters, brilliant though both Brooks and Benny were in the leading role.

However, having seen Jack Benny on the screen and heard him on the air, when he made his first post-war appearance at the London Palladium I was there. On stage he was mesmeric. The orchestra played 'Love in Bloom', his signature tune, and on to the stage sauntered this tall, mature, good-looking man in a well-cut suit. He was greeted with rapturous applause and laughter as he stood centre stage and just stared at us.

I remember little of his act. He cracked the oldie, 'People say I'm stingy but I've been in London three days and [*snap of the fingers*] 10 shillings has gone just like that.' No matter that it was a slight variation of a joke that had appeared in *Punch* in the 1890s, Jack Benny telling it made it mint fresh.

Phil Harris came on as part of the act, and in addition there was a would-be

201

singing group looking more like the three witches in *Macbeth* than a vocal trio. Jack politely asked their name. Came the answer in a high-pitched snarl: 'We're the Landru Sisters.' Jack asked: 'Isn't that a bit like the *Andrews* Sisters?' and was greeted by the harridan screech: 'We know what we're doing.' Jack's turn to the audience, the lift of his eyebrows and the slight shrug conveying that he had no connection with these three harpies was the master of comedy at his urbane best.

It was years before I actually met this wonderful comedian and the circumstances were somewhat curious. In 1956 I was appearing in a long-running revue, *For Amusement Only*, at the Apollo Theatre, Shaftesbury Avenue in London. Evening performances were booked solid but the Wednesday matinées were sparsely attended, mainly it seemed by deaf, elderly ladies up in town from the country for a day's shopping and who'd slipped into the theatre for a sit down and a chance to rest their feet.

One particular Wednesday the silent calm was broken by one raucous laugher. Anything remotely amusing in the script caused this unknown cackler out there in the dark further paroxysms of mirth, and even the less funny moments in the show were greeted with rapture. Members of the cast muttered to each other, *sotto voce*, various suggestions. 'It's a drunk,' 'It's a practical joke devised by the authors to needle us', etc. Several of the actors complained that this 'over the top' reaction was ruining their performance, others thought 'better one laugher than none at all'. By the interval the manager had been called and asked to evict or at least quieten the intrusive hysteric. While the cast waited on stage for the second-act curtain to go up the manager, white-faced but beaming, addressed us. 'It's Jack Benny,' he said, 'he *loves* the show!'

After the final curtain Jack came backstage and chatted to us all. He'd found the show delightful, particularly the performance of Ron Moody, who subsequently starred as Fagin in the musical *Oliver*. He swore he'd come again and bring friends, and sure enough he did. From then on our regular visitors included Van Johnson, Sam Goldwyn, and Tyrone Power, who was between marriages and assiduously courted our leading lady, Thelma Ruby. (Come to think of it, he snitched my dresser when he opened in a production of Shaw's *The Devil's Disciple*, but that's another story).

Jack Benny came often and wanted to ship the whole company to New York to appear on *The Ed Sullivan Show*, but the commitment to the London run made it impossible. When the show finally ended after a run of over two years I can remember Charles Laughton in tears at the end-of-run party. 'But why must it end', he sobbed. Thanks to Jack we'd become as well known in Hollywood as in London.

My next meeting with Jack Benny was when I was on the writing team of *Rowan and Martin's Laugh-In* in 1969. The following year, when I'd become an executive at London Weekend Television, I booked him to appear as the star guest in a chat show hosted by Simon Dee who then had a big following but whose show, I felt, needed a boost. The director nearly got himself fired for panicking in the middle of a long Jack Benny pause and cutting away for a reaction, thus ruining the tag line of the joke. However, the appearance was a success and afterwards Jack was his usual affable and enthusiastic self, telling us all with great animation his future plans.

When Jack Benny died in December 1974 he was 80 years old and he was working right up until the end. His 22 films, his countless radio and television shows, his innumerable public appearances all over the world, made him a major star. What made Jack Benny special was that he loved and was loved by everybody. In an era when stardom really meant moving in a different world to us mere mortals, and in Beverly Hills where everyone was a star (except the little old ladies who sold guides to the star's homes), Jack Benny was still the greatest comic talent of them all.

Frederick De Cordova, one of the top Hollywood TV producers, sums up Jack Benny better than most. Quoted in Mary Livingstone Benny, Hilliard Marks, and Marcia Borie's biography of Jack Benny, De Cordova says:

> Jack worked very hard to make what he did seem so casual and spontaneous. In truth he was concerned line by line with whatever he did. And while it was true that Jack was perpetually generous in seeing to it that other people got laughs ... that *wasn't* Jack being darling that was his professional evaluation of what looked best.
>
> He knew he was a big star but he didn't act like any other celebrity I've ever known. He appreciated things more than others. He was always *more* surprised. He was *happier* at someone else's success.

It's good to know that someone who gave such happiness was happy himself.

FILMS

Hollywood Revue of 1929   1929
Produced by Harry Rapf
Directed by Charles F. Reisner
Written by Al Boasberg and Robert E. Hopkins

Chasing Rainbows   1930
Produced by MGM
Directed by Charles Riesner
Written by Bess Meredyth

Medicine Man   1930
Produced by TIF
Directed by Scott Pembroke
Written by Ladye Horton and Eva Unsell, from a play by Elliott Lester

Transatlantic Merry Go Round   1934
Produced by United Artists

Directed by Ben Stoloff
Written by Joseph Moncure March, Harry W. Conn, and Leon Gordon

Broadway Melody of 1936   1936
Produced by John W. Considine Jr
Directed by Roy del Ruth
Written by Jack McGowan, Sid Silvers, and Moss Hart

It's in the Air   1935
Produced by E. J. Mannix
Directed by Charles F. Riesner
Written by Bryon Morgan

The Big Broadcast of 1937   1937
Produced by Lewis Gensler
Directed by Mitchell Leisner
Written by Edwin Gelsey, Arthur Kober, Barry Travers, Walter de Leon, and Francis Martin

College Holiday   1936
Produced by Harlan Thompson
Directed by Frank Tuttle
Written by J. P. McEvoy, Harlan Ware, Jay Gorney, and Henry Myers

Artists and Models   1937
Produced by Lewis E. Gensler
Directed by Raoul Walsh
Written by Walter de Leon and Francis Martin

Artists and Models Abroad   1938
Produced by Arthur Hornblow Jr
Directed by Mitchell Leisen
Written by Howard Lindsay, Russell Crouse, and Ken Englund

Man About Town   1939
Produced by Arthur Hornblow Jr
Directed by Mark Sandrich
Written by Morrie Ryskind

Buck Benny Rides Again
Produced by Mark Sandrich
Directed by Mark Sandrich
Written by William Morrow and Edmund Beloin

Love Thy Neighbour   1940
Produced by Mark Sandrich
Directed by Mark Sandrich
Written by William Morrow, Edmund Beloin, and Ernest Pagano

Charley's Aunt   1941
Produced by William Perlberg
Directed by Archie Mayo
Written by George Seaton

To Be or Not To Be   1942
Produced by Ernst Lubitsch
Directed by Ernst Lubitsch
Written by Edwin Justus Mayer, from a story by Ernst Lubitsch

George Washington Slept Here   1942
Produced by Jerry Wald
Directed by William Keighley
Written by Everett Freeman, from the play by George Kaufman and Moss Hart

The Meanest Man in the World   1943
Produced by Twentieth Century Fox
Directed by Sidney Lanfield
Written by George Seaton and Allan House, from a play by George M. Cohan

Hollywood Canteen   1944
Produced by Alex Gottleib
Directed by Delmer Daves
Written by Delmer Daves

It's in the Bag   1945
Produced by Manhattan Productions
Directed by Richard Wallace
Written by Jay Dratler and Alma Reville

The Horn Blows at Midnight   1945
Produced by Mark Hellinger
Directed by Raoul Walsh
Written by Sam Hellman, James V. Kern

A Guide for the Married Man   1967
Produced by Frank McCarthy
Directed by Gene Kelly
Written by Frank Tarloff

TELEVISION

The Jack Benny Show   1950–65

CHARLIE CHAPLIN

C haplin, like so many comedians of his generation, began his career in the British music-halls and subsequently the vaudeville circuits in the United States. He was born in 1889 at a period when the growing prosperity of a more or less literate working class accelerated the boom in centres of family entertainment, that's to say the music-halls. They hadn't reached their full flowering, which came at the start of the twentieth century and lasted until the arrival of talking pictures, but there were many halls and a great thirst for entertainment. Chaplin's mother and father were both entertainers — his father a singer and comedian ('Oui, trey bong', 'As the Church Bells Chime', 'She Must Be Witty' being three titles in his repertoire), his mother also a singer who worked under the name of Lily Harley and subsequently, in the 1890s, as Lily Chaplin.

In the nineties, Charlie's father (who was, incidentally, Sydney Chaplin's father too) deserted his wife and family, and the boys were sent first to the workhouse and later, in 1896, to school and, in Sydney's case, the naval training ship HMS *Exmouth*. The remaining years of the century were a time of upheaval for the young Chaplin — a succession of workhouses and schools, his mother ill both physically and mentally, and his father more or less on the run. It must have been with a certain amount of relief that Charlie joined the music-hall act The Eight Lancashire Lads, whose speciality was clog dancing, at Christmas 1898.

In 1901 Charlie Chaplin Senior died aged 37. Shortly after Charlie's mother was committed to a lunatic asylum. By 1903 Charlie's career changed direction when he joined H. A. Saintsbury in the Sherlock Holmes Company playing the page boy, Billy. Later, brother Sydney joined the company too. In 1906 Charlie joined the Caseys Court Company, a group of knockabout comedians. Brother Sydney signed a contract with Fred Karno, who ran a group of touring companies.

There was a vogue for knockabout acts in the music-halls at that time and Karno, although uncouth and in many respects, so eye-witness accounts affirm, something of a blackguard, had great comic inventiveness. His companies performed long comic scenes with such titles as 'The Mumming Birds' (called 'A Night at the English Music-Hall' in the USA), 'The Wow Wows' (or 'A Night in an English Secret Society'), which mocked the initiation ceremonies of the Masons, Oddfellows, or Elks types of society, and 'London Suburbia', in which Sydney

Chaplin appeared. He was paid three pounds a week, which would be increased to six pounds a week if required to work in the USA. Thanks to Sydney's urging in 1908 Charlie also signed with Karno at three pounds ten shillings a week.

He quickly made his mark appearing in many of the Karno favourites, for at that time Karno had as many as 10 companies on the road playing one or other of his 'Burlesques'. A famous one was 'The Football Match', which had a large cast and many special effects. It depicted a soccer game between two teams of no-hopers and was very popular in the pre-1914 era. In the sketch Charlie played the part of a villain who tries to bribe the goalkeeper, 'Stiffy' (the leading comic part), and in later versions played Stiffy himself.

In 'The Mumming Birds' the set depicted a theatre stage with boxes on either side, and in it Charlie played a drunk who criticizes the appalling acts and finishes up in a scrap with an alleged strong man, billed as 'The Terrible Turk'. This built up until everyone in the sketch, 'performers' and 'audience' alike, joined in for a finale of mayhem.

By 1910 a new contract with Karno guaranteed him six, eight, and ten pounds a week for the next three years. The year 1910 also saw Chaplin's first USA tour followed in 1912 by a tour of France, and a second American tour.

At the end of 1913, his contract with Karno completed, Charlie Chaplin signed a one-year contract for 150 dollars a week with the Keystone Film Company. In November 1914 he signed a contract with Essanay at 1250 dollars a week for 14 films to be made over the following 12 months. Thus his income had risen in three years from the equivalent of 48 dollars and 86 cents a week (the exchange rate at that time was 4 dollars and 86 cents to the pound sterling) to an astounding 1250 dollars a week. By 1916 that had become 10,000 dollars a week with a bonus of 150,000 dollars on signature. By 1917 Chaplin signed his first 'million dollar' contract with First National (actually 1,075,000 dollars). In a little over 12 years Charles Chaplin had risen from being a minor comedian in a vaudeville troupe earning 17 dollars a week to being an international star and a millionaire.

It was a rise as sensational as Chaplin's comic ability. It speaks volumes for his ingenuity, originality, and intelligence — a rare combination among international stars — that he could not only make this leap from obscurity to notoriety but behave in a reasonably modest and commonsense way while he was emerging as a star. Furthermore, although in these years he had produced a number of comedy classics, albeit brief ones, his best work both in short and long films was yet to come.

No other comedian had ever made this impact, but then no medium had the impact of the cinema in its early years. The lack of sound far from being a hindrance was a positive asset, for with a white sheet, a reel of film, and a projector you could set up shop anywhere. And people did, worldwide, and millions flocked to see this new phenomenon. In the USA the tidal wave of immigrants was beginning to subside, but many people in the large towns of America could only speak their native tongue, be it Italian, Latvian, or Yiddish. The cinema united these disparate groups and inability to speak English was no bar to entry. The only question asked was whether you had the price of admission to these so-called 'nickelodeons'.

While emotional dramas and large-scale historical epics such as *Way Down East* and *Intolerance* were popular, the poor, ragged, and deprived found in Chaplin a hero of their own kind, fighting for his existence in a world they understood and in which they too were struggling to survive.

In France Chaplin was dubbed 'Charlot' and became known by that name in many countries. Poverty is stateless, and his battered heroism and stoic jauntiness lifted the hearts of the poverty-stricken worldwide.

Today one tends to think that in films Chaplin only played the tramp with the bowler hat, moustache, baggy trousers, and cane, but though this character was invented in 1914 and first seen in the short film *Kid Auto Races at Venice*, making a second appearance in that same month (February 1914) in *Mabel's Strange Predicament*, in which Charlie starred with Mabel Normand, in later Keystone shorts Charlie's list of characters included a waiter, a pickpocket, 'Lord Helpus', and a great variety of drunks. He also played a boxing referee in *The Knockout* with Fatty Arbuckle, the wife(!) in *A Busy Day* with Mack Swain, and a dentist's assistant in a short which Chaplin also wrote and directed called *Laughing Gas*. The longest and most important film in Chaplin's early career was *Tillie's Punctured Romance*, which at the length of 6000 feet ran approximately one hour and 15 minutes. (I owe this information about the running time of silent films — 16 frames a second — to my old friend, the inspired film buff and collector, Philip Jenkinson. Film speed today is 24 frames a second and, of course, we are talking about 35 mm film. Another note on film speeds of silent movies is that in those days not only film cameras but also projectors were hand-cranked — thus the speed of any film could be varied at the whim of the projectionist. An old acquaintance of mine, a cinema projectionist in the early days, once told me: 'If I wanted to get home early — I'd crank a bit faster'!)

The length and the big cast of *Tillie's Punctured Romance* — which included, in addition to Chaplin, Marie Dressler, Mabel Normand, Mack Swain, Edgar Kennedy, and Slim Somerville, plus many others — made it something of a landmark in the making of comedy pictures and it was certainly the biggest Chaplin made with Keystone. When he changed studios to Essanay it was back to shorts and playing parts called 'Reveller', 'Aspiring Pugilist', 'The Fake Count', and 'Janitor', but mainly Chaplin played the tramp sometimes called just Charlie. His leading lady was invariably Edna Purviance, a charming and talented actress who provided ideal support and was moderately glamorous (at least by present-day standards; judged by the standards of the time she could well have been considered a great beauty). Obviously, she and Chaplin had a great rapport both on and off the screen. They made 35 films together and when, sadly, Edna left the movie business and took to drink, Chaplin was always ready to help her; in fact in 1946 he considered her for a part in his film *Monsieur Verdoux*, but decided with regret that she was not suitable. Edna Purviance died of cancer in 1958 at the age of 62.

By 1916 Chaplin had moved to the studios of Mutual Films and was entering what could be considered a 'golden' period. Some of those Mutual films are regarded by many experts as classics. They include *The Pawnshop*, where Chaplin, as the pawnbroker's assistant, takes apart an alarm clock with the delicacy and finesse of a surgeon performing a major operation. Having wrecked the clock he hands the dismembered timepiece back to the customer, refusing to accept it as a pledge as it is now broken. This typical Chaplin mixture of dexterity, charm, and cruelty has only been equalled in recent times by Barry Humphries who, as Dame Edna Everage, can somehow both cosset and destroy his guests simultaneously. (There are other similarities between Humphries and Chaplin which I explore elsewhere in this book.)

. In this period (1916–17) Chaplin also made the classic *Easy Street*, where, as a vagabond recruited into the police force, he subdues a tough slum neighbour-hood, and *The Cure*, where he plays an upper-crust drunk at a health hydro.

In 1918 Chaplin moved to First National Films where, for the first time, he had complete control over every aspect of production in his own studios built in the heart of Hollywood. The major films produced by this new set-up were *A Dog's Life*, where most of the action takes place in and around a dance-hall. Edna Purviance, as a singer of sentimental songs, causes floods of tears from all who hear her. (This was, of course, a silent movie so one has to guess at the sentiments expressed in the song — Mother and a home far away, one supposes!) Chaplin is a relaxed, louche tramp who, because he won't part with his dog, is repeatedly thrown out of the dance hall.

The film runs for about half an hour, and *Shoulder Arms*, made in the sum-mer of 1918, is even longer. It is a comedy war movie with Chaplin as the clumsy recruit who at the end saves the day and gets the girl. By way of contrast Chaplin's . next film was *Sunnyside*, a rural fantasy, then came *A Day's Pleasure*, set on an excursion boat, and then, taking a year to produce, came *The Kid*. It had an enor-mous cast of over 100 including extras and helped to make a star of Jackie Coogan who, as the Kid of the title, worked to brilliant effect with Chaplin.

The plot is full of sentiment and coincidence. Edna Purviance as the unwed mother leaves her infant in the back of a rich man's car. The car is stolen, the baby dumped in an alley. The baby is found and cared for by Chaplin who improvises feeding, sleeping, and hygiene arrangements. Five years pass and the baby is now Jackie Coogan. Charlie and the Kid have various adventures; the child falls ill, a doctor is summoned and insists that the child goes to an orphanage. Charlie gives chase, rescues the lad, but he is caught and dragged back into the arms of authori-ty. Charlie is alone and an outcast, and dreams he is in heaven — 'Too sentimental' said J. M. Barrie, the author of *Peter Pan*. However, the film ended happily especially in box-office terms: it was shown all round the world and made a for-tune for Chaplin and the First National Film Company. As I have noted, it also made Jackie Coogan a star, but that star soon waned and in Hollywood it was said that 'senility hit him at 13'. I owe most of the information about *The Kid* to David Robinson's exhaustive study of the master of comedy: *Chaplin — His Life and*

Art. It's a book that is full of meticulously researched detail and is refreshingly well written.

The world of Chaplin's films, and the principal reason for their success, was that they were, by and large, a true reflection of the world he saw and understood, but outside the studio gates the larger horrors of the twentieth century were mustering force. The First World War started with great displays of patriotism and ended in disillusion and the squalid carpetbagging of the Versailles treaty. The so-called 'Spanish flu' epidemic of 1918 killed more people than the combined firepower of Krupp and Vickers on the battlefields of Flanders and Gallipoli. The Russian revolution of 1917 changed the face of Eastern Europe for good, if not for better. The Blackshirts under Mussolini made Italy safe for Fascists and gave hope to the emerging right-wing extremists in the Balkans and Germany. By the 1920s France had lapsed into a kind of political coma, unable to lead and unwilling to be led.

In the USA prohibition created an underworld elite of bootleggers as people rushed to break the law. The midwest was fast becoming a dust bowl, and while Presidents Wilson, Harding, Hoover, and Coolidge mouthed pious platitudes or did nothing, the urban USA was carried away on an illusory tide of prosperity which ended when the Wall Street Crash of 1929 pointed to the fact that prosperity on paper is no prosperity at all.

While all these major events and others besides were making the earth a place of turmoil, rancour, and fear, Chaplin was consolidating his position as businessman and film-maker. In 1919 he joined forces with Mary Pickford, Douglas Fairbanks, D. W. Griffith, and William S. Hart, undoubtedly the most famous quintet of film-makers at that time, all earning astronomical salaries; Mary Pickford's even topped Chaplin's. To combat this the existing production companies planned to merge their interests in such a way that high salaries would no longer have to be paid to these box-office giants. The giants themselves countered by announcing that they were creating their own distribution company, to be called United Artists. When it came to the crunch William S. Hart (an early cowboy star) withdrew, but the other four went ahead and United Artists became a reality, distributing the films of not only the four founders but of any other independent film-makers who wished to join them.

Chaplin still had four films to make to complete his contract with First National, which included *The Idle Class*, in which Chaplin played a dual role — the drunken husband of Edna Purviance, and Charlie the tramp, the husband's double. After this came the provisionally titled *Come Seven* (later released as *Pay Day*), which starred Chaplin and Mack Swain, but after only a few days' shooting Chaplin decided to go to Europe. Five days later he left Hollywood bound for New York and the transatlantic liner. It was a surprisingly eccentric thing to do but Chaplin had been ill, and it's worth noting that in the previous seven years he had made 71 films. He was also feeling a nostalgic desire to see England again and, perhaps more to the point, *The Kid* was to be premiered in London when he would be there. He also felt for some strange reason that *The Kid* might be his last film (it was to that date one of his best) and wanted to bask in the applause of a London West End audience.

Like many comedians (John Cleese is a recent example) Chaplin felt that he was losing his comic power, although this was probably the result of overwork, and hectic comings and goings as a result of the problems surrounding the creation of United Artists. However, after a month-long European tour he returned to the USA refreshed and in November 1921 started work again on *Pay Day*, the film he'd abandoned in such a cavalier fashion in that August.

1922 and 1923 were fairly uninspiring years for Chaplin as he only produced *The Pilgrim* and *A Woman of Paris*, which was an attempt at serious filmmaking starring Adolphe Menjou and Edna Purviance, and in which Chaplin played only a cameo role as a porter. It was, to be frank, a pretty turgid film, but Chaplin's next movie was to be a classic — *The Gold Rush*. This tale of the Yukon, with its famous scene in which Chaplin and Mack Swain eat a stewed boot, and in which Chaplin does the much-applauded dance with the bread rolls, has become a landmark in movie comedy.

His next film, *The Circus*, was less successful and is almost forgotten now, but then in 1927 work started on possibly Chaplin's finest film, *City Lights*. In it Charlie the tramp befriends a blind flower-girl who mistakes him for a rich man. He raises the money for the operation to have her sight restored. The denouement when she sees the down-at-heel figure of Charlie and eventually recognizes that this was her benefactor is touching, if perhaps somewhat too maudlin for present-day tastes.

There were innumerable problems during the filming of *City Lights*, mainly caused by Chaplin's indecisions about script and casting, but eventually in early 1931 it was finished and was greeted by the cinema-going public of the day with rapture.

By now talking pictures had arrived (the first box-office success was *The Jazz Singer*, starring Al Jolson, in 1927) but Chaplin refused to change his style. His productions were now taking longer to prepare and shoot. *Modern Times*, his next big picture, started in production in September 1933 and was not completed until January 1936. *The Great Dictator* took from 1939 until October 1940 to complete, and it could be argued that this satire of Hitler and Mussolini (Chaplin played both Hitler, called in the film Adenoid Hynkel, and a humble barber) was the last good film that Chaplin made, for although *Limelight* has good moments in it (one scene of comic mime with Chaplin and Buster Keaton is one of the finest ever filmed), on the whole Chaplin's remaining output was mediocre to downright awful.

Monsieur Verdoux, a talkie based on the true story of a French mass murderer of the nineteenth century, *A King in New York*, the title of which tells the story, and *A Countess from Hong Kong* which, in spite of starring Marlon Brando and Sophia Loren, was conceivably among the 10 worst films ever made, completed Charles Chaplin's film-making career. He retired with grace and dignity to a life of domestic calm at Corsier-sur-Vevey in Switzerland.

In an extraordinary life crowded with as much drama in reality as there was in his stage and cinema career, Charles (in fact Sir Charles since he was knighted in 1975) Chaplin was rarely out of the headlines. Prodigiously talented he was none the less foolish in his private affairs, marrying four times and only at the fourth attempt, to playwright Eugene O'Neill's daughter, Oona, finding someone who was his emotional and intellectual match. His first three wives were all actresses — Mildred (née Harris), whom he married in 1918 when she was 17, Lita Grey (née Lillita McMurray), who was 16 and pregnant when they married in 1924, Paulette Goddard (née Levy) married Chaplin while on holiday with him in the Far East in 1934. They were divorced in 1942 and Chaplin was married for the fourth and last time to Oona O'Neill in 1943. He had had many lovers, and was much loved by almost everyone who came in contact with him. He was also moody and eccentric in his working habits, never happy until a scene was exactly to his liking.

He went through a period of great unpopularity in the USA in the early fifties mainly because of his internationalism, and this brought down upon him the displeasure of Richard Nixon, Senator McCarthy, and the wretched crew of mountebanks who sought to make political capital out of so-called un-American activities.

Through Chaplin and others of his outstanding talent the world saw some of the best of the USA in Hollywood's unrivalled skills at film-making. The presentation of a special Academy Award in 1972 showed that Hollywood could make sense after all. A little late perhaps, but like Chaplin's films — better late than never.

I was the film critic for *Punch* magazine when Charlie Chaplin passed away and it fell to me to write an obituary notice:

> When Sir Charles Chaplin died on Christmas Day 1977 it was almost as if it was an afterthought. He slipped out of the world as unobtrusively as he'd lived in it for the past twenty years: quietly, in Switzerland. In his life he'd been loved and loathed, feted and vilified, subject to violent abuse and praise that verged on deification. A contemporary of Henry Ford and Pierpoint Morgan, of Hitler and Mussolini, Stalin, Churchill, Roosevelt, Mao Tse Tung and General Franco, he was more famous and better liked than any of them and survived them all. Indeed Chaplin will survive as long as film survives and will be making people laugh through whatever eternity awaits the human race.
>
> He came into films before anyone really knew how to make them, and he left the world at a time when all but a handful had forgotten. In between he made half a dozen great films and a few stinkers. In recent years it became fashionable among the reach-me-down pundits who scrape a living from the rim of show business to compare Chaplin with Keaton, to Chaplin's detriment, which is as pointless as arguing about who won the battle of Jutland. In *Limelight* the two masters played a short scene together with such harmony and timing that you held your breath, never wanting the scene to end.

When someone is great, comparison is irrelevant; and Chaplin was a great comedian. Not only that; he was a great teacher. His tragedy was that so few bothered to learn.

FILMS

The Keystone Film Company Productions

These were all produced by Mack Sennett and released in 1914.
Making a Living
Kid Auto Races at Venice
Mabel's Strange Predicament
Between Showers
A Film Johnnie
Tango Tangles
His Favorite Pastime
Cruel, Cruel Love
The Star Boarder
Mabel at the Wheel
Twenty Minutes of Love
Caught in a Cabaret
Caught in the Rain
A Busy Day
The Fatal Mallet
Her Friend the Bandit
The Knockout
Mabel's Busy Day
Mabel's Married Life
Laughing Gas
The Property Man
The Face on the Bar-room Floor
Recreation
The Masquerader
His New Profession
The Rounders
The New Janitor
Those Love Pangs
Dough and Dynamite
Gentlemen of Nerves
His Musical Career
His Trysting Place
Tillie's Punctured Romance
Getting Acquainted
His Prehistoric Past

The Essanay Film Manufacturing Company Productions

These were all produced by Jesse T. Robbins and released in 1915–16
His New Job
A Night Out
The Champion
In the Park
A Jitney Elopement
The Tramp
By the Sea
Work
A Woman
The Bank
Shanghaied
A Night in the Show
Charlie Chaplin's Burlesque on Carmen
Police

Lone Star Mutual Productions

These were all produced by Charles Chaplin and released in 1916–17
The Floorwalker
The Fireman
The Vagabond
One a.m.
The Count
The Pawnshop
Behind the Screen
The Rink
Easy Street
The Cure
The Immigrant
The Adventurer

Chaplin–First National Productions

These were all produced by Charles Chaplin and released in 1918–23
How to Make Movies
A Dog's Life
The Bond
Shoulder Arms
Sunnyside
A Day's Pleasure
The Kid
Nice and Friendly

The Idle Class
Pay Day
The Pilgrim
The Professor

Regent–United Artists' Productions

These were all produced by Charles Chaplin and released in 1923–52
A Woman of Paris
The Gold Rush
The Circus
City Lights
Modern Times
The Great Dictator
Monsieur Verdoux
Limelight

A King in New York   1957
Attica–Archway Production
Produced by Charles Chaplin

A Countess From Hong Kong   1967
Universal Production
Produced by Jerome Epstein

BARRY HUMPHRIES

I t seems that when he was young his mother asked Barry Humphries what he
wanted to be when he grew up. He replied: 'A genius.' If genius means triumphant success in a chosen field, wide recognition, and a great deal of money, then
Barry Humphries has certainly achieved his early ambition. Today he can fill the
biggest theatres in Britain and Australia and has, since the late fifties, come to
epitomize the best in native Australian humour.

He's not the first antipodean entertainer to make his mark in the UK. Dick
Bentley was a star of radio in Britain just after the Second World War, and Bill Kerr
achieved fame on radio and latterly in movies as an accomplished character actor.
Rolf Harris too has been a frequent and popular visitor for many years now. Paul
Hogan in the movie *Crocodile Dundee*, the story of a backwoods Aussie in the
fleshpots of New York, has probably made more money than Barry Humphries
whose work in the cinema (to date) has not been particularly inspiring or
lucrative, but Barry Humphries on stage in any one of his many characterizations
is a world-beater.

In his native Australia — and Barry Humphries was born and grew up in
middle-class Melbourne — he is either loved or loathed. Those who loathe him
feel that in his parodies he is attacking Australian values and devaluing Australian
beliefs, and recently he's been the target of the Feminist lobby, who can't bear the
male chauvinist piggery of Sir Les Patterson.

Sir Les must be one of the grossest caricatures since the great satirical artists
Gillray and George Cruikshank were in action in the early nineteenth century.

Sir Les Patterson, sometime Minister of the Yartz, Ambassador to the Court
of St James, and permanent Chairman of the Australian Cheese Board, speaks to us
about the virtues of life down under and encourages us to visit the large and, on
the whole, delightful land from which he hails. What we get from this bloated,
filthy, priapic walking outrage is a stream of single-entendre jokes and a great deal
of self-confident boorishness. It takes a strong stomach to cope with Sir Les but if
you can subdue your revulsion for this epitome of antipodean vulgarity you can
see beneath the banter a portrait of a type that Barry Humphries loathes but who,
it seems to certain sections of Australian business (principally brewers), is a lovable

primitive. Paul Hogan in his pre-*Crocodile-Dundee* television shows is gross too, in the same way that the English Benny Hill is gross. They offer caricatures which are extensions of what we can see in our friends and neighbours and — if we have the insight and the honesty — ourselves.

No one on the face of the earth could be as appalling as Sir Les Patterson — and yet there's a glint of humour in it all, for while the audience is belly-laughing at the man's grotesque excesses, Barry Humphries's eyes twinkle with laughter at the shockwaves that echo round the theatre. Indeed, it would be easy to believe that Barry sees it as his mission in life to shock — to be outrageous and to belittle. This is what I suppose his denigrators seize on, his ability to belittle, and it offends them that he belittles little people.

When, as Dame Edna Everage, he invites people on to the stage to take part in a barbecue or to become chat show nonentities he is, claim his detractors, insulting the innocent and mocking those who have neither the wit nor the skill to answer back. But, as Wedekind pointed out in his play *The Singer*, written at the turn of the century, many people go to the theatre not for the quality of the play on offer but to be *seen* there. For these people a chance to feature even as a stooge on stage with Barry Humphries is the moment of a lifetime, and after all, they don't *have* to sit within range.

I guess that there must be a part of Barry Humphries's psyche that hates mankind (and in particular womankind, his detractors would say) and he certainly seems to hate organizations. ('Whenever you meet the words "democratic republic" expect tyranny' and 'The Arts [is] a phrase which reminds me of all the frauds, prigs, and scoundrels who sit on government culture committees', are both quotes from an article by Barry Humphries in the Australian magazine *The Bulletin*, 20 August 1977.) But whether this hatred is levelled at people or the things people allow themselves to become, there is undoubtedly a lot of venom in Barry Humphries's work.

Back in 1965 he edited a collection of articles and drawings from the French magazine *Bizarre* describing sado-masochistic acts, sexual perversions, and various kinds of freaks from Siamese twins to a three-legged Scotsman. Philip Toynbee in the London *Observer* attacked it as being 'a bestially vulgar collection'. Philip Higham in *The Bulletin* of 4 December 1965 says of *Bizarre*, 'We are evidently going to be spared nothing in exploring the horrors that go on behind the bland surface of life', although after that his review of the book is, surprisingly, quite favourable.

Early in his career Barry Humphries was asked: 'Are you *sure* you're not a flash in the pan?' Over 20 years later the answer is clearly 'no'. Something of a rebel at school and university, a taste for amateur theatricals soon became a major interest in his life. In the fifties he graduated to professional theatre, learning the business with a Shakespearean company touring his home state, Victoria. He then went through a surrealist period. Barry has always been keen on art and is no mean painter himself, and his Dada exhibitions caused a stir in their day.

From that it was a short step to revue and the creation of two major characters, Edna Everage and Sandy Stone. Edna was born at the time of the 1956 Olympic Games which were held in Melbourne. Edna, then known as Mrs Norm Everage, was Melbourne housewife offering to billet a foreign athlete. It was a local success and Barry was delighted when later the same sketch was popular in Sydney.

Mrs Everage is at the Olympic Information Bureau. The Games officer, Leslie Hopechest, is trying to be helpful.

HOPECHEST: Now, Mrs Everage, is there any particular nationality you would prefer?

MRS EVERAGE: Well, as a matter of fact, we were talking about that last night. We had quite a family conference — I made some of my savouries and Mother made one of her sponges, and we all sat round the dining room table and had a good old chin-wag about the whole thing.

HOPECHEST: And what seemed to be the general consensus of opinion?

MRS EVERAGE: (*Confidentially*) Look, little Kenny would really be tickled to death if you could let us have a real Red Indian.

HOPECHEST: (*Firmly*) I'm very sorry Mrs Everage, but the only Red Indian in the Olympic contingent has already been accommodated at Pascoe Vale.

MRS EVERAGE: Oh! The poor little kiddie will be disappointed. Never mind. I know it's not your fault. Well now, I'll read you our other choices. Valmai: Rhodesian, Dutchman, British. Norm: Canada, America or — Eerie. Merv — that's my son in law — said he was easy, but that he wasn't too keen on the idea of Mau Maus. Brucie suggested —

HOPECHEST: (*Hastily*) I think we have a Dutch weight putter on our files who might possibly suit you.

MRS EVERAGE: (*Abstractedly*) Have you? At the same time, I don't think it's fair of us to decide definitely until I have a word with Mother.

HOPECHEST: (*Exasperated*) But surely your mother attended the family conference?

MRS EVERAGE: Oh no, didn't I tell you? The poor old soul had a very bad turn last night in the middle of *Blue Hills*. She's marvellous, you know. Hasn't missed an episode in five years, but I'm afraid it makes her a bit excitable.

At about this time Barry wrote a short monologue called 'Sandy Stone's Big Week', which he describes as 'glowing with the inner cosiness of apricot jam' and which he recorded as the B-side of a record, 'Wild Life in Surburbia', which featured Edna.

In 1959 Barry came to Britain for the first time and appeared in several West End musicals in minor roles before finally and very successfully taking over the role of Fagin from Ron Moody, who had created the part in Lionel Bart's musical version of the Dickens novel *Oliver*. Barry played the part both in England and New York. He also wrote the 'Barry McKenzie' strip in the satirical magazine *Private Eye* (it was drawn by Nicholas Garland). In 1962 he returned to Australia with his one-man show — Sandy Stone now an established stage character, Mrs Norm Everage now fully Edna in her own right.

From then on Barry Humphries commuted from Australia to England and by the mid sixties had discovered Portugal, a country where he now lives when not working in the theatre or on television.

Although Dame Edna, Sandy Stone, and Sir Les are the best known of Barry Humphries's comic creations, he has invented many more. I am indebted to the Granada publication *A Nice Night's Entertainment* for glimpses of these characters.

One of Barry's trademarks is his boisterous use of language, and the politeness and curliques of suburban speech are present in this early creation, which he performed in an ABC television revue in Melbourne in 1959. The character's name is Jeff Pritchard, he's a coach driver giving a group of Melbourne ladies a high-speed commentary on a guided tour.

> Good morning, ladies. On behalf of the Pioneer people I should like to extend to you all a very warm and cordial welcome aboard your luxurious, air conditioned, twin diesel powered Pioneer Parlour Coach ... your itinerary includes a brief stop-off for morning tea and light refreshments at Ferntree Gully ... famed for the delightful sylvan setting from which it derives its name.

Then there's Colin Cartwright (vintage 1960), a Melbourne businessman trying to buy his children's affection. The monologue was written to appear on a record and has never been performed on stage.

> They're always crying out for what they haven't got, which isn't much I can tell you. Goodness knows, they've got enough toys to keep them out of mischief.
>
> Take a case in point:
>
> Young Duncan was on and on at me about bows and arrows, so I bought him the best archery set that money can buy. What happens? The first arrow he shoots goes through the new sunroom window. I don't need to tell you what a nine by six sheet of quarter inch polished plate glass cost me.
>
> Andrew decides he's interested in photography. Good enough. I fit up a darkroom for him under the stairs, have a sink put in and a red light; chappie comes all the way out from Kodak to give me a quote. Now, he's got a Leica twenty-six point retractable of his own, but he's always on my back about borrowing the movie camera I brought back from Japan on

my second trip. In the end the little tyke whips it behind my back and takes it down to Geelong for the boat races. Where is it now? Somewhere at the bottom of the Barwon. Seventy-eight guineas in the drink!

Then he tells me most of his school mates are learning carpentry, so carpentry it is! I buy him a year's lessons at eleven guineas a term, and I fit up a workshop for him at the back of the garage; a lathe, a handsaw, an electric drill, the works! What did he make with it? One bookend! Well one thing's for sure, they can't say they haven't had the lot!

On the same 1960 LP the character of Buster Thompson appeared. He's described as a loutish ex-public-school boy, and was to be the basis two years later of the cartoon strip character Barry McKenzie — temporarily domiciled in London.

There's quite a nice little hostelry just off the Strand near Australia House where some of the fellas usually get together. There's a fab atmosphere and you can get an ice-cold Fosters if you want it. A few poms go there of course, which is fair enough, but on the whole it's mainly an Aussie out-fit. I was taking a nice little Canadian bird to Covent Garden that night to pick up a bit of the old culture, so I didn't want to put away too much steam beforehand. Had a couple of ales with Bully Forbes, he was at school, and he told me he'd just got back from the States and had a fan-tastic time. He said they certainly had the poms licked when it came to the standard of living. It was absolutely phenomenal he reckoned. He asked me if I'd seen Brucie Mollison-Smith. He was at school and was pulling in quite a few notes over here as a quantity surveyor. Just got himself engaged to a Geelong lass apparently, and they were planning to go back to Melbourne via the States to get married in the school chapel. Well, I had to be pushing off about then on account of the opera that night so I told Bully if he saw Stringy Anderson later on, to give the old son a swift kick up the strides from me.

About this time the Australians in London formed a close-knit community centred on the Earls Court district, and Barry, in his only other female impression apart from Dame Edna, created the character of Debbie Thwaite — whom Barry describes as 'The type of Australian girl I kept meeting in London at the end of the fifties. They often succeeded in returning to Australia without having once met an English person.'

I'm sharing a flat in London with a few other Australian lasses, and it's really superb. I think it's the most economical way really. The really superb thing about it is that we all come and go exactly as we like and nobody cares.

Things have been a bit hectic in the flat just lately; particularly since June and Alwyn left to hitch round Belgium and the twins moved in. Pat-sie's leaving for Spain in a fortnight's time and I hope Migs will have got back from Scandinavia by then so as she can have the stretcher in the hall that used to be Norma's before she went back to Australia last October. As

223

it is, I don't know where we're going to put Janice when she arrives; she's hitching round France at the moment with Jeanie and I don't want to be in a spot like I was when Robyn and Gwenda descended on us out of the blue that time. We had to put sleeping bags down in the kitchen, and even then they stayed on for three and a half weeks. It is a problem.

Morrie Tate was a beatnik and appeared in Barry's repertoire in 1962. This excerpt gives you the flavour of the character.

Was anyone down the Cézanne Coffee Bar last night? It was a real swinging scene man. There was a group of cats had hitched over from Adelaide for the Snake's big farewell party and the place was stacked with guitars and sleeping bags and empty packets of No-Doz. Crazy man. Big Sonia and me and the Mouse and a real cool little raver from the Teachers' Training College went up the Greeks for a blow-out and we ended up at the Mouse's pad imbibing the old marsala and listening to a few really swinging Ella Fitzgerald sides with Clark Terry very interesting as usual on trumpet.

More characters followed: a government official engaged in creating the definitive Australian for overseas consumption, a surfer, and a middle-class skier. The first intellectual to appear in Barry Humphries's gallery of characters was Neil Singleton *circa* 1965. This is what Barry has written about the character:

Until the mid sixties, Neil's class of puritan, querulous, turtle-necked, elbow-patched, pipe-sucking, wife-cheating, wine-buffing, abstract-art-digging highbrow had been amongst my most enthusiastic fans, eager for a chuckle at the middle-class effusions of Edna, Sandy and the other Australians they never met at their own parties. Deep chagrin greeted this impersonation; it was only after the birth of Neil Singleton that the arty periodicals really got stuck into me.

Neil Singleton and his wife, Karen, are giving a party. The guests and the wife are invisible — it's a monologue.

Hello there, long time no see. Don and Verna, sweetie! Welcome to our private hell. Karen was last seen under the shower getting rid of a bit of the old psychic guilt. No, it's not a party, just a few old friends in for a drink. Should be pleasant. (*Pouring drinks*) My God Verna, look at that belly! What's the old sod given you — quins? Now then, what's it to be? There's Scotch or I can fix you a rather pleasant Oz burgundy. Coming up. Have you decided what you're going to call it yet? Well for your sake I hope you haven't got a father-in-law like mine. There was a rather Kafkaish interlude when her old man got it into his head we should call our first brat Karen after its mother. Imagine saddling some poor kid with a label like that. We've got three now. Sibion, Adam and Natasha. Rather pleasant don't you think? Glad you like the new place. Larry designed it and I must say we find it exceedingly pleasant. For a kick-off it's brilliantly sited and we think he's got a terrific feeling for materials *per se*. I mean, take that wall treatment in vertical clear varnished pine slap up against an area of good honest second-hand brick. What a statement. That wall says: I am brick — take it or leave it. I'm brick and I don't pretend to be anything else *but* brick. You run your hand over it sometime tonight and you'll see what I mean. I mean, why the hell shouldn't a wall be tactile?

An early version of Les Patterson appeared in 1968, in the person of Rex Lear, father of the bride. The monologue was in the form of a speech by the bride's father, which broadens into conversation with unseen guests, the caterer, a waiter, and so on. Barry Humphries says of this minor *tour de force*, 'It was an experiment to see if I could present singlehand on stage [at the Tivoli, Sydney, in the 1968 presentation of Barry's one-man performance *Just a Show*] an entire wedding breafast with bridesmaids, vicars, best man, caterers, and Italian waiters.' waiters.'

While it didn't altogether come off it's a major task to attempt in the first place and, like Neil Singleton, depended on the rapport between Barry and his audience. To anyone actually or potentially hostile to the Barry Humphries view of life these characters come over as unpleasant and without many redeeming features. The same is true of Colin Cartwright, the father who does too much for his children. The bitterness of the monologues outweighs the humour.

I said Barry had created only two female characters. In fact there was a third, a creature of the sixties protest movement — a folk singer, a feminist, and downright stupid. She was called Big Sonia and her opening words give you the flavour of the character.

> I'd like to sing you a little song that is still sung by some of the oppressed half-caste inbred descendants of the enslaved catnip spinners in south-west Kentucky, USA.

Also in the 1968 show was the avant-garde film-maker Martin Agrippa. It's another in the Humphries gallery of pseuds. Here's a sample.

> Hi there. My name is Martin Agrippa and it was my motion picture which ran off with the big prize in Helsinki this year for the best Australian entry in the experimental film section.

The film itself, containing every trick of awful avant-gardism, was scripted by Barry Humphries and filmed by Bruce Beresford, the Australian director who subsequently made several successful feature films (*Breaker Morant, Tender Mercies, King David*).

Another character in *Just a Show* was called Brian Graham, a young businessman who was a closet homosexual. Later came Morrie O'Connor, an art dealer with the patter of a used-car salesman; an operator who conned every government, state and national, out of any grant going was aptly named Brett Grantworthy, and lasted for only one performance.

Later still, in 1978, came Lance Boyle. This is what Humphries has to say about the character:

> This richly promising character emerged with the help of Maxwell Newton and Ian Davidson. Lance Boyle is as delightful to act as he is repulsive to watch. While performing him (in *Isn't it Pathetic at his Age*, in 1978), it was amusing to scan the stalls and pick out the pious pinkos gazing up estatically at the unsavoury opportunist on stage. Their poor little pinched faces always fell most entertainingly when they realised that the odious operator on the boards was one of their own sacrosanct self-sacrificing trade union lefties.

You can almost hear the snarl in Barry Humphries's writing when he penned that.

I once asked Barry why he'd not used Lance Boyle in the UK. His answer was to the effect that he didn't think the poms would understand the character. I suspect that he feels that it's just a little raw and anti-labour — that's to say anti-Australian labour — for it to register well in Britain.

The character of Lance Boyle is formed of the pure untreated effluent of corruption, hyprocrisy, bullying, and greed. In comparison Les Patterson is politeness and charm itself. Patterson is the most recent of the Humphries inventions. Sir Leslie Colin Patterson (int. cert. Parramatta High), Australian Cultural Attaché, was based originally on the entertainments officer of an RSL club in Sydney.

For the uninitiated, 'RSL' stands for Returned Serviceman's League, and these clubs spangle, if that's the word I'm looking for, New South Wales and Victoria. They date from the time when Australian licensing laws were such that pubs closed at 6 p.m. Any evening drinking had to be done at home or at a club. When the clubs added one-armed bandits to their attractions their revenues soared to great heights, and in terms of decor and facilities the average RSL club is opulent to a degree.

It's interesting to note that in his early days Barry had the unfortunate experience (common to anyone who has embarked on a career as a stand-up comedian) of playing to an audience at one of these clubs, which greeted him briefly with stony silence before returning to the fruit machines.

So, as the MC of such a club, Les Patterson first saw the light of day. 'Later', says Barry Humphries, 'Les inherited the suit and upholstered groin of Morrie O'Connor, the vehicle vendor, the baroque scatology of Barry McKenzie discourse, and the rodomontade of the Australian politician.'

Popular in Hong Kong, where Barry played in carbaret in 1974 and 1975, Sir Les, as he had by now become, was the hit of the 1976 production *Housewife Superstar* at London's Globe Theatre. This extract is from *A Night with Dame Edna* at the Piccadilly Theatre, London in 1978–9.

I'm a maverick, I'm a wag, I'm a hard-nosed carpet-bagging trouble-shooter and if ever there's any strife in the world that needs a bit of *finesse*, a little *savoir-faire* — what has become known in diplomatic circles as 'the Patterson touch' — they send for old Les. I'm a sort of Australian Henry Kissinger and I'm here on another whistle-stop tour at the moment. Just back from New Zealand, as a matter of fact, fronting up a Royal Commission there into these sightings, these saucers, these UFO's — Unidentified Fuckin' Objects.

Awh, I'm sorry. Please forgive me, ladies, that just slipped out — you know the feeling don't you, son? I'm under a terrific lot of pressure and I've got a confession to make to you and I'm going to make a clean breast of it now: I've had a drink tonight. I've had a couple of drinks as a matter of fact — who hasn't, for Christ's sake? To tell you the truth, I'm as full as a fairy's phone book. I'm as full as a state school hat rack. I'm as full as two race trains. I'm as full as a seaside shithouse on Boxing Day.

This is comparatively mild to some of Les Patterson's patter, and it must be said that it is not for the delicately reared. The fact that theatre audiences nearly explode with laughter at this walking outrage seems to justify the (fictional) existence of a character who on a recent sighting struck me as being like the late Max Miller without the subtlety. It's an interesting note on Australian attitudes that while Melbourne-born Barry's lovable characters come from Melbourne, Sir Les comes from Sydney!

Sandy Stone is a complete contrast. He started life as a dear old chap in poor health, living in the Melbourne suburb of Glen Iris, reminiscing about days gone by and the small details of his life. He hasn't changed much over the years except that he died some time back and now addresses us from beyond the grave, dressed as he was in life in pyjamas, a fawn woollen dressing-gown, and slippers.

Here is the opening of an early monologue of Sandy Stone. It was first heard on the record 'Wild Life in Suburbia' and later made a stage debut in a revue jointly devised by Barry, and Peter O'Shaughnessy at the New Theatre, Flinders Street, Melbourne, called *Rock 'n' Reel*.

I went to the RSL the other night and had a very nice night's entertainment. Beryl, that's the wife, came along too. Beryl's not a drinker but she had a shandy. She put in quite a reasonable quantity of time yarning with Norm Purvis's good lady and I had a beer with old Norm and some of the other chappies there. I don't say no to the occasional odd glass and Ian Preston, an old friend of mine, got up and sang a few humorous numbers — not too blue, on account of the womenfolk — so that altogether it was a really nice type of night's entertainment for us both. We called it a day round about ten-ish; didn't want to make it too late a night as Beryl had a big wash on her hands on the Monday morning and I had to be in town pretty early, stocktaking and one thing and another.

Well, we got back to Gallipoli Crescent about twenty past and Beryl and I went to bed.

Sandy's detailed description of the entire week followed and charted what must have been a recognizable routine to many elderly Melbournians.

On his death he recorded the event with great pride.

> In the days prior to and immediately preceding my internment Beryl was like a human dynamo, up to her eyes in paperwork ... putting a rocket under the solicitor and attending to my estate. My wife and I are without issue, to date, so Beryl is to all intents and purposes my sole executrix. She didn't skimp on my insertion either — if ever a man was given a decent long insertion by his wife it was me!
>
> (*He produces a newspaper cutting.*)
>
> 'STONE, Alexander Horace 'Sandy'. On April 7th, devoted son of Horace (deceased) and Enid (née Cockburn, deceased), beloved brother of Hector (deceased), Lance (deceased), Lorna (deceased), Phyllis (deceased) and Muriel (Western Australia). Much-loved husband of Beryl Eileen (née Pizzey), formerly of Koo-wee-rup. At his Residence, alone, suddenly. Brief service 9.30 a.m., April 14th, Springvale Necropolis. Family only please. In lieu of flowers, kindly remember the Holy Trinity Ladies' Auxiliary Jazz Ballet Stereo System Appeal.
>
> Memories of you I will always keep,
> God saw you were tired and put you to sleep.'

Sandy Stone may be dead but, as the song says, 'his soul goes marching on'.

Having quoted Dame Edna earlier in this chapter when she was just plain Mrs Norm Everage, it's interesting to chart her progress from cheery philistine through disapproving monitor of the sexual freedom of the sixties, the 'Put Australia First' matron with her gladioli and stories of her husband Norm, who 'was very big in dried fruit', to world traveller, name dropper and finally megastar (both fictionally and in reality) with thousands, if not millions, of adoring fans.

On TV Edna has scored many triumphs from her first 'Special' on BBC2 in 1969 to her highly rated chat shows of 1987. Barry Humphries, through the persona of Dame Edna Everage, is now up there with the big names of show business.

From drunken iconoclast (at one stage his drinking habits were so extreme that he was given six weeks to live — sensibly he stopped drinking) to sober pillar of the Establishment, thrice-married Barry Humphries has moved easily from obscurity to triumph. Today he's rich, and, one hopes, contented. He's certainly added something special to the entertainment of the world in the latter part of the twentieth century. For that he deserves, and on my part certainly gets, thanks.

FILMS

These include:
Bedazzled 1965

Produced by Stanley Donen
Directed by Stanley Donen
Written by Peter Cook

Adventures of Barry McKenzie   1972
Produced by Phillip Adams
Directed by Bruce Beresford
Written by Barry Humphries and Bruce Beresford

Barry McKenzie Holds his Own   1974
Produced by Reg Grundy
Directed by Bruce Beresford
Written by Barry Humphries and Bruce Beresford

The Getting of Wisdom   1977
Produced by Phillip Adams
Directed by Bruce Beresford
Written by Eleanor Witcombe, from the novel by Henry Handel Richardson
(Ethel Richardson)

Shock Treatment   1981
Produced by John Goldstone
Directed by Jim Sharman
Written by Jim Sharman, Richard O'Brien, and Brian Thompson, from the book
by Richard O'Brien

Les Patterson Saves the World   1987
Produced by Diane Millstead
Directed by George Miller
Written by Barry Humphries and Diane Millstead

TELEVISION

Several programmes for the BBC from 1968 to 1982 including:
The Barry Humphries Scandals
La Dame aux Gladiolus
Parkinson (1 hour 'special')

For London Weekend Television:
An Audience with Dame Edna Everage   1978
Last Night of the Poms   1981
Another Audience with Dame Edna Everage   1984
The Dame Edna Experience   1987
The Dame Edna Christmas Experience   1987
One More Audience with Dame Edna   1988

BARRY HUMPHRIES

STAGE SHOWS

These include:
Call Me Madman   1953
Rock 'n' Reel Revue   1958
A Nice Night's Entertainment   1962
Excuse I   1964
Just a Show   1968
A Load of Olde Stuff   1971
At Least You Can Say You've Seen It   1974
Housewife Superstar   1976
Isn't it Pathetic at his Age   1978
A Night with Dame Edna   1978–9
An Evening's Intercourse   1981
Songs of Australia   1983
Tears Before Bedtime   1985
Back with a Vengeance   1987–9

BIBLIOGRAPHY

Woody Allen, *Getting Even* (Warner Brothers, 1972).
____, *Without Feathers* (Warner Brothers, 1976).
____, *Side Effects* (New English Library, 1981).
Mary Livingstone Benny, Hilliard Marks, and Marcia Borie, *Jack Benny* (Robson, 1978).
Rudi Blesh, *Keaton* (Collier, 1971).
Eddie Braben, *The Best of Morecambe and Wise* (Woburn, 1974).
Kevin Brownlow, *The Parade's Gone By* (Secker & Warburg, 1968).
George Burns, *Living it Up* (Putnam, 1976).
____, *The Third Time Around* (Putnam, 1980).
Charlotte Chandler, *Hello I Must Be Going* (Sphere, 1986).
Alistair Cooke, *Six Men* (Bodley Head, 1977).
Donald Deschner, *The Films of W. C. Fields* (Citadel, 1968).
Peter Evans, *Peter Sellers — The Mask Behind the Mask* (New English Library, 1980).
William K. Everson, *The Films of Laurel and Hardy* (Citadel, 1967).
____, *The Art of W. C. Fields* (Allen & Unwin, 1968).
William Robert Faith, *Bob Hope — A Life in Comedy* (Granada, 1983).
W. C. Fields, *W. C. Fields by Himself* (W. H. Allen, 1974).
John Fisher, *Funny Way to be a Hero* (Paladin, 1973).
____, *Call Them Irreplaceable* (Elm Tree, 1976).
Ray Galton and Alan Simpson, *Hancock's Half Hour* (Woburn, 1979).
The Groucho Letters (Michael Joseph, 1967).
Leslie Halliwell, *Halliwell's Film Guide* (Granada, 1977).
____, *Halliwell's Filmgoer's Companion* (Granada, 1977).
____, *Double Take and Fade Away* (Grafton, 1987).
____ and Philip Purser, *Halliwell's Television Companion* (Granada, 1979).
Freddie Hancock and David Nathan, *Hancock* (Ariel/BBC, 1986).
Jim Harmon, *Great Radio Comedians* (Doubleday, 1970).
Barry Humphries, *A Nice Night's Entertainment* (Granada, 1981).
Pauline Kael, *When the Lights Go Down* (Holt, Rinehart & Winston, 1980).
Buster Keaton and Charles Samuels, *Buster Keaton — My Wonderful World of Slapstick* (Da Capo, 1982).

231

BIBLIOGRAPHY

Eric Lax, *Woody Allen and his Comedy* (Elm Tree, 1975).

John McCabe, *Mr Laurel and Mr Hardy* (Citadel, 1967).

Eric Morecambe and Ernie Wise, *There's No Answer to That* (Coronet, 1981).

Joe Morella and Edward Z. Epstein, *Lucy — The Bittersweet Life of Lucille Ball* (Dell, 1974).

David Nathan, *The Laughtermakers* (Peter Owen, 1971).

Parkinson — Selected Interviews from the Television Series (Elm Tree, 1975).

George Perry, *Life of Python* (Pavilion/Michael Joseph, 1983).

Punch at the Cinema (Robson, 1981).

Neil Sinyard, *The Films of Woody Allen* (Bison/Hamlyn, 1987).

Robin Skynner and John Cleese, *Families and How to Survive Them* (Methuen, 1983).

Tony Staveacre, *Slapstick* (Angus & Robertson, 1987).

Howard Teichmann, *George S. Kaufman* (Dell, 1972).

Barry Took, *Laughter in the Air* (Robson/BBC, 1981).

____, *Took's Eye View* (Robson, 1983).

Kenneth Tynan, *A View of the English Stage* (Methuen, 1975).

Roger Wilmut, *Hancock Artiste* (Methuen, 1978).

____, *From Fringe to Flying Circus* (Methuen, 1980).

____ and Jimmy Grafton, *The Goon Show Companion* (Robson, 1976).

Victoria Wood, *Barmy* (Methuen, 1987).

____, *Up to You, Porky* (Methuen, 1987).

Maurice Yacowan, *Loser Takes All — The Comic Art of Woody Allen* (Ungar, 1979).

INDEX

Films and shows are indexed if they appear in the text. References in lists only are not included.

INDEX

235

93
96
03